Contents

The Challenge of PROBLEM-BASED LEARNING

2nd Edition

EDITED BY
DAVID BOUD and GRAHAME I FELETTI

Kogan Page
London • Stirling (USA)

First published in 1991
Second edition 1997
First paperback edition published in 1998
Reprinted 1999, 2001, 2003

Kogan Page Limited
120 Pentonville Road
London N1 9JN

www.kogan-page.co.uk

© D. Boud, G I Feletti and named contributors, 1997

British Library Cataloguing in Publication Data

A CIP record for this book is available from the British Library.

ISBN 0 7494 2560 1

Typeset by Northern Phototypesetting Co Ltd, Bolton
Printed and bound in Great Britain by Biddles Ltd, Guildford and King's Lynn

Contents

Contributors

Stephen Abrahamson, Professor Emeritus, former Chairman, Department of Medical Education, University of Southern California, Los Angeles, USA.

Christine Alavi, Associate Professor, School of Nursing, Griffith University, Brisbane, Australia.

Alexander S Anderson, former Professor of Medicine and Director, Office of Medical Education, John A Burns School of Medicine, University of Hawaii, USA.

Elizabeth G Armstrong, Director of Medical Education and Associate Professor in Pediatrics (Medical Education), Office of Educational Development, Harvard Medical School, Boston, Massachusetts, USA.

Richard Bawden, Professor, Faculty of Agriculture and Rural Development, University of Western Sydney – Hawkesbury, Richmond, New South Wales, Australia.

Natalie Bolzan, Lecturer, Department of Social Policy and Human Services, University of Western Sydney – Macarthur, New South Wales, Australia.

David Boud, Professor of Adult Education, University of Technology, Sydney.

Ken Brown, Lecturer, School of Computer and Mathematical Sciences, The Robert Gordon University, Aberdeen, Scotland.

Hilary Burgess, School for Policy Studies, University of Bristol, England.

Susan M Case, Senior Evaluation Officer, National Board of Medical Examiners, Philadelphia, USA .

Peter Cawley, Department of Mechanical Engineering, Imperial College of Science and Technology, London.

Colin Coles, Professor of Medical Education, University of Bournemouth, England.

Debra Creedy, Senior Lecturer, School of Nursing, Griffith University, Brisbane, Australia.

David Dathe, Coordinator, Department of Problem Solving, Alverno College, Milwaukee, Wisconsin, USA.

Contributors

John Drinan, Director, Centre for the Advancement of Learning and Teaching, University of Newcastle, New South Wales, Australia.

Shirley E Earl, Staff Development Coordinator, Educational Development Unit, The Robert Gordon University, Aberdeen, Scotland.

Charles E Engel, Centre for Higher Education Studies, University of London, London.

Grahame I Feletti, Professorial Associate, Faculty of Health Sciences, University of Sydney, New South Wales, Australia.

Stephen F Foster, Professor of Behavioural Sciences, Maastricht School of Management, The Netherlands.

Alan Gilbert, University of Portsmouth Business School, England.

Janet P Hafler, Associate Director of Faculty Development, Office of Educational Development, Harvard Medical School, Boston, Massachusetts, USA.

Karen Heycox, School of Social Work, University of New South Wales, Australia.

Edward M Hundert, Associate Dean for Student Affairs, Harvard Medical School, Boston, Massachusetts, USA.

Shona Little, Principal Lecturer, Centre for Staff and Educational Development, Auckland Institute of Technology, New Zealand.

Stephen E Little, Department of Business Information Technology, Faculty of Management & Business, Manchester Metropolitan University, England.

Georgine Loacker, Professor and Director, Assessment Council, Alverno College, Milwaukee, Wisconsin, USA.

Jan Lovie-Kitchin, Associate Professor, School of Optometry, Queensland University of Technology, Brisbane, Australia.

Iain Mackenzie, The Robert Gordon University, Aberdeen, Scotland.

Peter J MacDonald, Director, Family Practice Residency Program, University of Illinois College of Medicine at Rockford, Illinois, USA.

Barry Maitland, Professor and Head, Department of Architecture, University of Newcastle, New South Wales, Australia.

Don Margetson, Griffith Institute of Higher Education, Griffith University, Queensland, Australia.

Mary Georgia Matlock, Coordinator, Department of Information Studies, Alverno College, Milwaukee, Wisconsin, USA.

Gordon T Moore, Associate Professor of Medicine, Harvard Medical School, Boston, Massachusetts, USA.

Geoffrey R Norman, Professor of Clinical Epidemiology and Biostatistics, Faculty of Health Sciences, McMaster University, Hamilton, Canada.

Kathleen O'Brien, Associate Professor and Chair, Division of Business and Management, Alverno College, Milwaukee, Wisconsin, USA.

R A (Bob) Ross, Professor Emeritus, former Director, Centre for the Advancement of Learning and Teaching, Griffith University, Queensland, Australia.

Greg Ryan, Senior Lecturer, Professional Development Centre, University of New South Wales, Australia.

Chris Sauer, Senior Research Fellow, Fujitsu Centre for Managing Information Technology in Organizations, Australian Graduate School of Management, University of New South Wales, Australia.

Peter Schwartz, Associate Professor, Department of Pathology, University of Otago Medical School, Dunedin, New Zealand.

David G Simmonds, Senior Lecturer, School of Computer and Mathematical Sciences, The Robert Gordon University, Aberdeen, Scotland.

David B Swanson, Senior Evaluation Officer, National Board of Medical Examiners, Philadelphia, USA.

Imogen Taylor, School for Policy Studies, University of Bristol, England.

John R Usher, Senior Lecturer, School of Computer and Mathematical Sciences, The Robert Gordon University, Aberdeen, Scotland.

Cees P M van der Vleuten, Professor and Chair, Department of Educational Development and Research, University of Maastricht, The Netherlands.

LuAnn Wilkerson, Associate Dean for Medical Education, UCLA School of Medicine, Los Angeles, California, USA.

Keith Winsor, formerly Senior Lecturer, New South Wales College of Law, Sydney, Australia.

Donald R Woods, Professor, Department of Chemical Engineering, McMaster University, Hamilton, Ontario, Canada.

Christel A Woodward, Department of Clinical Epidemiology and Biostatistics, McMaster University, Canada.

Chapter 1

Changing Problem-based Learning. Introduction to the Second Edition

David Boud and Grahame Feletti

Problem-based learning (PBL) is the most significant innovation in education for the professions for many years. Some argue that it is the most important development since the move of professional training into educational institutions. Why is this so? What are the characteristics of this approach to higher education which make it so attractive and yet so controversial?

Aim of the book

This book examines PBL, explores its significance, how it can be used and its strengths and limitations. It is directed to those who are interested in this form of teaching and learning and who wish to assess how it might address central issues in professional education. The book treats PBL both sympathetically and critically. Almost all its contributors have direct experience of the approach, and are firmly committed to the need to find alternatives to what they believe are indefensible practices in traditional teaching in higher education. However, they are not all wedded to a particular view of PBL. The contributors are very conscious of what can and cannot be achieved and they point to important directions for the further development of this approach.

> The principal idea behind problem-based learning is... that the starting point for learning should be a problem, a query or a puzzle that the learner wishes to solve. (Boud, 1985: 13)

PBL is a way of constructing and teaching courses using problems as the stimulus and focus for student activity. While there are different versions of what constitutes PBL, it does not, as is sometimes erroneously assumed, involve the addition of problem-solving activities to otherwise discipline-centred curricula. It is a way of conceiving of the curriculum as being centred upon key problems in professional practice. Problem-based courses start with problems rather than with exposition of disciplinary knowledge. They move students towards the acquisition of knowledge and skills through a staged sequence of problems presented in context, together with associated learning materials and support from teachers.

Although there is no universally agreed set of practices which must be found in problem-based courses to define them as such, the following features are characteristic of PBL as an approach to education:

- using stimulus material to help students discuss an important problem, question or issue;
- presenting the problem as a simulation of professional practice or a 'real life' situation;
- appropriately guiding students' critical thinking and providing limited resources to help them learn from defining and attempting to resolve the given problem;
- having students work cooperatively as a group, exploring information in and out of class, with access to a tutor (not necessarily a subject specialist) who knows the problem well and can facilitate the group's learning process;
- getting students to identify their own learning needs and appropriate use of available resources;
- reapplying this new knowledge to the original problem and evaluating their learning processes.

The origins of PBL

PBL as it is generally known today evolved from innovative health sciences curricula introduced in North America over 30 years ago. Medical education, with its intensive pattern of basic science lectures followed by an equally exhausting clinical teaching programme, was rapidly becoming an ineffective and inhumane way to prepare students, given the explosion in medical information and new technology, and the rapidly changing demands of future practice.

Medical faculty at McMaster University in Canada introduced the *tutorial process*, not only as a specific instructional method (Barrows and Tamblyn, 1980) but also as central to their philosophy for structuring an entire curriculum promoting student-centred multidisciplinary education as a basis for lifelong learning in professional practice (Neufeld and Barrows, 1974). Some key features of the McMaster model are evident in an earlier curriculum reform by medical faculty at Case Western Reserve University in the late 1950s, which incorporated a wide range of instructional methods and strategies. Their multidisciplinary laboratory was perhaps the forerunner to the PBL tutorial (Bussigel *et al*, 1988). The Case Western Reserve model heralded an equally legitimate and perhaps more feasible approach for developing problem-based curricula at larger and more traditional schools. Harvard Medical School's 'hybrid' model is a good example of the latter. It uses problem-based tutorials, lectures, conferences and clinical sessions to integrate teaching and learning around weekly themes (Tosteson *et al*, 1994).

The appeal of both the McMaster philosophy, which led to a worldwide spread of problem-based learning in many professional fields by 1980, and Harvard's hybrid model (which has influenced more traditional medical schools since 1990), is twofold. First, they revitalize classroom teaching and learning processes, and enable students to get the most from independent studies. Second, these curricula feature regular small group 'problem solving' sessions at which students discuss simulated but true-to-life problems, and a weekly schedule which facilitates integration of learning across disciplines, with very few lectures and more 'protected time' for electives or self-directed studies.

What is intriguing about these two models of PBL is their international appeal and influence despite their very specific contexts, particularly the academic confidence and capability of their students. The McMaster approach would seem only generalizable to a limited number of other medical schools – in terms of its relatively small number of students and dedicated faculty, its funding and learning resources, and its commitment to improving the health status of populations and communities in both developing and developed countries. Not content with producing generalist physicians for Canada's city hospitals and academic medical centres, McMaster made a shift of emphasis in its approach towards community-based learning which has been reflected in a growing trend elsewhere. It linked with a number of sister medical schools to form a Network of Community Oriented Educational Institutions for Health Sciences.

Its mission, and similar ventures funded by the W K Kellogg Foundation (USA), has been to support problem-based curricula which enable health profession students to spend significant periods of time learning from real experiences off-campus, in non-traditional practice environments in community settings (Richards, 1995; Richards *et al*, 1987; Magzoub *et al*, forthcoming). Curricula designed for other professions and vocations have adopted similar workplace orientations. In essence, as the context of professional practice changes so will the nature of the curriculum model.

PBL is not static. It is changing from the approach which arose from the unique context of medical education. Nevertheless, those original ideas were sufficiently robust that they have provided the foundations for many others elsewhere. Some of the compelling features of PBL which have generated interest are as follows.

- ☐ It takes account of how students learn. It is becoming increasingly apparent that learning takes place most effectively when students are actively involved and learn in the context in which knowledge is to be used.
- ☐ The expanding knowledge base of most professions means that it is impossible to include all the knowledge that is required for the beginning practitioner in the pre-service curriculum. It is more important for students to be able to learn quickly, effectively and independently when they need it, than it is for them to have assimilated (at graduation) all the information which their teachers believe is desirable.
- ☐ It supports the view of many professionals about what constitutes their field of activity, in contrast to the curriculum they experienced as neophytes in the profession. The problem-based course has high face validity for practitioners.
- ☐ It fits well with the political exigencies of higher education institutions: the need to respond to changes in professional practice, to update both content and method in the light of changing learning environments, and to regenerate enthusiasm amongst faculty in the face of a tight economic future.
- ☐ Most importantly, despite the apparent different demands that PBL places on an institution compared with the traditional lecture/lab/tutorial structure, it is sufficiently adaptable to fit within the rigidities of large educational institutions.

Changes to the second edition of this book

Since the publication of the first edition, there has been a substantial increase in the adoption of PBL in many different countries and in many additional professional areas. This has been accompanied by innovation extending the boundaries of a problem-based approach. There is a more sophisticated appreciation of the issues that underpin successful adoption. These important developments are discussed in the next section.

However, alongside the positive developments there have also been misapplications and misconceptions of PBL, some of which relate to the particular features of the approach, others which involve the challenges associated with instituting major educational change. Many of the difficulties have arisen because insufficient attention was given to issues raised in the earlier edition of this book. These include:

- confusing PBL as an approach to curriculum design with the teaching of problem-solving;
- adoption of a PBL proposal without sufficient commitment of staff at all levels;
- lack of research and development on the nature and type of problems to be used;
- insufficient investment in the design, preparation and ongoing renewal of learning resources. This is commonly associated with a lack of recognition of the additional resources for the start-up phase of a problem-based curriculum;
- establishing small elements of PBL in a context which rewards students for the kind of behaviour favoured in a traditional lecture-plus-examination environment;
- insufficient concern with staff induction and development, particularly for those staff who were not part of the original team which developed the programme;
- inappropriate assessment methods which do not match the learning outcomes sought in problem-based programmes; and
- evaluation strategies which do not focus on the key learning issues and which are implemented and acted upon far too late.

While there have also been difficulties associated with reduced funding levels for teaching and learning in higher education, it is interesting to observe that there is no simple connection between low resourcing for courses and unsuccessful implementation. Some of the best examples of problem-based practice can be found at modest levels of funding, while access to resources does not guarantee that they will be well used.

The second edition of this book has retained the best features of the first while incorporating a number of changes throughout. It aims to address the misperceptions mentioned above. There are several new chapters and authors. Greg Ryan reports on first year students' development of knowledge structures, problem solving and self-directed learning skills in an undergraduate curriculum. Imogen Taylor and Hilary Burgess discuss how PBL courses can be designed to meet the needs of non-traditional students. Debra Creedy and Christine Alavi discuss some of the major developments and issues for nursing education, which has seen a huge increase in PBL initiatives. Of particular importance in the light of questions about the value and effectiveness of problem-based curricula is Christel Woodward's chapter, which reviews what research studies have revealed about the impact of PBL courses on a wide range of outcomes.

A number of previous authors have completely revised their chapters as their courses have evolved or their thinking about PBL developed: Don Woods and Geoff Norman at McMaster, Shona Little, Janet Hafler, Natalie Bolzan and Karen Heycox, Keith Winsor, John Usher and his colleagues, Alan Gilbert and Stephen Foster, and faculty from Alverno College. In most other chapters there has been an updating of material and incorporation of new references. Many of the original chapters that have been retained express views that are as current now as when they were written.

The new challenges of PBL

As we have seen, the notion of PBL is not new, nor is it unique to the health sciences despite their major contribution to its origins and literature. PBL in its very many manifestations does, however, attempt to link a sophisticated analysis of professional practice to a humanistic technology of education, to develop highly competent practitioners who will continue to learn effectively throughout their lives. This last statement seems just as valid six years after publishing our first edition, but a number of new developments and challenges have emerged.

First, the definition of PBL is now *international* property rather than the publicized impressions of any one profession or institution.

Up to the mid-1980s the PBL literature was more descriptive of process than analytical of either process or outcome. Research mostly related to student perceptions and to some extent student performance within certain aspects of courses. There were very few impact studies on graduates, the faculty, the institution or the profession. With most evidence coming from only a handful of medical schools, and with few examples of coherent PBL curricula for any other profession, curriculum designers had little choice in finding an appropriate model. And so the mid-70s to -80s saw schools struggling to develop and implement a curriculum appropriate for their particular context. Perhaps this concentrated effort – to make 'it' work – diverted attention from concurrent evaluation research, in particular, from whether effort might be better directed towards critically analysing their paradigm of problem solving and whether their curriculum model served their intended goals.

In common with other educational innovations (eg, computer-based learning and distance education) international acceptance of PBL has distinct benefits for educators in the professions who, in turn, have taken advantage of new information networks. Critical analysis of PBL and problem-solving approaches has been greatly facilitated by access to the Internet, e-mail communication via PBLIST, PBL-dedicated journals such as *PROBE* (Australian Problem-based Learning Network), and a growing number of conferences and books devoted to PBL theory and practice – all helping to balance the earlier evangelism and intuition with broader based experience and healthy scepticism.

Second, the more recent PBL literature has embraced broader perspectives. These include contemporary learning theories and reflections on curriculum experiences from different disciplines and professions (Wilkerson and Gisjelaers, 1996); more quantitative research studies from these disciplines enhancing our understanding of the dynamics of problem-based curricula (Bouhuijs *et al*, 1993); integrated studies on the psychological basis for PBL as a teaching and learning phenomenon (Norman and Schmidt, 1992; Schmidt and Moust, in press); and the outcomes and challenges remaining for evaluating its impact on professional practice and standards (Berkson, 1993).

Paradoxically, as the number of vocations, disciplines and professions contributing to the PBL literature increases, the nature of PBL has become both more explicit and controversial (Feletti, 1993). Health sciences like medicine, occupational therapy, physiotherapy, orthoptics, nutrition and dietetics have developed curricula and heuristic models that emphasize relatively well-defined problems – ones that could be resolved. Other applications in areas such as agriculture, architecture, community nursing and social work are more field or community based. Their 'problems' are less well defined, and 'solutions' are less predictable in terms of specific factors, strategies and outcomes. Some disciplines have even adopted a version of PBL while rejecting the term 'problem' (eg, enquiry and action learning or issues-based learning in social work, and situation improvement in agriculture). Their curricula may incorporate systems thinking, social theory, and models of critical thinking that make different assumptions about the nature of problem solving and the roles of student and teacher (Checkland, 1981; Paul and Heaslip, 1995). They can be regarded as having features in common with PBL as they base their curriculum design around key issues from practice and students learning collaboratively.

The relative merits of tutors' facilitation versus 'case' expertise is an ongoing concern for some; providing the flexibility for both to occur in tutorials is of more interest to others. For example, in legal training it is important for students to learn how to see and argue cases *from different perspectives*. The kind of practice simulation used, the contested nature of evidence, the way it is revealed, and the merits of using other teaching methods such as role play or debate in class will be different from the tutorial process developed for medical education.

A third major change in context since our first edition is that many academic institutions have experienced severe resource constraints and budget cuts for education, resulting in adverse conditions for curriculum innovation. Older and newer schools in public and private universities differ greatly in their competing priorities, resource needs and constraints. The size of the class, the available numbers of teaching and support staff, and available physical space will each affect decisions on the size of tutorial groups and the model of PBL adopted. With even the best of intentions these factors dictate whether a school can start directly on, or must work steadily towards an integrated, coherent curriculum over a number of years.

There is mounting anecdotal evidence, from both schools in rapid transition and those changing more slowly, that the students themselves are a valuable curriculum resource quite capable of promoting and hastening the development of PBL. For instance, at the Zamboanga Medical School in the Philippines students contributed substantially to development of PBL modules by generating learning objectives and case materials, writing clinical abstracts and patient simulations, and formulating examination questions based on their objectives for subsequent classes (Joson, 1996). This is well beyond the typical evaluation of tutors, resources and learning experiences.

Fourth, the philosophy and practice of PBL, and its impact on higher and professional education has received closer scrutiny from contemporary learning theorists. While in agreement on the advantages of involving students in authentic problem-solving activity, some theorists are less convinced that curricula should have a *major* focus on practical problem solving. One intrinsic danger is that students will equate learning solely with its practical or instrumental value, which comes from too narrow a construal of the problem. This approach may also downplay the *transformative* role of students' experience – in terms of subverting their own perceptions and internal information-processing aspects of cognition. Instead of taking an executive role in their learning, they may become more analytical, reflexive critical thinkers – with the curriculum defining the world for them, or professional practice, as a series of problematic situations which can be interpreted and resolved by using *existing* schemata and available routines.

An alternative approach, called 'idea-based social constructivism', focuses less on problems and more on the teaching value of concepts and possibilities inherent in a given situation (Prawat, 1993). In this way community and workplace learning experiences become just as important as classroom simulations of professional practice for stimulating inquiry. This approach challenges both campus and practice-based faculty to develop new teaching and learning skills, so that off-campus or field activities are not treated as glorified apprenticeships where students conduct the same old surveys or memorize service protocols, observe and practise interaction skills, or write log diaries of time spent on task. Instead, some academic-community partnerships are committed to the principle that undergraduates should benefit from doing something worthwhile for others, supervised at an appropriate level, and guided to ensure it is a meaningful experience (Feletti and Lum, 1997; Oneha *et al*, in press).

The continuing evolution of PBL

Researchers have intensified their efforts to establish the scientific basis of PBL practices, particularly in health sciences education. Up to the mid-1980s those interested in adopting a problem-based course had to rely more on the stated philosophy and unique experiences of a handful of institutions than on robust curriculum evaluation data. Since then there has been far greater emphasis on empirical research and reviews, plus recognition of the need for good qualitative studies. However, much of this research seems to have concentrated on teaching technology and curriculum control issues, aimed at achieving stated course objectives or national examination standards, and justifying the cost and intensity of this new approach.

There are a number of areas of current research and faculty development. These include:

- □ problem selection and case writing,
- □ tutorial group dynamics and composition,
- □ tutor background and training,
- □ classroom architecture,
- □ library resources,
- □ relative costs including faculty teaching time, and
- □ appropriate problem-solving methods for student assessment.

Recent experimental studies and literature reviews (described earlier) have attempted to identify:

- □ what learning principles are transferable to new 'problem' areas, and from classroom to clinical or other practice contexts;
- □ how well designed a problem-based curriculum has to be in terms of rigorous objectives (and computer databases for monitoring changes and their effects); and
- □ the kind of learning resources (including senior students, 'process' expert tutors) that are optimal for particular levels of student.

But has there been too much emphasis put on 'teaching technology' and research efforts to quantify what makes PBL work – ie, to test the many assertions of the original theory? Despite considerable scientific advancement in the last decade, some 'big picture' evaluation questions remain. What principles of curriculum design and implementation are non-negotiable or unchangeable if a curriculum is to sustain its PBL status? How can we best measure problem-solving processes and outcomes before and after graduation? What difference can we confidently say it makes to the learners, the faculty, the institution and/or the profession in the short- and longer-term?

The experience of the authors of this book suggests that through critical appraisal of many forms of PBL now in use, it is possible to design courses which equip students well for the world of practice. It is rarely possible to translate a given approach from one context to another without considerable modification. However, if sufficient attention is given to building on solid educational foundations and understanding student learning, effective new courses can be established and old programmes significantly improved. In the process, new forms of PBL will emerge which will stimulate further innovation.

Rationale for the book

We aim to present a view of this major innovation in teaching and learning in higher education, to discuss its strengths and limitations, to explore how such an approach can be implemented and to give examples of PBL in practice. Clearly, PBL is not the solution to all curriculum design problems in professional education. At the present time, however, it is the most fully articulated and trialled alternative to traditional practices and it can provide a means of tackling some of the challenges of professional education which have appeared to date to have been quite intractable. These challenges include linking initial education with professional practice, bringing professional skills into the curriculum in a meaningful way and enabling students to develop an holistic view of the practice for which they are being prepared.

In this volume, the experiences are drawn from many countries (Australia, Canada, The Netherlands, New Zealand, the United Kingdom and the United States) and from many fields of practice (architecture, economics, engineering, the health sciences, information science, law, mathematics and computer science and social work). They also come from a variety of higher education institutions: the large and small, some world famous, others known mainly in their local area. The one characteristic the authors share is that they have all been actively involved in either implementing or studying the effects of implementing problem-based and similar kinds of approach to learning. The book draws on much practical expertise as well as the quite extensive research literature, much of which has been reported only in the last decade.

Structure of the book

The book is organized in six major parts, each of which includes chapters from different perspectives. Some contributors are undoubted enthusiasts, others report on how they have found ways to solve problems which confronted them in their particular situation, others are more sceptical and critical of what they see being implemented. All are concerned with how to meet the challenges of professional education and with this approach.

We start Part I by addressing the question: what is problem-based learning? Is it just another method to add to the repertoire of teaching methods which are available? Or is it a much broader approach, encompassing a view of what constitutes professional knowledge and its utilization? Also, is there a best or an optimal way of doing PBL or is there a variety of 'methods' within the overall approach?

Getting started – Part II – is often the major challenge. There is now a great deal of reported experience available on how to design and conduct problem-based courses. Practitioners of PBL who have introduced this approach in often quite hostile circumstances provide guidance on the issues involved and how the approach might be adopted. How is it possible to move from the existing curriculum to one which is different in so many ways? While it might be relatively straightforward in a new institution or a new department, what can be done when there is a weight of tradition and an existing course to be accommodated?

Many issues and questions are raised in Part III. These include: how are problems selected? How should cases be written? How can courses foster the development of students' knowledge structures over time? How can teachers used to traditional methods be trained to cope with very different demands on them? How can we deal with very large classes or funding levels which do not appear to allow us the luxury of small-group teaching? How can the needs of non-traditional students be addressed?

While the sections on introducing PBL concentrate on its extensive use for the whole or large parts of the curriculum, we also include a section which examines some applications of PBL which are more modest in scope, ranging from a single subject to a subject sequence. In Part IV we also explore the many variations on the theme of PBL which can be found in different subjects. The application of PBL is not necessarily the same in those fields of practice in which the focus of study is not the health of a person, but a system or other body of knowledge. Engineering not only has different subject matter from medicine, but it is also organized quite differently and engineers seek different kinds of outcomes from their work.

It is not sufficient to have a teaching approach which is problem-based; assessment of students' performance needs to be consistent with the teaching method. New approaches to student assessment have been developed and existing ones have been adapted to suit the context. One of the main emphases has been on the use of self- and peer-assessment for the reason that it is only when students take responsibility for assessing themselves, can they develop problem-solving skills to use throughout their career (Boud, 1995). Work in PBL contexts has also been responsible for reinvigorating interest in the assessment of professional competence. The evaluation of problem-based approaches is also particularly important. Not only have they been used in fields where the cost of incompetence is high, but substantial innovations always seem to require more justification than traditional practice. Part V discusses the close connection between student assessment and programme evaluation and suggests that it may be timely to develop new ways of thinking about the latter.

Finally, it would be naive to regard PBL as having reached some final stage of development. Indeed, the problem-based approach is certainly not the end of innovation in professional education. Problem-oriented strategies are but one set of examples of the broader category of systemic educational thinking and approaches which emphasize learning from experience. Part VI starts to take us beyond PBL into some speculation about where future trends might lie. There is much unfinished business: what curriculum design issues has PBL not solved? Does it imply a professional world full of 'problems' which have solutions? If learning occurs best in context, how do we prepare ourselves for future contexts which are unknowable? We do not pretend to resolve these questions here, but to lay the foundation for the next challenge.

References

Barrows, H S and Tamblyn, R M (1980) *Problem-Based Learning: An Approach to Medical Education*. New York: Springer.

Berkson, L (1993) Problem-based learning: have the expectations been met? Invited Review, *Academic Medicine*, 10, S79–88.

Bond, D (1985) Problem-based learning in perspective, in D Bond (ed.) *Problem-Based Learning in Education for the Professions*. Sydney: Higher

Education Research and Development Society of Australia.

Boud, D (1995) *Enhancing Learning through Self Assessment*. London: Kogan Page.

Bouhuijs, P, Schmidt, H and van Berkel H (eds) (1993) *Problem-Based Learning as an Educational Strategy*. Maastricht: Network Publications.

Bussigel, M, Barzansky, B and Grenholm, G (1988) *Innovative Processes in Medical Education*. New York: Praeger.

Checkland, P (1981) *Systems Thinking, Systems Practice*. New York: John Wiley.

Feletti, G (1993) Inquiry based and problem based learning: how similar are these approaches to nursing and medical education? *Higher Education Research and Development*, 12, 2, 143–156.

Feletti, G and Lum, C (1997) Ke Ola O Hawaii: a community partnership for health and new challenges for faculty. *Pacific Health Dialog*, 4, 1, 14–21.

Joson, R (1996) Student empowerment and participation in the development of a problem based learning medical curriculum in the Philippines. A poster presentation at the 3rd International Symposium on Problem-Based Learning, Durban, South Africa, 24 September 1996.

Magzoub, M, Schmidt, H, Feletti, G and Nooman, Z (eds) (in press) *Handbook of Community Based Education: Theory and Practices*.

Neufeld, V and Barrows, H (1974) The McMaster philosophy: an approach to medical education. *Journal of Medical Education*, 49, 1040–1050.

Norman, G and Schmidt H (1992) The psychological basis of problem-based learning: a review of the evidence. *Academic Medicine*, 67, 9, 557–565.

Oneha, M, Magnussen, L and Feletti, G (in press) Ensuring quality nursing education in community based settings. *Nurse Educator*.

Paul, R and Heaslip, P (1995) Critical thinking and intuitive nursing practice. *Journal of Advanced Nursing*, 22, 40–47.

Prawat, R (1993) The value of ideas: problems versus possibilities in learning. *Educational Researcher*, 22, 5–16.

Richards, R (ed) (1995) *Building Partnerships: Educating Health Professionals for the Communities they Serve*. San Francisco, CA: Jossey-Bass.

Richards, R, Fülöp, T, Bannerman, J, Greenholm, G, Guilbert, J and Wunderlich, M (1987) *Innovative Schools for Health Personnel*. Offset Publication No. 102, Geneva: World Health Organization.

Schmidt, H and Moust, J (eds) (in press) *Essentials of Problem Based Learning*, Hillsdale, NJ: Lawrence Erlbaum Associates.

Tosteson, D C, Adelstein, S J and Carver, S T (eds) (1994) *New Pathways to Medical Education: Learning to Learn at Harvard Medical School*. Cambridge, MA: Harvard University Press.

Wilkerson, L and Gisjelaers, W (eds) (1996) *Bringing Problem-Based Learning to Higher Education: Theory and Practice*. New Directions for Teaching and Learning No. 68. San Francisco, CA: Jossey-Bass.

Part I
What is Problem-based Learning?

Introduction

Is it possible to provide a prescription of what is and is not problem-based learning? We suggested in Chapter 1 that it is possible to do so at the most basic level. Problem-based learning is an approach to structuring the curriculum which involves confronting students with problems from practice which provide a stimulus for learning. However, there are many possible forms that a curriculum and process for teaching and learning might take and still be compatible with this definition.

Charles Engel sets problem-based learning in the context of an approach to learning rather than a teaching technique. The traditional curriculum suffers from overloading students with an excessive emphasis on memorization. Engel sees problem-based learning as a means of developing learning for capability rather than learning for the sake of acquiring knowledge. He is sympathetic to Barrows' (1986) analysis which associates problem-based learning with a particular strategy based upon small groups with a supportive tutor. This method is, he argues, consistent with adult learning principles and takes account of the need for courses not only to 'teach' well, but also to lay the foundations for a lifetime of continuing education, formal and informal. Engel outlines some of the options, but also emphasizes a particular variant which he helped to develop as one of the pioneers of the University of Newcastle medical curriculum.

An effective curriculum is not just a matter of having a collection of well-designed subjects. There is a need for a clear conceptual map of the domain of learning, a curriculum structure, a means for students to progress through the material and a way of checking to see if both the students and the course are achieving what is intended.

Bob Ross pursues the idea of a framework for the curriculum in more detail and describes a broader framework for problem-based learning. In his view, the tutorial-centred model is self-fulfilling and needs to accommodate a great variety of activities. He is not wedded to a particular model, having been involved in a variety of innovative course designs in different discipline areas at Griffith University. He offers a clarification of terms, referring to problem-oriented, problem-based and problem-solving curricula as a way of distinguishing levels of specification and approach to the role of problems. Ross makes the important point that problem-based learning is one of few approaches to study which makes active use of students' existing knowledge.

Why does problem-based learning generate so much strong feeling, both for and against the approach? Don Margetson, from his philosophical background, sees this as closely connected with a conception of knowledge in problem-based learning which is profoundly different to that found in subject-centred learning. The knowledge which is valued in problem-based learning is that which can be used in context, rather than that which justifies the structure of particular disciplines.

The emphasis of problem-based approaches is on learning processes of enquiry which proceed by asking what needs to be known to address and improve a particular situation. This is quite different from some of the garbled versions of discovery learning which imply that students are supposed to invent knowledge which is already known. The knowledge which students use needs to be identified and applied in the context of the presented situation. Margetson stresses that students will be ill-served if they are given only the products of enquiry without learning how they were derived or how to pursue enquiry. Critical reflection is central to effective action and an enquiry-oriented approach is a useful means of promoting this vital skill.

Reference

Barrows, H S (1986) A taxonomy of problem-based learning methods. Medical Education, 20, 481–486.

Chapter 2

Not Just a Method But a Way of Learning

Charles E Engel

'Pedants sneer at an education which is useful. But if education is not useful, what is it?' Whitehead (1950) wrote in the Foreword to his book *The Aims of Education and Other Essays*. In 1978 the Royal Society of Arts devoted three Cantor Lectures to Education for Capability. This initiated a movement in educational circles in Britain that culminated in 1987 in a programme designated 'Higher Education for Capability'. While higher education has a long tradition of fostering scholarship and of valuing knowledge for its own sake, the primary responsibility of Higher Education for Capability is to assist students in their development of the capability to benefit from and cope with modern life, and to contribute productively to their society. Higher education is thus seen as responsible for producing capable agriculturalists (Bawden and Valentine, 1984), anthropologists, doctors (Neufeld, 1984), engineers (Cowan, 1984) and lawyers (Duncan, 1984). The same is also true for any profession.

However, in order to be capable of benefiting from and coping with modern life and of contributing to society, students need to acquire much more than a store of knowledge in the subjects that relate to their future profession. Those who embark on higher education now will still be in active professional practice well towards the middle of the next century. They will practise during a period of accelerating and massive change. Change, as it relates to their profession, will make self-directed learning throughout their life a *sine qua non*. However, to adapt to change and to participate in change *within* their profession will perhaps be the least demanding of their tasks. They will have to adapt to numerous economical, political, scientific and technological changes and, as members of their profession, to participate in advancing, moderating or retarding changes as they affect their own society and, increasingly more frequently, as they affect the whole of our world. Adapting to, and participating in, change and self-directed learning are composite competences. Each will require the development of a number of component competences, such as the skills of communication, critical reasoning, a logical and analytical approach to problems, reasoned decision making, and self-evaluation.

How, then, are institutions of higher education to meet their challenge of creating capable citizens for the next century (Engel, 1985)? As long ago as 1913, Sir William Osler argued cogently against too great a reliance on courses of lectures and on students' capacity to memorize a growing number of items of knowledge. More recently, Dornhorst (1981) warned with even greater urgency against information overload. Medicine is perhaps one of the most conservative professions where education of its next generation is concerned, but it has also provided some of the fiercest critics of present-day higher education, for example Maddison (1978) and Bok (1984). Bishop (1983) summarized his view of contemporary medical education by saying 'What emerges are physicians without enquiring minds, physicians who bring to the bedside *not* curiosity and a desire to understand, but a set of reflexes that allows them to earn a handsome living'. Can the liberal arts, the natural and physical sciences, or any of the other professions lay claim to a more positive epitaph for their educational practices? However, medicine has also been among the pioneers in the application of problem-based learning as a means towards rectifying the existing situation in undergraduate medical education (Spaulding, 1969) and postgraduate medical education (Jack and Engel, 1976).

Where problem-based learning has been adopted as the mainstay of the curriculum, its application is expected to fulfil two quite distinct purposes. One aim is to use problem-based learning as a method that will assist students towards achieving a specific set of objectives, that is to become capable in a set of competences (Table 2.1) that will be important to them throughout their professional life, irrespective of the precise branch of the profession in which they come to practise.

Table 2.1 *Examples of generalizable competences*

☐ Adapting to and participating in change.
☐ Dealing with problems, making reasoned decisions in unfamiliar situations.
☐ Reasoning critically and creatively.
☐ Adopting a more universal or holistic approach.
☐ Practising empathy, appreciating the other person's point of view.
☐ Collaborating productively in groups or teams.
☐ Identifying own strengths and weaknesses and undertaking appropriate remediation, eg through continuing, self-directed learning.

The second aim is to use problem-based learning as the method of choice, because it is particularly suitable to support the conditions that influence effective adult learning (Table 2.2)

Barrows (1986) has analysed the various educational practices that use the appellation 'problem-based learning'. Only one method of problem-based learning can be expected to contribute optimally to the achievement of the generalizable competences cited above. This is also the only problem-based approach that will consistently support effective adult learning. Tables 2.3 and 2.4 present a condensed illustration of the 'pure' form of problem-based learning (Barrows and Tamblyn, 1980) and may serve to support Barrows' contention.

Table 2.2 *Examples of conditions for effective adult learning*

☐ Active learning through posing own questions and seeking the respective answers.
☐ Integrated learning, learning in a variety of subjects or disciplines concurrently through learning in the context in which the learning is to be applied in real-life situations.
☐ Cumulative learning to achieve growing familiarity through a sequence of learning experiences that are relevant to the student's goals, experiences that become progressively less straightforward but more complex, as well as less non-threatening but progressively more challenging.
☐ Learning for understanding, rather than for recall of isolated facts, through appropriate opportunities to reflect on their educational experiences, and through frequent feedback, linked with opportunities to practise the application of what has been learned.

Imagine a group of some seven first-year students sitting around a table with their tutor. This two-hour session (Table 2.3) is scheduled for early in the week so that a follow-up session (Table 2.4) can take place before the end of the week. The group has elected a scribe who will record the main items of the group's discussion on a flipchart, chalkboard or white board. In some institutions the group will also elect a chair. The tutor is not necessarily an expert in the topic to be

Table 2.3 *The first problem-based group session*

The process	The goals	The outcomes
The tutor starts the session with the presentation of a problem that a new graduate might be faced with. He or she may show a short videotape, play a brief audio recording or distribute a written account.	The students are stimulated to attempt to tackle a realistic problem in the field in which they wish to become competent.	Learning in the context in which it is to be applied is remembered longer and can be retrieved more easily for application in the context in which it is to be used. Relevance to the goals of the learner provides an incentive to learning.
The students are expected to organize their thoughts about the problem and to attempt to identify the broad nature of the problem and the factors or aspects involved in the problem.	The students practise observation and succinct presentation of what has been observed. The students are challenged to begin by applying their existing knowledge and experience.	Learning is cumulative, leading to increasing familiarity. Stimulation of existing knowledge facilitates anchoring of the new knowledge.
After a period of brainstorming in relation to underlying causes, mechanisms and solutions the students are encouraged to examine each of their suggestions more critically.	The students are given constant practice in a logical, analytical, scientific approach to unfamiliar situations.	This facilitates the progressive development of a mental process for the storage, retrieval and application of knowledge.
Throughout the discussion the students will quite naturally pose questions on aspects that they do not understand or need to know more about. These questions will also be recorded by the scribe.	The students are consistently encouraged to identify what they do not yet understand or know and to regard this as a challenge to further learning (not as a disgrace).	Adults find it easier to learn if they can ask their own questions and seek answers to their own questions.

Table 2.3 *Cont.*

The process	The goals	The outcomes
Before the end of the session the tutor will help the students to concentrate on questions that are particularly important at this stage of their studies. The students decide which of these questions they will all want to follow up and which questions they will leave to individuals who will subsequently teach their fellow students.	Students are helped to recognize that nothing is ever learned completely, and that learning in a variety of subjects/topics is concurrent in order to be applied in an interrelated fashion. Also that when a great deal has to be learned, the task needs to be shared with other students.	Integration of learning assists integrated application. Cooperation is fostered instead of competition with colleagues.

Table 2.4 *The second session*

The process	The goals	The outcomes
The tutor starts the session by encouraging the students to reflect on what they have learned towards answering the questions that are still on the flipchart or board. They will start by exploring each others' answers to the questions which all the students had decided to follow up. The next step is to invite individual students to pass on to their peers the insights they have gained from their study of questions which they alone had agreed to tackle.	The students practise exchanging information on the usefulness of various sources of information. They practise sharing new learning by presenting it to their peers and by questioning each other.	They learn how to obtain information from various sources, including consultation of experts. They learn how to convey information and how to question others critically but without causing offence. Active use of what has been learned and feedback on how well new learning has been assimilated help to embed new information in long-term memory. Students learn how to compare their performance with that of their peers and to identify their own strengths and weaknesses.

Table 2.4 *Cont.*

The process	The goals	The outcomes
New knowledge and understanding is applied to the original problem. The students consider whether their earlier conjectures or hypotheses can be reordered or refined, and what further information about the problem will assist in its further exploration. Throughout both sessions the tutor can provide further data about the problem when the students have advanced cogent reasons for access to such information. A definitive resolution of the problem may not be necessary, particularly early in the course.	The students practise the application of new knowledge to the original or a similar problem.	They practise transfer of knowledge through application in a realistic context.
Perhaps, once every two weeks, at the very end of a second session, the tutor will call 'time out' and stimulate the group to reflect on how their studies are progressing, what they have learned, how their learning fits together, how they, as individuals, are progressing and how they have functioned as a group.	Students are encouraged to reflect on what they have learned, how they have learned and how they have contributed to the group's work.	Reflection on recent experiences is an effective method of learning: wisdom through reflection.

explored by the students at this early stage in the course and will thus be spared the temptation to lecture or to give ready answers the students. The tutor's role is to guide and help the students through each of the successive and iterative stages of their discussion and decision making. The tutor will also prevent or remediate difficulties that arise in the dynamics of the group's interaction.

Problem-based learning is thus particularly suited to assist students towards mastery in a range of generalizable competences and to support effective adult learning in the cognitive and affective aspects of a course in higher education. However, the full potential of problem-based learning as an educational approach is dependent upon the design of the curriculum. The quality of the educational environment (Clarke *et al*, 1984) is equally important if the curriculum is to be implemented by the academic staff as it was designed, and if it is to be perceived and used by the students in the spirit in which it was planned (Engel, 1989). Table 2.5 includes perhaps the four most important aspects to be built into a problem-based curriculum.

Table 2.5 *Important components of a problem-based curriculum*

☐ *Cumulative learning*
No subject or topic should be studied in finite depth at any one time, rather it should be reintroduced repeatedly and with increasing sophistication whenever it contributes legitimately to reasoned decision making in a problematic situation.

☐ *Integrated learning*
Subjects should not be presented separately but rather be available for study as they relate to a problem.

☐ *Progression in learning*
As the students mature so the various aspects of the curriculum (eg working in groups, relationship between theory and practice) must change and progress.

☐ *Consistency in learning*
The aims of problem-based learning must be seen to be supported in every facet of the curriculum and in the way it is implemented (eg students must be treated throughout as responsible adults. It should never be perceived as merely the sugar on a bitter pill; summative assessment should be used sparingly and should test for application, not merely recall of knowledge (Feletti *et al*, 1983); adequate human and material resources must be available to support individual, self-directed study).

What are the consequences?

First, it is not possible for separate, subject-centred groups of academics to plan, organize, implement and evaluate a problem-based curriculum. For example, a medical curriculum will need to be faculty-centred, a mechanical engineering curriculum will need to be department-centred. Subject-centred groups will thus need to relinquish some of their power. This loss of power will need to be replaced or appropriately compensated, and budgetary reorganization will be required where financial resources were previously linked to subject-based teaching.

A central education committee will need to ensure that the overall curriculum, with its progression through the years of the course and its philosophy, is implemented through sub-committees that are *not* staffed on the basis of subject representation (Clarke, 1984). Evans (1970) described the overall administrative pattern as matrix management, a well-established system in industry.

Second, each subject needs to develop a 'discipline map' that provides a hierarchical overview of the principles and concepts which the subject experts expect students to learn. When this content has been justified in terms of the curriculum objectives, to the satisfaction of the education committee, it can be transformed into a 'road map' that shows when the principles and concepts are studied, repeatedly, in relation to the agreed progression of problems.

The third and perhaps most difficult task is to devise an overall curricular structure that allows students to progress towards mastery in each of the generalizable competences. The curriculum must help students to do so in the *context* of progress towards mastery in the specific objectives that delineate the responsibilities to be assumed on graduation. The curriculum must also accommodate the concomitant and relevant study of basic subjects which enable students to make reasoned decisions in dealing with the problems that are presented to them.

Fourth, and last, the academic staff need time to become informed about the need for change, the nature of the change and its consequences (Mennin and Kaufman, 1989). They will need opportunities to contribute to the new curriculum, whether for the entire intake of students (Richards and Fülöp,1987) or for a parallel track with a limited number of students in the first instance (Kaufman, 1985; Kantrowitz *et al*, 1987). They will also need opportunities to practise skills that are specific to planning, implementing and evaluating problem-based learning, but especially the skills required for the tutorial process (Barrows, 1988). How better to let problem-based learning be seen to be practised than to place these academics in situations where they are required to deal with problems of planning, implementing or assessment, where they can identify for themselves what they need to learn and are then able to apply their new insights and skills?

One other task remains. As responsible academics we are bound to encounter the questions: Have we planned, implemented and assessed in ways that teachers and students find acceptable? Have the objectives been achieved effectively and efficiently – with an affordable expenditure of time, effort and resources? The new curriculum needs to be evaluated so that it can be improved and refined. It also needs to prove itself, if the heterodox of today is to become the orthodox of tomorrow (Schmidt *et al*, 1987).

Problem-based learning is not a mere method to be taken up and discarded as just another passing fashion. As an essential means for higher education into the next century it is an exacting taskmaster. The reward rests in the intellectual stimulus provided by the high motivation and enthusiasm of our students and graduates (Rolfe, 1984; Boyd *et al*, 1984; Barbeau *et al*, 1990).

References

Barbeau, D, Quesnel, J and Des Marchais, B (1990) Students' perceptions after one year of problem-based learning at Sherbrooke, in Engel, C, Schmidt, H and Vluygen, P (eds) *Annals of the Network of Community Oriented Education, Vol 3*, Maastricht: Network Secretariat, Rijksuniversitcit, Limburg.

Barrows, H S (1986) A taxonomy of problem-based learning methods, *Medical Education*, 20, 481–486.

Barrows, H S (1988) *The Tutorial Process*, Springfield: Southern Illinois University School of Medicine.

Barrows, H S and Tamblyn R M (1980) *Problem-Based Learning: An Approach to Medical Education*, New York: Springer.

Bawden, R and Valentine, I (1984) Learning to be a capable systems agriculturalist, *Programmed Learning and Educational Technology*, 21, 273–287.

Bishop, J M (1983) Speech delivered at the Annual Meeting, American Association of Medical Colleges, 8th November.

Bok D (1984) *President's Report 1982–83*, Boston: Harvard University.

Boyd, H, Adeyemi-Bero, A and Blackhall, R (1984) Acquiring professional competence through learner directed learning, *Occasional Papers No 7*, London: Royal Society of Arts.

Cantor Lectures on Education for Capability (1979): Barnett, C – Technology, education and industrial and economic strength, *Journal of the Royal Society of Arts*, 127, 117–130; Handy, C – The challenge of industrial society, *Journal of the Royal Society of Arts*, 127, 131–142; Burgess, T – New ways to learn, *Journal of the Royal Society of Arts*, 127, 143–153.

Clarke, R M (1984) Organizing an institution to deliver educational programmes designed to achieve capability, *Programmed Learning and Educational Technology*, 21, 301–306.

Clarke, R M, Feletti, G I and Engel, C E (1984) Student perceptions of the learning environment in a new medical school, *Medical Education*, 18, 321–325.

Cowan, J (1984) Learning from mistakes: a pragmatic approach to education for capability, *Programmed Learning and Educational Technology*, 21, 256–261.

Dornhorst, A C (1981) Information overload: why medical education needs a shake-up, *The Lancet*, 2, 513–514.

Duncan, R M (1984) Education for capability: a professional model for practical legal education, *Programmed Learning and Educational Technology*, 21, 288–293.

Engel, C E (1985) Change: a challenge for higher professional education, *Interdisciplinary Sciences Reviews*, 10, 199–201.

Engel, C E (1989) Change in medical education, in Schmidt, H, Engel, C and Schoenmakers, P (eds) *Annals of Community-Oriented Education, Vol 2*, Maastricht: Network Secretariat, Rijksuniversiteit, Limburg.

Evans, J R (1970) Organizational patterns for new responsibilities, *Journal of Medical Education*, 45, 988.

Feletti, G I, Saunders, N A and Smith, A J (1983) Comprehensive assessment of final-year medical student performance based on undergraduate programme objectives, *The Lancet*, 2, 34–37.

Jack, R D and Engel, C E (1976) An analytical approach to postgraduate medical education, *British Journal of Anaesthesiology*, 48, 495–498.

Kantrowitz, M, Kaufman, A, Mennin, S, Fülöp, T and Guilbert, J-J (1987) Innovative tracks at established institutions for the education of health personnel, *WHO Offset Publication No 101*, Geneva: World Health Organisation.

Kaufman, A (ed) (1985) *Implementing Problem-Based Medical Education: Lessons from Successful Innovations*, New York: Springer.

Maddison, D C (1978) What's wrong with medical education? *Medical Education*, 12, 97–102.

Mennin, S P and Kaufman, A (1989) The change process and medical education, *Medical Teacher*, 11, 9–16.

Neufeld, V (1984) Education for capability: an example of curriculum change from medical education, *Programmed Learning and Educational Technology*, 21, 262–267.

Osler, Sir W (1913) Examinations, examiners and examinees, *The Lancet*, 1047–1050.

Richards R and Fülöp, T (1987) Innovative schools for health personnel, *WHO Offset Publication No 102*, Geneva: World Health Organisation.

Rolfe, I (1984) Graduation through education for capability, *Programmed*

Learning and Educational Technology, 21, 268–272.

Schmidt, H G, Dauphinee, W D and Patel, V (1987) Comparing the effects of problem-based and conventional curricula in an international sample, *Journal of Medical Education*, 62, 305–315.

Spaulding, W B (1969) The undergraduate medical curriculum (1969 model): McMaster University, *Canadian Medical Association Journal*, 100, 659–664.

Whitehead, A N (1950) *The Aims of Education and Other Essays*, 2nd edn, London: Williams and Norgate.

Chapter 3

Towards a Framework for Problem-based Curricula

Bob Ross

Barrows, one of the major contributors to the field, defined problem-based learning as:

> ... the learning which results from the process of working towards the understanding of, or resolution of, a problem. (Barrows and Tamblyn, 1980)

Problem-based curricula, then, are those designed to facilitate such learning.

Some time ago I developed a framework for problem-based curricula to use in a course design activity with my colleagues. In this chapter I complement that framework with ideas from a taxonomy reported by Barrows (1986) and apply this expanded framework to two examples of problem-based curricula reported from the Lincoln Institute of Health Sciences in Melbourne (McKenzie, 1987; Svendsen and Wallis, 1987). This results in further additions to the framework. The framework contains a set of ideas and categories for use during the early stages of a problem-based curriculum design activity; it might also serve as a diagnostic tool for examining a problem-based programme in practice.

However, before describing the initial framework, I will put problem-based curricula in a wider context of some other ways in which the terms problem and curricula are related.

Elsewhere (Ross *et al*, 1985) I have drawn a distinction between problem-oriented, problem-based and problem-solving curricula. This was done in the context of some confusion over these terms – particularly as applied to the approach that Griffith University took to curricula in its early days (mid to late 1970s). Very briefly:

- problem-oriented curricula are ones where problems are used as selection criteria for content (and method);
- problem-based curricula are ones where students work on problems as (part of) the course;
- problem-solving curricula are ones where students are given specific training (or development experiences) for solving problems.

Problem-oriented curricula can be presented in an entirely traditional manner, or can involve some (or all) problem-based learning and can (but don't necessarily) involve problem-solving techniques. The latter can, of course, be used in courses that are neither problem oriented nor problem based (in the above meanings of these terms).

I would expect that any degree or diploma (or equivalent) that was made up of sections that contained entirely problem-based curricula could be stated in problem-oriented terms. However, it is quite possible that such a programme would not have been explicitly a problem-oriented one – that is it may not have been focused around a stated problem (or set of problems).

The level of detail of problems will generally vary between the three categories. The problem (or problem set) for a problem-oriented curriculum is likely to be used at the level of a complete programme or at the level of large units (course, subject – depending on terminology – lasting one term/semester/year at least), whereas an individual problem for a problem-based learning curriculum is more likely to be found at the sub-unit level – being used for a section of student work lasting one to five weeks or so. Hence, a number of problems would be employed in a problem-based curriculum that covered a complete unit. The term problem-oriented (although not problem-oriented curricula) could be used at a broader level than a degree or diploma programme. For example, a faculty or even a whole educational institution could be problem-oriented, although at this level the specificity of the problem would decrease considerably.

Problem-solving techniques, on the other hand, are likely to involve problems at the other end of the spectrum – in terms of specificity. They will vary from problems that would be more appropriately described as puzzles or exercises to problems that might approach the level of those used for problem-based sections of a unit. At this latter level the distinction between the two types of curricula may well become blurred, as will be seen from one of the examples given later.

In what is probably the most significant educational approach to problem-based curricula, student work on the problem is explicitly used to get students themselves to identify, and search for, the knowledge that they need to obtain in order to approach the problem. This turns the normal approach to problem solving found in university and college programmes on its head. In the normal approach it is assumed that students have to have the knowledge required to approach a problem *before* they can start on the problem; here the knowledge *arises from work* on the problem. (I will use the term 'problem' throughout, but it should be clear from what follows that this can be a quite misleading description for some of the 'prompts' that are selected to initiate student activity.)

The advantages of this alternative approach will appear throughout this volume, some of them being covered in this chapter. Most of the advantages relate to effective student learning; it is certainly one of the only approaches that makes appropriate use of the knowledge that students bring to any programme (at any level!).

Let me now concentrate on problem-based curricula. I start by distinguishing the following factors that can be treated more or less independently:

- the person or group who selects (designs, devises...) the problem(s);
- the purpose for which the problem is selected;
- the form in which the problem is presented to students;
- the way the resources students require are identified; or
- the processes that students follow in their work.

I identify alternatives for each of these factors in turn below.
  Problems can be selected by:

- the curriculum design team (or individual);
- the curriculum design team, from problems listed by students; or
- students as a group or as individuals.

The problem can be selected:

- in order to ensure that students cover a pre-defined area of knowledge;

- to help students learn a set of important concepts, ideas, techniques;
- for its suitability for leading students to (parts of) the 'field';
- for its intrinsic interest or importance; or
- because it represents a typical problem faced by the profession.

In the first of these alternatives one might ask on what basis the pre-defined area of knowledge is selected. This could obviously be from using a problem-oriented approach – using a (broader) problem to guide the selection. It will be clear that these alternatives are not mutually exclusive for any one problem and certainly they could all play a role in a single curriculum. The same, of course, would be true of the alternatives listed under the first factor.

The form that the problem takes could be:

- an event (or 'trigger');
- a descriptive statement; or
- a set of questions.

In fact, the range of ways in which 'the problem' is presented to students can vary enormously, clearly including a mixture of the three alternatives above.

The resources students will use can be selected by:

- the design team;
- the students, from a resource 'package' (accumulated by the design team); or
- the students from any sources available to them.

Again, many other alternatives could be listed and in approaching any particular problem a mixture of all of them could be employed. Finally, students can work:

- in groups with a tutor (facilitator);
- in groups without a tutor; or
- as individuals.

In most curricula one would expect that students would work in all of these ways on any particular problem. In fact, in all the factors the alternatives are not mutually exclusive and mixtures, or variations, can be as wide as the ingenuity of the design team (and the students) and the resources will allow.

One (but only one) route through these different sets of alternatives is as follows:

- □ The design team selects a problem (as orientation for the unit say),
- □ and uses this to define the area of knowledge to be covered.
- □ Within this and relating to that problem, the team selects an *event* to place before the students,
- □ who (as a group) *define* the problem from the event,
- □ then express the problem as a *question*, or set of questions
- □ which they use to define the *resources* needed, collect these and apply them to the problem.

This last step can involve a considerable amount of iteration: students returning to and redefining the questions a number of times. In like manner, students will return to the original event a number of times before the section is completed. There are, of course, other ways than problem orientation of defining the area of knowledge that is to be covered; external accreditation requirements being one.

Barrows' 'taxonomy' has an explicit medical orientation but, in fact, corresponds fairly closely to the above framework. What he adds is an emphasis on the educational objectives. His four categories for this 'variable' are:

- □ structuring of knowledge in Clinical Contexts,
- □ the development of an effective Clinical Reasoning Process,
- □ the development of effective Self-Directed Learning Skills, and
- □ increased MOTivation.

(The capitals indicate Barrows' acronyms.) These categories can readily be generalized from the clinical context in which Barrows developed them. By a rather self-fulfilling analysis Barrows concludes that problem-based tutorials are the most appropriate procedures to achieve all four objectives.

To some extent Barrows' analysis is as much a taxonomy of teaching-learning methods, within which problem-based learning fits, as it is of problem-based learning itself. I myself have some worry about the use of the term 'tutorial'. I fear that even with the 'problem-based' qualifier it could be a misleading term. For example, the activities covered in Charles Engel's chapter – Tables 2.3 and 2.4 – would not be adequately described as 'tutorial'; they are much more a parallel to (equivalent to?; a simulation of?) a professional planning/strategy meeting. This, indeed, is one of the major advantages of problem-based learning (using this approach) as covered by Barrows' second 'objective' and clearly demonstrated by Cowdroy and Kingsland (1990) in the field of architecture.

From his outcomes emphasis it is not surprising that Barrows adds a brief warning about the importance of the procedures used for assessing student achievement ('evaluation' in Barrows' terms). Assessment plays an important role in determining what students actually *do* in any type of programme; in non-traditional approaches it is extremely easy to find inappropriate assessment methods seriously subverting the intentions of the designers (and of their students).

Barrows also (briefly) draws attention to the 'skill of the teacher' (in the unusual role of 'facilitator') as an 'unplanned variable' (implying that he sees the other variables as planned – a somewhat optimistic view in many cases) and adds a reminder that 'cost and feasibility are also important variables'.

How useful, then, is the above extended framework for examining the two examples of problem-based learning mentioned earlier?

The example of problem-based learning that Linda McKenzie (1987) describes occurs in the final year of a programme. The objectives listed incorporate the final three from Barrows but add an additional category. The problems relate to a (two-week) section of student learning; are selected by the design team; and presented in a form that appears to lie in between 'an event' and a description. Students work as a group with a tutor (as facilitator) supplying additional information on request. As in the framework example students return with information, define the need for more, and return again. As a final-year course one purpose included in selecting the problems is the integration of previous knowledge (which will also, of course, lead to a deeper understanding). This adds a further objective to the framework. The assessment procedure that was selected for this course is one that has been explicitly tested on problem-based learning courses in medicine (Feletti, 1980).

In this example it is clear that the emphasis of the problem-based process is on integration of knowledge (and reinforcement) rather than developing the knowledge initially. If the process had been slightly differently designed this could be categorized appropriately as an example of problem-solving curricula rather than problem-based curricula.

Diana Svendsen and Barbara Wallis (1987) describe a pilot problem-based learning experiment in which 'two of eight groups of first year physiotherapy students … were given a slightly changed schedule of practical classes'. From the brief description in their article this appears to incorporate another use of problem-based curricula. Some of the problem-based sessions are used as motivators and 'advanced organizers' for practical sessions (presumably shared with the other groups of students). Others of their problem-based sessions were of the integrating/applying/reinforcing type identified in the McKenzie example, above. Clearly this idea (using problem-based sessions to prepare for traditional teaching experiences) can be generalized, adding another category to the framework

Describing this pilot programme using the framework, would be as follows:

- □ students are given a description (task) from which to prepare questions as a group or are given a trigger from which to define a problem;
- □ resources are preselected by the design team and the objectives include motivation and integration;
- □ assessment (as in the other example) has used a procedure that has been tested in a problem-based learning context, and in these cases facilitates learning as well as assessing achievement.

The framework has been modified from these two examples and can incorporate a wider range of problem-based curricula than initially covered.

How do developments since the first edition of this book affect the 'framework' presented above? PBL has continued to evolve with many new applications of the idea adding to our understanding. For a good illustration of the evolutionary process, see Alavi (1995). One reason for using 'Towards' in the title of this chapter was to recognize this healthy continuing evolution; the framework needs to adapt to incorporate these developments. As indicated in the description of the framework this has indeed been a feature of its development. So, keeping that necessity in mind, the framework is still a useful tool in the initial development stages of the PBL application or as an analytical tool for examining PBL applications.

Acknowledgements

I acknowledge the contributions of my colleagues from the Centre for the Advancement of Learning and Teaching and Barbara Wallis from the Newcastle Medical School with whom I have discussed these ideas.

References

Alavi, C (ed) (1995) *Problem-Based Learning in a Health Science Curriculum* London: Routledge.

Barrows, H S (1986) A taxonomy of problem-based learning methods, *Medical Education*, 20, 481–486.

Barrows, H S and Tamblyn, R M (1980) *Problem-Based Learning: An Approach to Medical Education*, New York: Springer.

Cowdroy, R and Kingsland, A (1990) Assessment of complex multiple criteria, in *Teaching for Effective Learning, Research and Development in Higher Education*, 13, Sydney: HERDSA.

Feletti, G I (1980) Reliability and validity studies on modified essay questions, *Journal of Medical Education*, 49, 666–72.

McKenzie, L (1987) Problem-based learning at Lincoln Institute of Health Sciences: PBL in the final year of orthoptics, *HERDSA News*, 2 (9), 3–4.

Ross, B, Abel, D, Margetson, D and Sauer, C (1985) Designing academic programs with a problem orientation, in Boud, D (ed) *Problem-Based Learning in Education for the Professions*, Sydney: HERDSA, 69–79.

Svendsen, D and Wallis, B (1987) Problem-based learning at Lincoln Institute of Health Sciences: piloting PBL in first year physiology, *HERDSA News*, 2 (9), 5–6.

Chapter 4

Why is Problem-based Learning a Challenge?

Don Margetson

Why does the idea of problem-based learning evoke remarkably strong, even vehement, reactions? Why does the idea often generate a surge of passionate hostility which tends to swamp what should be the *care*-ful consideration of an educational issue? What is problem-based learning that it generates such reactions? A host of reasons for reactions to problem-based learning may be identified – for example, dislike of evangelistic presentations of the claimed benefits of problem-based learning; anxiety that the outcomes of problem-based learning will not be very tangible; a disruption of habitual and comfortable patterns of work; and, more widely, a general fear of change.

Here, I shall concentrate on only one of the reasons underlying resistance to problem-based learning: a belief about expertise arising, in part, from a conception of the nature of discovery. In the space available here I want to suggest, first, that education has inherited a mistaken understanding of discovery which has led to an impoverished notion of expertise; second, that this understanding is associated with a questionable conception of knowledge, learning and teaching which many have adopted unreflectively and uncritically; third, that this conception has had a pernicious effect on education generally but especially that it has generated ill-founded antagonism to problem-based learning; and, fourth, that part of the explanation for the depth of feeling often manifested in reactions to problem-based learning lies in the implicitness of the conception about the nature of discovery.

By implicitness here I mean, roughly, that teachers on the whole tend unreflectively and uncritically to employ the conception – usually they do not reflect on it. Therefore when something challenges the conception, as problem-based learning does, the conflict between implicit conception and an explicit alternative is experienced more as a felt tension than as a clearly articulated set of sensitively reasoned considerations. This gives rise to emotionally charged reactions, especially as some of the beliefs associated with the conception and its alternative are deep-seated.

The complexity of the issue

Emotionally charged reactions, however, are not the only source of resistance to problem-based learning. It is important to guard against over-simple one-factor explanations. Let us, therefore, note briefly some of the richly interactive, complex influences on individual reactions that have occurred in educational practice. Personal matters can influence an individual's attitude to any kind of education. These include, for example, interest in, beliefs and feelings about, and attitudes towards, education, particularly its purpose and value; approaches to learning and views of teaching; educational and academic background; and personal ambitions and career prospects.

Any or all personal matters may interact with the particular characteristics of the institution in which an individual finds him or herself. Universities, for example, and different parts of the same university, differ in their organization, operation and ethos. Differences are multiplied across national boundaries: there are major differences across cultures and political systems. At any particular time, international political or economic climates, or these climates in a particular country or region, can further complicate an individual's reaction to education.

Against a background of extensive, complicated, and interrelated influences, an individual's reaction to problem-based learning is likely to be anything but simple. Bearing in mind the complexity of issues affecting views of problem-based learning, let us begin by considering what problem-based is.

What is problem-based learning?

At a fundamental level, problem-based learning is a conception of knowledge, understanding, and education profoundly different from the more usual conception underlying subject-based learning. The difference can be seen in the notion of expertise. On a subject-based conception, expertise tends to be seen in terms of content: to be an expert is to know a lot of content; it is to have 'covered' much in one's learning; typically, one has a great deal of propositional knowledge, 'knowledge *that*... (such and such is the case)'. This is a tendency, often strong, but it is not exclusively so. Especially in professional areas 'knowing *how*... (to do something)' is also important. None the less, the often overwhelming tendency in subject-based knowledge is to concentrate on content.

An alternative understanding of expertise may be put this way. Expertise is an ability to make sound judgments as to what is problematic about a situation, to identify the most important problems, and to know how to go about solving or at least ameliorating them. Dealing with problems *presupposes* propositional knowledge but does not equate expertise with it, as subject-based views tend to do. Problem-based learning places emphasis on what is needed, on the ability to gain propositional knowledge as required, and to put it to the most valuable use in a given situation. It does not, therefore, deny the importance of 'content' – but it does deny that content is best acquired in the abstract, in vast quantities, and memorized in a purely propositional form, to be brought out and 'applied' (much) later to problems. Problem-based learning requires a much greater integration of knowing *that* with knowing *how*. Nor does it, as does subject-based learning, prejudge what is relevant subject-matter; there is a sense (but this needs careful interpretation) in which problems select the subject-matter needed to deal with them.

Thus, for example, the problem of global warming raises questions for the special subject-matters of politics, social organization, culture and economics, no less than for chemistry, physics and meteorology. Global warming is a phenomenon which cannot be realistically restricted to some specialist subject-matter although it will require contributions from various specialist areas if it is to be overcome.

Now, it may be thought that this could be conceded while denying its relevance to education. Undergraduates, for example, are not seriously expected to tackle the whole problem of global warming. But this would be a misunderstanding of problem-based learning. In effect, problem-based learning proceeds by asking what needs to be known in order to solve or at least mitigate or manage a problem or improve a problem-situation. Subject-based teaching would begin with a subject – meteorology, say – and require the learning of a great deal of general knowledge of meteorology. In the course of this it might indicate to learners the relevance of some of that knowledge to problems such as global warming. Problem-based learning, by contrast, could begin with the problem of global warming, and in the process of tackling that problem identify what needed to be known (including knowledge of meteorology) in order to deal with the problem.

Three important characteristics of problem-based learning flow from this, and each can represent a significant challenge to some orthodox beliefs about education. Problem-based learning:

☐ *encourages open-minded, reflective, critical and active learning.* This can be a threat to those who prefer passive students in circumstances where the teacher has maximum control over what is to be learned, and who see the loss of this control as a loss of personal power.

☐ *is morally defensible in that it pays due respect to both student and teacher as persons with knowledge, understanding, feelings and interests who come together in a shared educational process.* This can be a threat to those who conceive of education as a largely one-way process of direct information transmission from the knowledgeable teacher to the ignorant student (in contrast to educative processes of a more indirect, guided rather than didactic, nature). It can also be a threat to those who feel uneasy about treating other human beings as persons of equal worth *as persons* irrespective of differences between them, in this case differences concerning knowledge.

☐ *reflects the nature of knowledge – that is, knowledge is complex and changes as a result of responses by communities of persons to problems they perceive in their worlds.* This can be a threat to those holding conceptions of knowledge simply as bodies of information to be transmitted, of teaching as a process of information transmission, and of learning as merely an information-absorption process. It can also be a threat to those who see the notion of 'problem' as restricted, at least in educational contexts, to comparatively small, atomistic, single difficulties.

These are, in Woods' (1985) terms, exercises not problems. In fact, the notion of a problem is relational in that it is always part of a *problem-situation* (as Dewey, 1916, conceived it). 'A problem' refers to what is *problematic* about a situation; it is generally shorthand for a cluster, network or set of interrelated problems and related contextual conditions.

However, it must be observed that problem-based learning sometimes itself attempts to deny this relatedness, when, for example, it attempts to de-contextualize a problem. In academic situations, for example, the cognitive aspects of problems are often regarded as central and are artificially separated from emotional aspects which are sometimes regarded as not relevant to education.

This approach to learning raises the question of discovery, for the learner appears to have to discover knowledge (that is, discover knowledge new to the learner, even though it is well known to experts). Problem-based learning therefore seems to put the learner in a position akin to that of the scientist tackling a problem and making a discovery in the process. But to put a learner in this position is, on one conception of discovery, irrational. To see why this is so, we must consider the conception in question.

A myth of discovery

A widely held conception of discovery is that it is an inexplicable, unpredictable and uncontrollable process (eg Nickles, 1980; Langley *et al*, 1987). Apocryphal stories such as that of Archimedes leaping from his bath shouting 'Eureka!' epitomize this belief. For this is taken to be a paradigm case of discovery. There is no rational process involved. The idea which solved Archimedes' problem is believed to have come to him somehow, almost magically, in a mental flash quite without his trying at the time consciously to solve it. While ideas may indeed suddenly and unpredictably come to mind, the conception neglects any possibility of a connection between knowledge underlying a discovery and that discovery.

The impact of this conception in education is evident in the hostile reactions to problem-based learning often voiced by practitioners of the more traditional subject-based learning. If, they assert, discovery is an unpredictable and uncertain process then how could any responsible educator suggest a form of learning which relies on students' discoveries of solutions to problems? For, surely, wouldn't such an approach to learning lead only to an occasional, random, piece of learning by only a very few students? Wouldn't most students be condemned to learn nothing but frustration and disappointment? And does this not show problem-based learning to be irrational, even absurd?

There is a veritable morass of questionable assumptions in this sort of reaction to problem-based learning. However, the conception of the nature of discovery is important, for if the 'mental flash' theory were an adequate account of discovery, then the hostile reactions to problem-based learning might carry weight. But the account is seriously inadequate. While some discoveries are undoubtedly serendipitous, many are not.

Discovery and justification

The idea that processes leading to discovery are open to rational considerations has undergone a comparatively recent revival. Nickles (1980) recounts the decline of the notion of a 'logic of discovery' by the mid-19th century and the separation of discovery from justification. In this century the separation was significantly reinforced by the distinction between 'the context of discovery' and 'the context of justification' made by Reichenbach in 1938 (Nickles, 1980). Nickles argues against the separation view, ie the separation of discovery from justification that Reichenbach's distinction has been taken to support; the view has, especially as part of a more general logical positivist view, been influential. I want to suggest that education has inherited the separation view, that this is reflected in beliefs about education, and that its effect in education has been seriously harmful. We therefore need to consider the separation view.

Briefly summarized, the argument in support of the separation view is as follows. Any process leading to discovery appears to follow no rational pattern – there is nothing rational about, say, Archimedes deciding to take a bath and thereby accidentally discovering his Principle. All that can be done in such cases is to describe what happened; no norms can be laid down as to how to proceed in order to discover something. Therefore, as factual, descriptive matters, investigations into discovery are matters for psychology, not logic. Justification is different. It is a normative matter, for here we can say what ought logically to be done. Scientific theories ought to be coherent, explain data relevant to them, etc. Justification applies to the products of scientific discovery – typically, published theories. Processes leading to discovery precede this, for they are processes resulting in the product to be justified. Discovery and justification are therefore temporally as well as logically different.

But this raises a key issue in discovery, for, while it may be true that discovery cannot be programmed on the model of programming a computer to achieve exactly what the programmer intends, some discoveries are certainly made systematically as part of a routine search process. The great voyages of discovery of the past were not strictly serendipitous; Magellan, da Gama, Cook and others followed some kind of search pattern or plan just as, for example, in current genetic research a great deal of systematic searching of genetic structures is pursued in order to discover the genes responsible for specific traits.

Nickles criticizes the separation of discovery from justification, arguing that processes of discovery and justification are closely linked. While some discoveries, especially the most radical, will always be serendipitous and confound prevailing norms, many discoveries can be facilitated by appropriate structures of enquiry and critical reflection on progress. Consequently, there can be a methodology of discovery without this amounting to a requirement that there be algorithms for discovery which guarantee success.

The related educational conception

The conception of knowledge, learning, and teaching associated with the separation of discovery from justification is part of a questionable conception of education. And it is incompatible with problem-based learning.

On the conception associated with the separation view of scientific discovery there can be no taught process of educational discovery, for discovery is, by definition, a serendipitous process about which no normative guidance can be given. But the teaching of products which have survived a due process of justification is possible. Teachers are authorities on what has passed the tests of justification, and this authorized material can then be safely transmitted to students. On this view, the task of students is simply to learn as many of the justified products ('knowledge') as possible in order to gain possession, in advance, of the prerequisites for solving problems. There is, on this view, no alternative to learning subjects and trusting that subject-based knowledge will be relevant to any problems that arise.

The conception also has moral implications that are important to education. It does nothing to discourage questionable attitudes towards persons. It is a conception preoccupied with the *products* of enquiry processes, not the processes in relation to the products. In this way it is one-sided. Consequently, it largely ignores the learner as a person, treating him or her instead as a passive object to be filled with products that have passed the justification tests – and it often leads to expressions of impatience (or worse) with the perceived recalcitrance of the 'object' in absorbing the precious information transmitted to it.

The conception lays itself open to what Popper (1979) has disparaged as 'the bucket theory of the mind', the theory which regards the mind as an empty bucket which has to be filled with information before it can 'know' anything; it echoes the misleading model that has plagued education for centuries, the Lockean model of the mind as a *tabula rasa* waiting for the teacher to write on it. This implies a conception of teaching as little, or nothing, other than the transmission of information from active teacher to passive learner.

Problem-based learning stands in contrast to this, and is consistent with Nickles' criticism of the rigid separation of discovery from justification. Discovery by students is possible without this being a haphazard uncontrollable process. Indeed, on Nickles' argument the implication for education is clear: students will be ill-served if they are given only the products of enquiry without learning how actually to pursue enquiry. Identifying, tackling and – where possible – solving problems is a process of discovery that is much more open to sensitive and reasoned activity than that which is envisaged by the conception of knowledge and education inhibited by a separation of discovery from justification.

Conclusion

One source of the strength of reaction to problem-based learning lies in a misleading conception of the nature of discovery, the conception taking discovery to be logically and temporally different from justification. This misleading separation view leads to a narrow notion of expertise as essentially a matter of content. This is reflected in educational practice as an undue emphasis on didactic forms of teaching, and an ill-conceived resistance to problem-based learning deriving from a lack of understanding of what problem-based learning is.

Problem-based learning does not deny expertise; rather it is a way of gaining a vitally important form of expertise. Nor does it deny the importance of subject-matter, or 'content'; rather it places content in an active perspective which *renders* it important.

Problem-based learning is of literally vital significance, in the sense that some problems are of the utmost importance to the very future of human life. The challenge to education is to give those problems the place that their importance merits in human understanding, and to bring the necessary, smaller-scale, detailed aspects of knowledge and understanding into relation with them. Problem-based learning, especially when given fuller scope as problem-based *education*, has a built-in capacity to respond to the challenge. It *enables* discovery – by both learners and teachers – of whatever is most important in the improvement of knowledge and understanding.

References

Dewey, J (1916) *Democracy and Education*, New York: Macmillan.

Langley, P, Simon, H A, Bradshaw, G L and Zytkow, J M (1987) *Scientific Discovery*, Cambridge, Mass: MIT Press.

Nickles, T (1980) Introductory essay: scientific discovery and the future of philosophy of science, in Nickles, T (ed) *Scientific Discovery, Logic, and Rationality*, Dordrecht: D Reidel.

Popper, K R (1979) *Objective Knowledge*, revised edn, Oxford: Clarendon Press.

Woods, D (1985) Problem-based learning and problem-solving, in Boud, D (ed) *Problem-Based Learning in Education for the Professions*, Sydney: HERDSA, 19–42.

Part II
Getting Started

Introduction

This Part describes five personal academic experiences in trying to introduce a problem-based approach to higher education. Each chapter uniquely reflects a different stage of development and varied strategies for getting started. Together, and with some insights from other literature, these chapters begin to outline some important features for guiding future efforts in this direction.

Four chapters are about medical education, and the challenge of changing well-established rites of passage to an omnipotent profession. By contrast, the fifth chapter describes the evolution of a new curriculum for the rapidly emerging profession of information science, within a relatively traditional academic milieu.

In reading these chapters, three key questions emerge. They may help us to broaden our awareness of how challenging the 'getting started' process is, and to see whether we can identify the more crucial elements for 'success' at this stage.

1. Is there a generally useful process for getting any innovation started?

Some helpful ways of thinking about this emerge from literature taken from the disparate realms of commerce and higher education. Kanter (1985), for example, identifies various stages which characterize successful innovations in the business world. First, assess the need for change (within the market or profession), identifying the organizational factors which need to be dealt with in order for any innovation to begin; see how ready the organization itself is for the kind of change being contemplated. The second stage is often much more melodramatic, since it involves strategic planning and specific tactics or options to achieve the desired goals. Effective communication, flexible and autonomous decision making, and frequent monitoring and evaluation of progress are vital operations. More often than not, a special organizational group (unit or task force) is constituted, with the necessary powers and dedication to 'see the innovation through'. Such task forces are typically headed by carefully selected 'mid-level entrepreneurs' (executives), with a remit enabling them to operate across departments in temporarily recruiting a project team, and with a budget that should at least get the project comfortably started. Clear communication channels to a designated senior executive ensures that normal operating routines don't frustrate the team's efforts, and that the company's investment is essentially buoyant.

However, there are some important differences between businesses and higher education institutions (professional schools) in their capacity to promote innovation. Some of these differences may relate to the typical nature of their respective innovations (ie graduates vs hardware), but not all. Commercial organizations rely heavily on innovations for their financial survival. Professional schools do not, although innovative education may be linked to maintaining standards by attracting more, good quality students and faculty (Mangan, 1988). Companies are more autocratic and potentially able ruthlessly to reorganize their management structures, goals and budgets to pursue new directions or innovations. Deliberation and consensus are more integral elements of higher education and its politics. Such features pose substantial inherent resistance to educational innovation, particularly in more traditional settings where other priorities and processes have operated 'successfully' in the past (Fullan, 1982). And, since businesses survive on their profits (ie the new product must prove better than the last) they use more quantifiable methods for evaluating their efforts. This is much less apparent for higher education generally although, as mentioned earlier, it may be due to inherent differences in the innovations themselves and what is being measured. More useful comparisons might be made with organizations providing innovative public services rather than specific products or hardware.

In this respect, a number of questions emerge as common ground. Does the innovation have a simple and clearly stated purpose? Does it have the active support of a senior executive, thereby ensuring sufficient resources to proceed? Does the innovation have an accepted project leader, with enough autonomy to get essential support and negotiate appropriate timelines for progress?

Two chapters in this Part dramatically illustrate the importance of these questions. As the former Director of the New Pathway Project in General Medical Education at Harvard University, Gordon Moore shows the relative merits of applying business principles to such an educational innovation, particularly when dealing with an established faculty. By contrast, the experiences of Steve Little and Chris Sauer, in introducing a Bachelor of Information degree at Griffith University, show the relative disadvantages of not having adequate autonomy, support or confidence from colleagues in the traditional curriculum structures.

How does starting a problem-based approach compare with other educational innovations?

This question may benefit from a two-part answer although, as the respective authors in this Part dramatically illustrate, it is not easy to separate them in practice. The first part relates to other innovative *educational* approaches.

Some useful ideas emerge from a comprehensive report on the introduction of a programmed system of physics instruction at the Massachusetts Institute of Technology (Friedman *et al*, 1976). That report described the rapid translation of a small-scale, well-accepted project within a department to a school-wide programme. Considerable development by a few senior faculty contrasted with the secondary, and less creative, roles that teachers themselves played as students methodically worked their way through the multitude of self-contained instructional units. Despite students' favourable reactions overall to this system, and the acknowledged refinements by the dedicated few, its demise lay with the faculty at large. We might raise further questions from this report alone. Was the transition from project to school-wide programme too rapid? Was it crafted by too few (albeit well-meaning) faculty? Was there sufficient educational support (to help develop and implement the transition)? Were faculty at large committed to trial and improvement – in other words, to making the innovation work? Ultimately, it seems, any educational innovation must be mutually engaging and satisfying to students and their teachers.

The second part relates more specifically to *problem-based* learning which, by its very nature, relies heavily on the above thinking, and more. It challenges teachers' philosophy of how we know things and therefore what and how best to teach students (as elucidated in Don Margetson's chapter in Part I). Traditional, didactic curricula for the technologically oriented professions seem preoccupied with teaching *what* is known, rather than how we know. The scientific method is hailed as a model for research, but not as a way of learning by enquiry based on *students'* personal experience. Consequently, the conflict for those wanting to introduce problem-based learning is how to persuade colleagues to change their attitude from efficient teaching to effective learning.

If there is such a fundamental difference in attitudes, then some further questions arise. Is it even possible to demonstrate or present a balanced view of this new approach? Would faculty be willing to observe or try this experience for themselves? Can they give honest, open-minded reactions and be willing to give student education a higher priority? The respective chapters by Steve Abrahamson and Shona Little illustrate many teachers' hesitancy even in spite of their personal experience or observation of this approach to learning. One reason for their apparent distrust of problem-based learning is their belief that students won't achieve the same old 'gold standards' of knowledge.

The 'gold standards' notion introduces another hazard for those advocating problem-based learning. It relates to faculty's own competence and confidence in teaching their specialization, compared with learning new approaches, in related subject areas. This is not an easy matter to resolve – particularly when problem-based learning appears to devalue academic expertise (normally demonstrated by lecturing to the masses) and replaces it with a softer currency (of guiding small group discussion on a range of issues). Obvious questions emerge. For example, can it be tried on a limited basis, say, in conjunction with other teaching methods? Will there be adequate support (nurturance) for faculty and students when difficulties arise? Will both groups have regular opportunities to plan and review the curriculum together?

Peter Schwartz's chapter clearly describes the mutual satisfaction of faculty and students resulting from his carefully organized and evaluated, discipline-based curriculum. For several years his school was not prepared to take the next step, but Schwartz's patience and steady accumulation of supportive data from students' examination results and perceptions of the coursework won through. They are now developing interdisciplinary, or integrated, curricular subjects. The chapter by Gordon Moore, and that of Chris Sauer and Steve Little, illustrate the same apprehensions from a different perspective. Their respective degree programmes were given the opportunity to develop as integrated, problem-based curricula. However, the same time, effort and inevitable personal frustrations occurred in trying to establish 'new gold'.

One further hazard relates to faculty apprehensions over problem-based learning – namely, pragmatism and benefit. Given the intensive effort required to get started properly, more questions emerge. What facilities or opportunities will teachers have to plan and implement this approach? Will their efforts have the nominal support of the curriculum committee and head of department? LuAnn Wilkerson's research, outlined in Part III and more recently in another volume (Wilkerson and Gijselaers, 1996), not only clarifies our understanding of faculty's motivation for trying PBL but also describes some useful strategies for helping tutors learn from each other's experiences.

Alexander Anderson's chapter introduces another perspective on this 'pragmatism-benefit' issue. Both the Harvard and the University of Hawaii medical school deans very actively supported their respective problem-based programmes. At face value this itself seems important – particularly given the apparent reversal for the other two medical schools described in this Part, whose programmes are struggling for faculty-wide support. Of particular interest here, the Harvard and Hawaiian programmes have adopted quite different curriculum development approaches, but similar initiatives for faculty development. Briefly, Harvard mustered sufficient resources to introduce a pilot project which devised a new curriculum and trained its volunteer faculty concurrently. Hawaii decided to temporarily adopt a well-tried and accepted version (from McMaster), thus focusing its efforts on effective delivery – through intensive tutor training programmes. However, both of these schools now have procedures for the progressive growth and formal recognition of teaching excellence, for consideration in the promotion and tenure of faculty.

What other dimensions seem important in getting a problem-based curriculum started?

Two dimensions spring to mind, incorporating many of the questions raised earlier. One dimension relates to the inertia anticipated in getting started. It is interesting to consider the inherent differences between introducing problem-based learning in an existing curriculum (which also means in an existing faculty or school), and starting a new programme entirely. In rare instances, such as occurred at the University of Newcastle Faculty of Medicine, a newly appointed faculty may dedicate themselves to such a task. More likely, as described by Moore, and Little and Sauer respectively, the new approach must develop under the guiding influence or watchful eyes of a well-established system (eg a school, a department or curriculum committee). The simplest and most likely option, characterized by Peter Schwartz as the Otago Medical School experience, is a problem-based subject controlled by one or more departments. Each chapter in this Part uniquely describes a different model for getting started, the inherent resistance or inertia, and the strategies and effort required at different stages and in various directions. A tentative feeling for the relative inertia, or alternatively the confidence in getting problem-based learning started, can be gauged from the crude aggregate of responses to the checklist of elements, presented in Figure II.1.

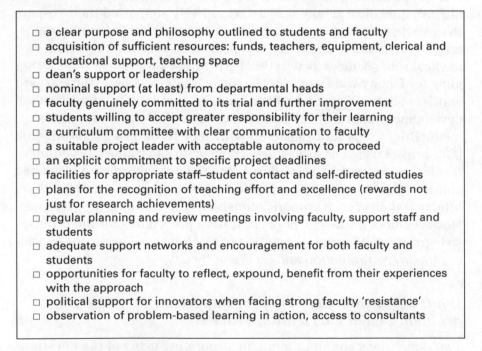

□ a clear purpose and philosophy outlined to students and faculty
□ acquisition of sufficient resources: funds, teachers, equipment, clerical and educational support, teaching space
□ dean's support or leadership
□ nominal support (at least) from departmental heads
□ faculty genuinely committed to its trial and further improvement
□ students willing to accept greater responsibility for their learning
□ a curriculum committee with clear communication to faculty
□ a suitable project leader with acceptable autonomy to proceed
□ an explicit commitment to specific project deadlines
□ facilities for appropriate staff–student contact and self-directed studies
□ plans for the recognition of teaching effort and excellence (rewards not just for research achievements)
□ regular planning and review meetings involving faculty, support staff and students
□ adequate support networks and encouragement for both faculty and students
□ opportunities for faculty to reflect, expound, benefit from their experiences with the approach
□ political support for innovators when facing strong faculty 'resistance'
□ observation of problem-based learning in action, access to consultants

Figure II.1 *Some elements in getting a problem-based curriculum started*

The second important dimension for getting started is the relative resources required. This may be linked to the first dimension, for example in terms of the urgency and extent of the impending change. But a further consideration seems to be the sheer size of the institution involved, and hence the concurrent processes and resources needed to get started. Three of the most prolific and internationally acclaimed schools to have introduced problem-based medical education have relatively small annual intakes of students. Together with faculty dedication to this educational approach, the administration of their respective programmes (eg staffing, teaching areas, educational support, learning resources, timetabling) is relatively much simpler in their context. McMaster, New Mexico and Newcastle medical schools have demonstrated that the tutorial process is technically possible (and sustainable) for class sizes up to 80 students. Harvard Medical School appears to have successfully engineered a new curriculum for twice that many students, ably assisted by a revamped office of educational support and a new office of educational development.

There is no simple answer to the optimum range or recommended maximum student numbers, nor the ratios of faculty and educational support staff needed. These and other resource issues have been particularly challenging to nursing and social work faculty intending to adopt PBL (Feletti, 1993). There will be inevitable frustration and inertia in bringing a new approach to fruition in a large school. However, good leadership and a broad base of dedicated faculty can have an extraordinary impact. But there are also disadvantages in being a relatively small school or programme. For example, the preparation, teaching and evaluation of subjects is labour-intensive for faculty – unless strategies, such as those described in Alexander Anderson's chapter, are adopted to reduce this load. Anderson's new postscript to his chapter indicates that regular opportunities for curriculum revision by faculty at all levels have enhanced their sense of ownership of the new curriculum. Put another way, 'getting started' has been an exercise in problem-based, faculty development.

In summary, some key questions emerge from our collective wisdom about getting educational innovations started. Other questions relate specifically to introducing problem-based learning. Paradoxically, higher education institutions and their faculty are not geared well for introducing substantial curriculum change. The difficulties seem even more pronounced for initiatives like problem-based learning in traditional settings. However, this does not mean it is impossible. More schools are making serious attempts, and reporting their endeavours

– warts and all. From this literature emerges a broad range of strategies and structural approaches appropriate to particular contexts, from which principles can be derived by an institution wishing to adopt problem-based learning. Hopefully, the unique profiles depicted in the following chapters will encourage institutions and faculty alike to consider more flexible administrative arrangements supportive of such innovations.

References

Feletti, G (1993) Inquiry and problem-based learning: how similar are these approaches to medical and nursing education? *Higher Education Research and Development*, 12, 2, 143–156.

Friedman, C P, Hirschi S, Parlett, M and Taylor, E F (1976) The rise and fall of PSI in physics at MIT, *American Journal of Physics*, 44 (3), 204-211.

Fullan, M (1982) *The Meaning of Educational Change*, New York: Teachers College Press, Columbia University.

Kanter, R M (1985) *The Change Masters*, London: Unwin Paperbacks.

Mangan, K S (1988) Decline in medical school applications seen as damaging quality of health care, *The Chronicle of Higher Education*, June 15, 24 (40), A29-31.

Wilkerson, L and Gijselaers, W H (eds) (1996) *Bringing Problem-Based Learning to Higher Education*. New Directions for Teaching and Learning No. 68. San Francisco, CA: Jossey-Bass.

Chapter 5

Good Planning is Not Enough

Stephen Abrahamson

The history of American medical education suggests that it is difficult at best and impossible at worst to change the curriculum. Two different waggish commentaries state it very well. In the early 1950s, the statement was that 'changing curriculum in the medical school is like trying to move a graveyard.' Nobody knew (or apparently cared) whose bones they were, but surely they were somehow to be revered and not disturbed. Late in the 1960s, a new statement emerged: 'changing curriculum in the medical school is like rearranging the lifeboats on the Titanic' – a reference to the fact that many schools were busy with curriculum change, but that the changes were largely cosmetic and would contribute little to avoiding potential educational disaster.

The history of American medical education also suggests that a strong central administrative action offers the best hope for significant curriculum development. As a start, one need only consider the dramatic outcome of the famous Flexner Report and its application and implementation by deans of the medical schools. And the next major change – chronologically 40 years later – took place at Case Western Reserve University School of Medicine as a result of the actions of the dean, including the fortuitous replacement of a significant number of department chairmen by the dean at that time. The late 1950s and the 1960s became a time of institutional self-study and cosmetic curriculum change. The University of Southern California School of Medicine (USC) was one of the many American medical schools caught up in the excitement and enthusiasm of that era and in 1969 it implemented its own curriculum change.

In the following 15 years the curriculum at USC was not studied or significantly changed from the organ-system programme which was introduced in 1969 after five years of study and deliberation. Then in 1985, a new medical school administration encouraged the newly appointed Associate Dean for Curriculum to consider possibilities for a new curriculum. (It should be noted parenthetically that there had not been an Associate Dean for Curriculum, or any other administrative officer in such a capacity, for 20 years!) Interestingly enough, the five years spent on the 1969 change had fallen just short of being adequate for that change to fulfil what planners had hoped for. Thus, in considering what might need to be done for the future, planners in 1985 recognized that adequate time for planning, deliberation, evaluation and decision making was essential – even more so when the change might be in the direction of a problem-based curriculum.

Consequently, planners took a number of steps to enhance the possibility of success:

1. Department chairmen were interviewed by the new Associate Dean for Curriculum.
2. New members were appointed to the Medical Education and Curriculum Committee.
3. A 'Long-Range Curriculum Planning Committee' was established to consider alternatives.

Out of the deliberations of that last Committee came the idea that USC ought to offer medical students a choice between several different curricula, one of which could be a problem-based curriculum. The strategy was to encourage faculty to consider a 'package' of curriculum options.

That 'package' included 'something for everybody' in an effort to generate broader enthusiasm and support. Four separate working groups were established to plan these disparate curricula:

1. a special curriculum for medical students interested in academic medicine (not an MD-PhD programme);
2. a combined BA-MD course for students committed to medicine at the point of graduation from secondary school;
3. a special MD-residency programme which might minimize (or elim-

inate) the 'pre-residency syndrome', a nationally recognized problem; and

4. the problem-based curriculum. Working groups were asked to consider a number of questions dealing with optimum number of students, faculty time-and-effort required, institutional resources needed, and the like.

The working group on the problem-based curriculum began its work with several principles in mind.

1. Faculty had to learn what the problem-based curriculum really is.
2. Political allies had to be located and recruited.
3. A key cadre of enthusiasts had to be developed.
4. Funds for implementation had to be obtained.

Members of the working group were asked to visit the University of New Mexico and participate in one of their training programmes for tutors. In addition, several other interested faculty also went to New Mexico. In all,10 different faculty members attended and returned all visibly impressed. Following those visits, three demonstrations of problem-based tutorials were conducted at USC for a number of invited faculty. Those invited to the demonstrations included all department chairmen, all associate and assistant deans, all members of the Education Policy Committee, and several other 'key' faculty members. In all, almost 60 faculty members had the opportunity to observe a problem-based tutorial conducted by tutors from the University of New Mexico. The 'students' in the demonstrations were pre-medical students from the University of Southern California – students who had never studied medicine or any of its basic sciences. Each demonstration involved an initial tutorial at which students considered a clinical problem and identified 'learning issues' and a second tutorial one day later at which the students shared the results of the work they had done overnight. Observers then had the opportunity to ask questions and discuss the experience with the tutor and the students.

While all of this was taking place, bibliographies, reprints of key articles and other reference material were circulated to faculty members. Discussions were held in committee meetings and particularly in the Faculty Executive Council. Videotapes of all demonstrations had been made and were available for review by any interested faculty members. Thus, the planning group believed that orientation had been treated as well as possible.

In the spring of 1989, almost four years after the initiation of the long-range planning effort, the Faculty Executive Council, including all 23 department chairmen, held one more – last – review; they concluded the discussion by 'tabling' the motion for implementation of all four curricula and requesting that the newly formed Educational Policy Committee take it under advisement. Clearly, the usual sources of resistance were in evidence. For instance, one chairman was overheard remarking to another chairman as they left the meeting, 'I don't understand this problem-based curriculum, but I know it won't work' – a wonderful example of xenophobia. Another chairman, who almost never attended these meetings (because they bored him) did make an effort to be present for this meeting after he learned what was on the agenda in order to announce that his department was unanimously opposed to the problem-based curriculum, although he had not made the effort to observe a demonstration tutorial – a good example of inertia. Still one other chairman asked, 'How do we know such a curriculum would even work?' When the answer came, 'McMaster has been doing it for 20 years and reports of their programme were distributed to everybody here', the response was, 'Yes, but how do we know whether it works?' ('I don't care about the facts; my mind is made up.')

Clearly, much more orientation and education ought to have been provided. Additionally, much more diplomacy ought to have been included: building of support, enlisting of favourable reviews, and the like. Finally, stronger administrative statements might have helped, along with broad student support. On the other hand, what steps could have been taken to make a difference in persons who are so closed-minded, as the following illustrates? One of the basic science teachers who visited the University of New Mexico returned so visibly impressed that he reported – gratuitously – that he had 'never seen medical students so "turned-on" and so enthusiastic and so wrapped up in learning activities'. When the committee then tried to enlist his continuing support of the efforts to promote an alternate curriculum track (for 24 students) at USC, his comment was, 'Oh, those students were really enthusiastic about learning and about basic sciences, but it would never work on our students!'

Once again, the tragic side of curriculum planning is revealed: in the final analysis, curriculum planning is not a logical or educational process; curriculum planning is an emotional and political process.

Any number of important insights were gained through this experience. The most important, of course, is verification of the observation that curriculum development in a medical school is a political and emotional process. It was interesting, for instance, that the chairman of one department, who believed that his department should have had two more faculty members, tried to use the consideration of the problem-based alternative curriculum as a political weapon. A member of his department was named chairman of the problem-based curriculum committee because of his excellence in teaching and his concern for medical students. He arrived at the second meeting of the committee with the announcement that his chairman had informed him that his name would not be submitted for consideration of promotion unless he resigned from the committee (not just the chairmanship) 'in order to devote time to his research'. However, had the dean 'restored' one or both of the faculty slots the chairman believed were due to him, that little incident would not have taken place.

It was fascinating to hear the reaction of one of the most highly regarded (and dedicated) basic science teachers who observed the problem-based tutorial. He commented that he would not be able to be a tutor because he did not know the content well enough in all the areas students were discussing. When students, tutor and educationists present at the demonstration explained that being a specialist in the content areas was not necessary – in fact, perhaps a handicap – the teacher replied that he would not be comfortable, would not try it out, and would resent the perceived 'subservient' role of a resource person. He eventually cast a negative vote and was used by the resistance as an example of just how 'bad' the whole idea was, considering the fact that the teacher annually voted 'the best basic science teacher' by the students was so adamantly opposed to the idea!

It would be an error – nay, a disservice – to leave the reader on such a negative note. Those involved in planning and promotion learned much about both the problem-based curriculum and the politics of curriculum change. The idea is far from 'dead' and the concept is indeed alive and well. Some of those who became committed to the virtues of problem-based tutorials are quietly introducing this form of instruction in their own respective areas of teaching. Changes in department chairmanships offer hope of a more favourable review in the future. Like any other significant innovation, this curriculum approach is bound to meet with mixed reviews and will require careful emotional nurturance and political dexterity. Indeed, it is only through emotional nurturance and political dexterity that this educationally sound and logically correct problem-based curriculum can be successfully introduced.

Chapter 6

Persevering with Problem-based Learning

Peter Schwartz

Problem based learning *here*? That was a question I asked myself on a number of occasions about the course I teach in clinical biochemistry. But it was also a question that was asked seriously at faculty level in 1987. The Otago Medical School (in Dunedin, New Zealand) would seem an unlikely place even to consider such an approach: it has a history dating back to 1875; a traditional curriculum with a heavy emphasis in the pre-clinical years on lectures and laboratory classes; a definite break between pre-clinical and clinical components; and a predominantly departmental organization. Yet both the faculty and I asked the same question, although the histories and outcomes were very different.

The history of my asking and answering the question spans 20 years. (For details and references, see Schwartz, 1989b, 1990.) The first stage involved simply recognizing that something was wrong with my teaching and then discovering what I might do about it. When I arrived at Otago Medical School in the early 1970s, the course in clinical biochemistry was the traditional mix of lectures and laboratory classes. Although I introduced popular innovations to both these types of session, I became dissatisfied as I learned about education and grappled with the question of what medical education was all about. I decided that it was not merely the transmission of masses of information to passive students, to be recalled or recognized on examination and then mostly forgotten.

I read about problem-based learning and was immediately attracted by the ideas of using cases as the appropriate context for learning basic as well as clinical sciences and of having students learn actively and cooperatively in small groups. However, I saw no prospect of the introduction at Otago of an innovation as far-reaching as problem-based learning. Nevertheless, I introduced to my own teaching some of the features of problem-based self-directed learning. I abandoned lecturing, had the students learn independently (from study guides, books and articles) and, in classes and examinations, had them apply the material they were learning to clinical cases and problems.

This early phase required considerable perseverance. Because I was the only teacher in the Medical School actively developing independent learning, many students complained about my approach. On evaluation forms my ratings fell and comments like the following appeared: this lecturer doesn't lecture, so he should be fired; this idea of getting us to learn on our own will be important later, but not now, so we should have lectures to present what we need to know. I despaired because, while I had long since realized that colleagues and administrators were at best indifferent to my ideas on medical education, I had always counted on the students to appreciate my efforts. Now that even they were not supportive I was tempted to give in and go back to a traditional approach.

However, even as I despaired I learned some important lessons. I saw that despite their complaints our students *could* do the work and that they *could* learn without depending on me to pre-digest and feed them everything. My use of the Keller plan (an individualized, self-paced, mastery learning system that I used with a small group of students each year from 1979 to 1987) demonstrated that they were much more capable and thoughtful than I had realized.

By the mid-1980s I had reached the stage where I hoped that I could demonstrate what I had observed to my colleagues. For many years I had felt confident that a successful demonstration of a working programme was more likely to convince others than would any amount of theoretical argument. In any event, by this time I had been able to implement in my own course a method which involved a large class in independent learning, small group activity, and problem solving (Schwartz, 1989a). I began to hope that, at least for a part of this one course, a form of problem-based learning could be further developed.

It was at about this time that rapidly developing events at faculty level had an influence (Schwartz, Heath and Egan, 1994). In the early 1980s, more teachers, students and administrators in the School became interested in the curriculum and in medical education. We had just about reached a critical mass of concerned people when, early in 1985, the medical faculty began a series of retreats and workshops on the curriculum. Deficiencies were identified, change was seen as necessary, and teachers listened attentively to students' forthright complaints about the current course. These included student boredom; an overemphasis on examinations; the lack of staff/student contact; the lack of coordination in the course; the impediment which depart mentalization provides to change and to integration; and the lack of feedback on progress. Faculty members generally agreed that the curriculum was overloaded: too much formal teaching time and too much material.

At these meetings faculty members perceived problem-based self-directed learning to be a likely solution to many of the defects in the curriculum. A Medical Education Development Unit was established and several working parties were given the task of investigating the feasibility of introducing problem-based self-directed learning into the first pre-clinical year of the medical course as early as 1988. During a hectic (but uniquely satisfying) interval, groups worked to write objectives for the course, to plan the types and sequence of problems that could be used in such a course, to design a programme of early clinical contact, and to decide the place of elective work in the new course. Substantial numbers of faculty from a wide variety of disciplines were involved. Meanwhile, some of us who were particularly interested in the practical aspects of problem-based learning proposed and organized a series of activities in which students and faculty could experience problem-based self-directed learning in small groups. During 1986 and 1987, large numbers of staff and students took part in activities that ranged from two highly concentrated single-day exercises (which we called case-based learning days – Schwartz, Fiddes, and Dempster, 1987), through a 50-hour programme where Barrows' (1985) problem-based learning modules were used, to a week-long trial where a prototype integrated problem, which we had designed ourselves for possible use in our proposed course, was used with a group of incoming medical students. This latter exercise was recorded in its entirety on videotape and extracts were shown to staff members in interested departments.

The culmination of this whirlwind of activity was the preparation and circulation in July 1987 of a lengthy discussion paper which considered whether there should indeed be problem-based self-directed learning at Otago Medical School. So what were the consequences?

On the one hand, while a lot of enthusiasm remained and there was clear recognition of the effort that had gone into the preparation of the discussion paper, it was obvious that departments would not accept a wholesale change in the curriculum to problem-based self-directed learning. However, departments did look at their own teaching practices and they incorporated a few ideas consonant with those expressed in the discussion paper. All the same, the most substantial initial change towards a form of problem-based learning (by the Physiology Department in 1987 for the first pre-clinical year – Heath, 1988) was more a response to positive experiences by staff during the demonstration exercises in problem-based learning than to the ideas in the discussion paper. The physiology programme was so well received by staff and students that other pre-clinical departments began to develop their own modifications. Although only ours has been as successful as physiology's, the faculty decided to build on the various departmental initiatives and to abandon any thought of introducing an integrated, full-scale course of problem-based learning across departments.

On the other hand, the discussion paper on problem-based learning unexpectedly provided the stimulus for a profound change to our second pre-clinical year course in clinical biochemistry. My departmental colleagues considered the discussion paper, the early success of the programme in physiology and the markedly positive student response to that programme, and their own experiences in the exercises in problem-based learning. As a result, they agreed that I and one other staff member should prepare a proposal for a course emphasizing small group work with cases and problems. We suddenly moved in one gigantic step to the limit I felt we could achieve within a departmentally based curriculum.

Since 1988, we have replaced our previous lectures and laboratory classes with our version of small group, problem-based learning (Schwartz, 1989b). In it, we encourage the students to use the cases and problems which we provide as guides to what to study in preparation for each of 13 two-hour sessions. At a session, the students work in small groups in a relaxed atmosphere, sharing their knowledge and cooperating to help each other in their understanding by applying what they have learned to the cases and problems. The tutor takes a facilitative role and contributes mainly by introducing brief new cases or problems to be tackled on the spot and by helping clear up any misunderstandings of important concepts.

There have been compromises, so that our course is closer to 'case method' than to optimal 'problem-based learning' as defined by Barrows (1986). We had to 'go it alone' as a department because the faculty could not agree on any integrated programme of problem-based learning. My colleagues wanted our sessions to be discipline specific, partly because of their concern about clinical biochemistry as a coherent discipline and partly because of their feelings of insecurity about working in other disciplines. We have provided limited guidance to the students (brief statements of objectives for the various topic areas, lists of possible references, and self-assessment quizzes on the content of the topics raised by the problems and cases) because of their lack of experience of full self-directed learning and to provide them with a basic source of security in their study.

The results have been amazing. Students and faculty were delighted with the method from the outset and student performance on assessments improved immediately (Schwartz, 1989b; 1990). Both of these positive outcomes have been maintained (Egan *et al*, 1994; Schwartz *et al*, 1994). Compared to the old course, we have observed more positive attitudes towards clinical biochemistry, more enthusiasm among the students, and more cooperation among the students and between staff and students. Student ratings of the course and of *every one* of the tutors have been extremely high. Written and oral comments by the students have been overwhelmingly favourable. Newly appointed staff have slotted into and accepted the course with ease. Other courses (in clinical chemistry for medical laboratory science students, in pathology and in pharmacy) have adopted key elements of our course with similar successful outcomes (Egan *et al*, 1994; Schwartz *et al*, 1995).

My impression is that the key reasons for the success of our course include:

□ the careful planning of the programme from the outset and then the contribution by all teaching staff to the preparation of the new course;

□ the inclusion in the programme of compromises to suit the concerns of faculty and students;

□ a willingness by all teaching staff in the department seriously to try the innovation and to keep an open mind about it while doing so;

□ a tradition in the department of experimentation with teaching methods so that change was not perceived as threatening;

□ the decision to have our new course *replace* the old one rather than be an addition to it.

One of the most important outcomes has been the demonstration that an effective type of problem-based learning can be used successfully in a single discipline within a predominantly departmentally structured medical school. Whether our model (or indeed any of those currently operating at Otago) will lead to an integrated curriculum incorporating problem-based learning remains to be seen. There are promising signs, with the incorporation of more small-group, problem-based work into a new integrated modular curriculum scheduled to begin at Otago in 1997. In any case, I agree with Anderson (this Part) and am more convinced than ever that participation by staff and students in a well-designed programme of problem-based learning is more likely to be persuasive than is theoretical argument.

References

Barrows, H S (1985) *How to Design a Problem-Based Curriculum for the Preclinical Years*, New York: Springer.

Barrows, H S (1986) A taxonomy of problem-based learning methods, *Medical Education*, 20, 481–486.

Egan, A G, Schwartz, P L and Heath, C J (1994) Program components that encourage students in a traditional medical curriculum to accept innovative teaching methods. *Teaching and Learning in Medicine*, 5, 154–60.

Heath, C (1988) Recent developments in the Otago Medical School curriculum, *Bulletin of the Australasian and New Zealand Association for Medical Education*, 15, (3), 18–22.

Schwartz, P L (1989a) Active, small group learning with a large group in a lecture theatre: a practical example, *Medical Teacher*, 11, 81–86.

Schwartz, P L (1989b) The right place at the right time: an example of innovation in medical education, *Teaching and Learning in Medicine*, 1, 171–175.

Schwartz, P L (1990) The changing face of medical education at Otago Medical School: the contribution of clinical biochemistry, *New Zealand Medical Journal*, 103, 269–271.

Schwartz, P L, Fiddes, T M and Dempster, A G (1987) The case-based learning day: introducing problem-based learning into a traditional medical curriculum, *Medical Teacher*, 9, 275–280.

Schwartz, P L, Heath, C J and Egan, A G (1994) *The Art of the Possible: Ideas from a Traditional Medical School Engaged in Curricular Revision*. Dunedin : University of Otago Press.

Schwartz, P L, Lovell-Smith, C J and Loten, E G (1995) Small group, case-based clinical biochemistry course for a medical laboratory science curriculum, *Clinical Chemistry*, 41, 1193–1195.

Chapter 7

Conversion to Problem-based Learning in 15 Months

Alexander S Anderson

Introduction

The John A Burns School of Medicine at the University of Hawaii converted from its traditional curriculum to problem-based learning for the entire incoming class of 56 students in 1989. We adopted the McMaster model of small group, self-directed, tutorial-based learning. That process of change was accomplished in 15 months. This case history will focus on the major events in the chronology of change, and the strategy and tactics which were successful in our situation.

Background

The School of Medicine was established at the University of Hawaii in 1967 as a two-year programme in the biomedical sciences. Students then transferred to mainland schools in the United States for their clinical education, much as one did to the finishing schools of Europe at the turn of the century.

By legislative mandate, the programme expanded to a four-year, degree-granting status in 1973, and graduated its first class in 1975. Since then more than 1,000 physicians have obtained their MD degree in Hawaii. Many are from ethnic groups who are under represented in medicine, including native Hawaiians, locally born Filipinos, and residents of American Samoa, Guam and the recently federated states of Micronesia.

That developmental process, however, entrenched a traditional curriculum of departmental offerings. Students were in residence at the biomedical sciences building on the main campus for two years of linear, lecture-oriented, basic science courses. Abruptly, they moved to a geographically separate two years of clinical clerkships, preceptorships and electives. These were distributed throughout six community hospitals and clinics in urban Honolulu.

Table 7.1 *Chronology of change*

	1988
May	AAMC San Diego workshop on problem-based learning
	University of Hawaii Task Force on Problem-based Learning appointed
September	Proposal to faculty for curricular change
	General faculty meeting and discussion
October	University of New Mexico problem-based learning workshop
November	Demonstration of tutorial process and consultation 1
December	Executive Committee approval to proceed with planning
	1989
March	Executive Committee approval to implement problem-based learning tutor-training workshop 1 and consultation 2
June	Tutor-training workshop 2 and consultation 3
	Dr Gulbrandsen appointed Dean
September	Onset of problem-based learning

Chronology of change

In 1988, Christian L Gulbrandsen, MD was appointed Acting Dean of the School of Medicine. In May of that year he attended the Association of American Medical Colleges' (AAMC) Management Education Programme in San Diego. The emphasis at that workshop was on managing institutional change and introducing problem-based learning. He selected to take with him four faculty who were the influential teachers and prime movers in gross anatomy, biochemistry, pathology and internal medicine. Upon their return I joined that group, and we were appointed as a Task Force on Problem-based Learning. It was chaired by the Acting Dean. That Task Force identified the problems in our traditional programme, studied existing curricular models, and in September 1988 presented a written proposal to the faculty for conversion to problem-based learning as a solution to these problems. In

December, the Executive Committee of the School of Medicine directed us to proceed with the planning of that new curriculum. In March 1989, the Planning Group, which I chaired, presented the curricular outline with a plan for implementation.

We were authorized by the Executive Committee to begin the new programme with the entire incoming class in September 1989. This rapid change was accomplished by an early strategic decision to concentrate our resources on faculty development, specifically on tutor training. That decision acknowledged the tutorial process as the core experience in problem-based learning. It recognized that faculty endorsement of this change required both acceptance of and skill in performing the tutorial role. The tactics employed were consultation, demonstration and broad interdepartmental participation. Persuasive and substantive consultation was obtained from McMaster University under the leadership of Dr Bill Shragge, Chairman of the McMaster MD Program. Curricular materials (Health Care Problems) were purchased and adapted to our local needs. A two-day demonstration of the tutorial process by Dr Shragge with six first-year students in front of 90 University of Hawaii faculty converted many sceptics. They saw that our students could perform impressively in a self-directed, participatory, problem-based format!

Participation has been the most effective vehicle of change. First, four faculty leaders accompanied Dr Gulbrandsen to the AAMC workshop. Next, five others, including the chairmen of anatomy, biochemistry, physiology, pharmacology and myself, attended a University of New Mexico workshop on problem-based learning. This interdepartmental group led the subsequent planning and implementation process. Thirty-five additional faculty joined on-site tutor-training workshops in March and June of 1989. These faculty development workshops were skilfully led by a three-man team from McMaster, and utilized University of Hawaii students for the tutorial practice sessions. Most faculty agreed that experiencing the tutorial process, like basic training in the military, created a sense of commitment to the new educational philosophy. That participation also provided the necessary critical mass to begin the new curriculum.

Strategies for change

Several key decisions which were made early in our planning have continued to provide direction at moments of uncertainty. Others emerged after we had gained some experience, and, indeed, are continually evolving as the problem-based curriculum develops. I would identify the following factors as those which have been most influential.

Leadership of the Dean

Early in his tenure as Acting Dean, Dr Gulbrandsen pointed the way to problem-based learning, but referred the decision to the faculty. He demonstrated that innovation in education was not only acceptable but his first priority. He proposed that those who selected education as their career choice would be rewarded. He supported the change process by his enthusiasm and participation, and by fiscal measures which provided for consultation, faculty development, curricular materials and learning resources. He approved the establishment of an Office of Medical Education for central development, coordination and ongoing assessment of the programme. He recruited me, a long-time ally in the Department of Medicine, to direct that office and head the planning and implementation process. He even served as a tutor in Unit I of the new curriculum. His educational philosophy was perhaps the prime reason for his selection by the faculty and the university as Dean in June 1989.

Successful choice of consultant

The relationship between the home team and our consultant, Dr Shragge, gelled quickly. He had been one of the faculty at the AAMC workshop who tutored the group from Hawaii. He was dynamic, inspirational and substantive. He provided a clear blueprint, but also knew when to step aside and let us introduce our own ideas. His first visit resulted in continuation of the analysis of our political structure and development of a plan for change which had started in San Diego. Continuing consultations have provided review of interim progress, reassurance and the opportunity to address problems as they emerge.

Early decisions

A number of early decisions influenced our rate and direction of change. We studied and used the experience of others to make decisions, to anticipate problems, and to make choices when alternatives existed. The most available prototypes for us were the McMaster and

University of New Mexico models (Neufeld *et al*, 1989; Kaufman *et al*, 1989).

Total conversion to problem-based learning was chosen rather than a dual-track system. Ours is a small school with insufficient faculty to sustain two parallel programmes (224 students, 109 state-funded faculty positions). We also wanted to avoid dividing faculty and student allegiance between competing educational processes.

Recognizing that early momentum might wane, we decided not to plan forever. Rather, we developed a critical mass of interested and key faculty, and began the new programme. My intuitive feeling was that faculty enthusiasm about their experience with students would induce others who harboured initial reservations to join us. That hunch was accurate.

We purchased the McMaster curriculum, ie Health Care Problems, learning resources and evaluation instruments, and implemented these with minimal changes. We decided to use a proven curriculum which resulted from 20 years of experience rather than burden our faculty with the development of new problems at the outset. We installed a mechanism to monitor the programme and to gather information regarding omitted objectives, content areas and learning resources in order to modify or introduce new problems in the future. Effort and resources were invested in faculty development, and specifically in tutor training. This focus provided the opportunity for them to acquire the necessary knowledge and skills for participation in problem-based learning. It effectively addressed the fear of the unknown, and the fear of becoming unskilled in an area of previous self-esteem.

Role of the major stakeholders

We identified the major stakeholders in the process of change, including those with most at risk from the loss of esteem, control or position (Grant and Gale, 1989). Many were involved early in our planning process, were assigned major roles in the implementation phase, and consequently have a sense of ownership of the new programme. Some hold important administrative positions in the problem-based curriculum and others have become tutors. Indeed, the roster of tutors for the opening unit of the curriculum demonstrated enormous support. It included the chairmen of the anatomy, biochemistry and pathology departments, the coordinators of the former courses in gross anatomy and histology, the Dean of the School of Medicine, and senior clinicians from the medicine, surgery, obstetrics and gynaecology, paediatrics and psychiatry departments.

Dissemination of information about problem-based learning was a necessary and important first step. It was met at times by intellectual argument and heated confrontation between those with differences of opinion. It seldom persuaded people to change. We decided to minimize the hardening of negative attitudes by providing early positive experiences. We found the use of demonstration of the tutorial process, participation in tutor training, and the experience of success to be the point of conversion for many.

Changes in the social structure of the school

The social structure of the school was reorganized (see Bloom, 1989 for an in-depth discussion). The Task Force on Problem-Based Learning (five members) was enlarged to become the Planning Group (10 members) for the new programme. With augmentation, that group evolved into the MD Program Committee (15 members) and was charged by the Dean with the implementation and monitoring of the educational programme. This evolution removed problem-based learning from the purview of the traditional curriculum committee which was organized to uphold departmental representation, control and autonomy.

By contrast, membership on the MD Program Committee was constructed to secure accountability for the integrated components of the programme. These are the Unit Chairmen (curricular Units I–V), the chairpersons for student evaluation, learning resources, tutor training, the advisor programme, discipline representation, community medicine, and clinical skills. Many of these were the same people who sat on the former curriculum committee, but now they had different roles.

This administrative system of chairpersons for functional rather than structural units has sub-committees for the implementation of each function. It provides for interdepartmental team building and faculty development. It offers recognition and increasing administrative responsibility based on successful performance, leadership and commitment. It is a training programme that supports the continuation of change.

Organizing these observations about the process of change at the University of Hawaii has in itself brought insights. Some of these events and decisions were carefully planned with prospective control. Many, however, are valued for their impact only after retrospective analysis. This suggests that we can take credit for some of this achievement, but should acknowledge the contribution of good luck, circumstance, intuition and timing. I do not believe, however, that serendipitous factors can facilitate change without high-level support and charismatic leadership, investment in faculty development, and adept consultation with those who have years of experience with problem-based learning.

Postscript

Several reviewers have urged me to identify my personal role in this change process. It has been that of providing enthusiasm, reassurance, persuasion and, at times, mild coercion. I have recruited faculty to participate (in tutor-training and administrative functions). I have outlined the steps and timetable for the planning and implementation process, defined and delegated the component tasks, and, on occasion, picked these up when the action faltered. I have written grant proposals to secure funds in areas where resources were lean. I have badgered our Dean and Department Chairs for their support and their resources during this process of change from departmental to central governance of the curriculum. I have worked on building an interdepartmental, multidisciplinary team committed to the continuation of this new curriculum and learning process. Finally, I have taken a personal risk. I left my secure (and somewhat monotonous) base of 17 years in medical education within the Department of Medicine for the uncertainties of a central Office of Medical Education and Chairmanship of the MD Program Committee. It has been worth that risk!

Postscript 2 (January 1997)

Our PBL curriculum has now been in full operation for seven years. Five classes of medical students will have successfully completed that programme by May 1997. At this distance from the initial frenzy of activity, I can reflect on PBL as an enabler of change at our institution, in four main ways:

1. All aspects of curriculum are now *centralized* and integrated throughout the course, rather than operated as independent departmental fiefdoms. The MD programme committee has identified a wide range of roles and expectations for faculty, and has been well served by the office of medical education in areas of PBL tutor training, curriculum and assessment initiatives and computer-based distance education;
2. Learning activities in all four years have been *decentralized*, and now incorporate PBL tutorials, community health projects and clinical experiences at a range of rural and inner city health centres (not just doctors' offices or hospitals).
3. Granting agencies (federal, state and private) view our school as quite capable of change and have invested in subsequent innovations involving PBL. Major contributions over the last six years have come from:
   – the Kellogg Foundation; it supports local education partnerships with medically underserved communities, enabling students from different health professions to do team projects at academic health centres from the campus;
   – the Robert Wood Johnson Foundation; it has supported extending PBL into the clinical clerkships and developing 'longitudinal experiences', in which students see and deliver continuity of care, mainly based in ambulatory settings;
   – Area Health Education Centers (AHECs); this federal agency is helping to develop more academic learning sites in medically underserved areas on the Big Island (Hawaii), Maui, Kauai and rural Oahu – to improve access to health services and to encourage more students to pursue primary care careers.
4. 'Young' faculty are engrossed in the excitement of such initiatives in medical education, and are bonding into interdepartmental alliances to develop their ideas. The initial change process has become self-sustaining.

(No doubt, a fitting tribute to both the dean, Christian Gulbrandsen MD, and the director of the Office of Medical Education, Alex Anderson MD, both of whom retired from the University of Hawaii at the end of 1996. *Editors' note.*)

References

Bloom, S W (1989) The medical school as a social organization: the sources of resistance to change, *Medical Education*, 23, 228–241.

Grant, J and Gale, R (1989) Changing medical education, *Medical Education*, 23, 252–257.

Kaufman, A, Mennin, S, Waterman, R, Duban, S, Hansbarger, C, Silverblatt, H, Obenshain, S S, Kantrowitz, M, Becker, T, Samet, J and Wiese, W (1989) The New Mexico Experiment: educational innovation and institutional change, *Academic Medicine*, 64, 285–294.

Neufeld, V R, Woodward, C A and MacLeod, S M (1989) The McMaster MD Program: a case study of renewal in medical education, *Academic Medicine*, 64, 423–432.

Chapter 8

Initiating Problem-based Learning at Harvard Medical School

Gordon T Moore

In 1984, after two years of extensive discussion and planning, Dean Daniel C Tosteson presented the curriculum committee with his final plans for the radical reform of medical education at Harvard. The committee agreed that an experimental, fully redesigned curriculum called the New Pathway would start about one year later for a volunteer group of students and faculty. The New Pathway curriculum (see Armstrong's chapter in Part III) featured problem-based learning in tutorial groups as its central educational approach.

Challenges

The use of problem-based learning, while supported by a small group of faculty, was by no means universally acclaimed by the HMS faculty. Considerable resistance, scepticism and outright hostility emerged during the planning process. These concerns arose in four categories: theoretical issues related to problem-based learning; practical and logistical concerns; personal factors; and significant questions about this educational approach even among those who were committed to using it.

Theoretical issues

Three issues dominated the theoretical discussions about problem-based learning. First, many faculty members were profoundly concerned that the approach was unsystematic and that students would not adequately cover the necessary learning objectives for a general education. Second, many faculty doubted that the students would learn what they needed if left to their own devices in a student-directed curriculum. Third, problem-based learning appeared to many faculty members to be like a clinical diagnostic reasoning exercise. Some basic science faculty could not imagine that students could learn the scientific basis of medicine if they were concerned with diagnosis. Clinical teachers worried that the curriculum would favour primary care medicine, since pre-clinical students could only handle the most simple of cases.

Practical concerns

Among the practical concerns, the department chairmen were most worried that the new curriculum would raid the faculty, leaving too few good teachers to cover both the new and the traditional tracks. In addition, many questioned whether the faculty would be adequately motivated for such a wholesale change in teaching. Inadequate finances, lack of academic recognition, and competing research priorities were raised as critical practical issues to be solved before moving ahead. Friends of this new approach to teaching cited the importance of faculty development, while those more resistant to the change indicated that this method of teaching was unlike any that most faculty had done in the past and that, as well as requiring more time, it might well require new skills that were in short supply.

Personal biases

The advent of a major new curricular effort unveiled diverse faculty attitudes towards the teaching of medical students. Many argued that the lecture method was efficient and adequate. Others, comfortable with teaching the old way, were resistant to any change. Most faculty viewed medical student education as among their lowest academic priorities.

Methodologic concerns among the committed

There were serious concerns and debates about how to proceed even among those faculty members committed to change. Early debates were about whether to use problems or teacher-directed topics for tutorials. Later, the locus of discussion shifted to the relative balance between lectures and problem-based tutorials, revealing significant conflict over the role of lectures in a problem-based curriculum. Later still, the desire to preserve time for electives conflicted with the need for independent study time in the new curriculum. Finally, debates emerged about the proper length of cases, the degree of integration between biologic and psychosocial issues, whether Harvard should develop its own cases or use those developed elsewhere, whether problems should be exclusively clinical or include research, and whether the case should adhere carefully to reality or be modified to achieve desired learning objectives.

Approaches utilized

We used a variety of approaches to implement the New Pathway and to overcome many of the problems identified in the prior section. Our approaches generally fell into the following categories: structure – how we organized getting the work done and dealing with the identified problems; process – how we communicated with and involved faculty in the development and implementation of the programme; and outcomes – the specific actions and products that were the building blocks and milestones leading to delivery of the curriculum.

Structure

The two most important structural steps were to initiate the new curriculum as a separate, experimental track and to develop an organization that could manage the process of development. Starting the New Pathway as a separate track was a strategy to bypass the resistance of many members to significant PBL change in the curriculum. Several prior attempts to change the Harvard curriculum for the entire medical school class and faculty had faltered or failed. Those responsible for initiating the New Pathway concluded that far-reaching alterations could only be achieved by starting with a volunteer sub-set of students and faculty. By using a separate track, we were able to approach the innovation as an experiment and encourage radical thinking and far-reaching alteration. We attracted the relatively small number of faculty who were dissatisfied with the traditional curriculum and excited about the prospect of change (Wilkerson and Maxwell, 1988) and enrolled students who voluntarily welcomed a different kind of educational approach. An important benefit of the separate track was the pioneering spirit, collegiality and enthusiasm generated by a small, tightly knit group of faculty and students.

At HMS, the separate track was never conceived by the planners as a permanent second pathway for medical education. Rather, it was envisaged as a way to pilot new ideas, determine which were most attractive in our setting, and use this information to design a single curriculum for all medical students.

The organizational structure for the New Pathway was designed to enhance project management and to encourage interdisciplinary integration and collective oversight for the entire curriculum. An explicit educational budget was developed and core staff (including administrative, curriculum development and faculty development experts) were recruited. This staff provided administrative and educational support to the faculty groups planning the blocks that comprised the four-year curriculum. Led by a single broad-based faculty leader, scientists and clinicians from the relevant disciplines developed, designed and delivered each block. The block chairmen met regularly in an interlocking directorate called the Core Planning Group, which oversaw the development of the entire curriculum and discussed and adopted policies and procedures. This Core Group, which was also attended by the central educational staff, achieved important compromises regarding gaps and redundancies in the curriculum content and experiences, as well as trade-offs that were required in order to fit the entire curriculum within the allotted time.

Process

Starting with a parallel track risked isolating the new curriculum from the majority of the faculty. Since their final goal was faculty approval of the ideas of the new curriculum, the planners recognized the importance of communication in fostering understanding and, ultimately, support for the innovations. Many of the objections to the new curriculum would be overcome by clarifying the tutorial method through discussion, through citing the available literature and through direct contact with the pilot group. The project staff set up a variety of mechanisms to inform the faculty and persuade them of the value of the problem-based approach:

1. The new programme reported frequently on its progress to the Curriculum Committee.

2. A special Steering Group, formed by the Dean, met monthly to review important decisions and monitor progress. This committee consisted of influential members of the faculty, including many who were sceptical about the new approach to education.
3. Department chairmen were asked to designate key faculty to lead and participate in the curriculum.
4. Each department was asked to designate a liaison to the new curriculum to serve as a channel of communication.
5. Faculty development programmes brought interested faculty together and communicated reactions to the new curriculum and tips for teaching to each succeeding faculty group.
6. The project director met individually with important faculty leaders to address their concerns about problem-based learning.

Initiating the curriculum as a separate track had another benefit for the educational process which was to create a sense of excitement, and even competition, about curricular methods. Having two curricula, each with its own avid supporters, drew attention to the New Pathway and stimulated each group to do its best. As the shape of the new curriculum emerged, faculty members engaged in lively discussion about the strengths and weaknesses of each approach. These discussions were formalized in year-end workshops in which topics relating to the educational changes underway served as the focus of discussion. Many faculty members commented that the sense of competition between the two student and faculty groups created an environment at once stimulating and distressing. This energy sometimes got out of hand but probably improved the effort of both the traditional and the new curriculum during its early stages of implementation.

The personal, positional and political influence of the advocates of the new curriculum were, of course, important elements in the process of change. Several department chairmen, a few respected and influential faculty members, and the Dean and his staff were enthusiastic participants in the New Pathway and effective behind-the-scenes forces in generating sufficient momentum to extend problem-based learning to all the medical students.

Specification of guidelines, milestones and outcomes

We utilized guidelines, timetables and careful specification of educational products to guide the development of the new curriculum and keep it on schedule. The curriculum committee created the first timetable by confirming a start date, specifying the number of students, and agreeing to a redesign of all four years. These actions guaranteed that discussion would be limited and actions would follow. Deadlines focused the debate and forced the planners to identify alternative options and make decisions quickly.

When we developed and brought options to faculty groups for discussion, we always pushed for closure on specific critical parameters. Among these were such important matters as the balance of time between electives and the required courses, the purpose and frequency of lectures (ultimately limited to one per day), and the goals and methods for student evaluation. These recommendations became guidelines that then set the necessary conditions for the development and design of the courses. These and other clear specifications allowed multiple design groups to work semi-independently but with a common understanding about what was to be included and how the course was to be taught.

Procedural guidelines shaped the expectations of students and faculty. We developed a programme guide that described the reasons for the new curriculum, the theory underpinning the educational approaches used, the general objectives and a detailed description of the problem-based tutorial methodology. A fourth-year student, on leave to work as a fellow with the project, developed a student guide to problem-based learning. As mentioned, the Director of Faculty Development initiated a series of courses about the approach as well as offering to improve lecturing and other educational approaches that might be used in both the traditional and the new curriculum.

We identified specific and tangible products to be achieved according to a developmental timetable for the project. Having these 'building blocks' focused the actions of all parties on concrete outcomes. In the curriculum development process, for example, a specified set of case materials was designated for each problem. The educational staff and faculty chairmen for each block were expected to develop a course book consisting of a description of the curriculum, general course objectives, and the set of problems for that block.

For the first time, we linked medical school funding to explicit educational outcomes. A specific educational budget was developed to support the New Pathway project, using programme budgeting to identify important milestones and the resources needed to achieve them. A funding campaign identified potential outside sources of support for the new effort and resulted in a number of grants to develop designated aspects of the new programme. Each award provided the opportunity to describe the project both inside and outside the medical school and to create a sense of momentum for the project's development.

Several other ventures removed barriers to or reinforced the new methods. As an example of reducing a barrier, a special task force identified methods of documenting excellence in teaching and using this information in the academic promotion process (see also Wilkerson and Hundert's chapter in Part III). Specific faculty evaluation procedures, once developed, were instituted on a trial basis during the first years of the new curriculum. This effort led to the development of clinician-teacher tracks in several key departments. An opportunity to facilitate the new curriculum arose during the development phase. A new educational facility was to be developed, and the funding campaign and the design of a facility specifically suited to problem-based learning focused considerable attention on this method both within and outside the faculty.

Perhaps the most important aspect of the approaches listed above was the goal-directed management of the entire process. Strong central management was needed to balance the heavy commitment to discussion and review by faculty and the decentralized organization used in the development of the curriculum blocks. In a project as complex as curricular change, effective project management is critical. Business approaches have much to offer through such techniques as programme budgeting, strategic planning, the use of critical path methods to specify milestones and develop timetables, and project monitoring to assure progress.

General principles

A handful of principles emerged from the experience of implementing problem-based learning at Harvard Medical School. These included:

1. take a 'do it and fix it' approach that limits discussion and moves towards action;
2. develop a strategy to isolate and protect the initial development of an educational innovation if one expects significant change;
3. find a means to counterbalance the centripetal force of strong, decentralized departments. Most successful schools have decentralized financial and operational organizations. This structure makes integration and collective action difficult. To achieve comprehen-

sive curricular change, leaders must create a centralized, inter-disciplinary group to provide an overview and integration of the entire span of medical education;

4. find and use the creative energy and commitment of the relatively small numbers of students and faculty interested in the early adoption of new approaches, without derailing their efforts by forcing them to work with nay-sayers. This principle can be achieved by segregating functions and authority among the faculty. The entire faculty need to gain agreement to the overarching goals and purposes of education, but operational implementation can be confined to a relatively small group of planners and workers. The review and comment function can be widely shared among the faculty while the authority for important detailed decisions can be reserved for smaller groups or responsible individuals. Balancing this tension between freedom to experiment while preserving faculty participation through the important functions of evaluation, review and comment is a critical dimension of success in educational innovation.

Acknowledgements

The author gratefully acknowledges the contributions of the Josiah Macy, Jr and the Kaiser Family Foundation to this work.

Reference

Wilkerson, L and Maxwell, J (1988) A qualitative study of initial faculty tutors in a new problem-based curriculum, *Journal of Medical Education*, 63, 892–899.

Chapter 9

Organizational and Institutional Impediments to a Problem-based Approach

Stephen E Little and **Chris Sauer**

Introduction

Any educational innovation will face a variety of hurdles. A radical problem-based programme confronts special difficulties beyond the usual academic matters of content and delivery. This chapter describes how organizational and institutional impediments affected the team developing the Bachelor of Informatics (BInf) degree at Griffith University in Brisbane in the mid-1980s.

Griffith University imposed critical elements of organization upon the BInf team. The inappropriateness of the structure impeded progress on the core tasks of developing the programme and establishing the necessary infrastructure to support it. It resulted in delays, conflict and low morale. It also failed to buffer the BInf team from its institutional environment, ie those norms which affect a task without being directly relevant to its effective completion. Thus, in universities, research is institutionalized as the critical determinant of tenure and advancement, regardless of the principal task for which academic staff are employed. (Scott, 1987, provides a review of institutional theory.)

Three differences between traditional and problem-based approaches

Traditional courses tend to consist of accepted gobbets of subject matter from a single discipline. They enjoy three significant advantages. One, they are routine. Content is defined by published curricula and standard textbooks, and their delivery consists of a mix of lectures, classes, seminars, field trips, laboratories and directed study. Two, they scale easily to varying student numbers by changing the size of the lecture room or the number of labs. Three, they have automatic legitimacy, being widely accepted by the academic community.

Problem-based courses are less conventional, and hence have special costs. First, to the extent that they are innovative, emphasizing problem solving and integrating material from several disciplines, as well as developing new modes of delivery and assessment, problem-based courses are not routine to design or present. Second, they are often lecturer intensive and require uncommon staff skills. Third, where content and delivery deviate from the traditional norms, courses may lack legitimacy in the eyes of academic peers.

Griffith University

From its inception in the early 1970s Griffith University set out to offer problem-oriented, interdisciplinary degree programmes. They varied in the extent of their commitment to problem orientation, some programmes assuming that to be interdisciplinary was sufficient, others designing some coursework around major problems. Initially there were four degree programmes each housed in a semi-autonomous organizational structure, a school. Subsequently a fifth degree was established and a new school created. One-degree-programme-one-school was the norm. Griffith's educational philosophy and organization have been discussed elsewhere (Topley and Willett, 1976; Abel *et al*, 1985).

In the 1980s Griffith found its environment changing. It faced central government pressure to expand. It also recognized increasing demand for programmes relevant to business. It was particularly weak in new technology. One obvious solution was a programme based around computing.

The Bachelor of Informatics development

The Bachelor of Informatics was intended to attract students wanting to learn how to apply computing in business and administrative organizations. It would respect Griffith's problem-based philosophy. Senior university planners intended it to be cheap. They therefore made two major organizational decisions. They housed the BInf within an existing school rather than creating a new one, and appointed a senior lecturer rather than a professor to lead the development. The BInf team was thus denied the autonomy it needed to manage the various organizational and institutional impediments it would encounter.

The working group overseeing the BInf development rapidly realized that computing was ideally suited to a problem-based treatment. They recruited a core of committed staff who designed a programme centred around problem-based and closed loop problem-based project courses, supported by further courses using a mixture of techniques ranging from traditional lectures to case-based and modified case-based tutorials (our terminology follows Barrows, 1986). The University authorities did not prevent this, apparently accepting the rationale advanced under its standard programme and course approval procedures (Abel *et al*, 1984). They thereby created a contradiction. The academic team was committed to an educational agenda which it had to implement under an organizational structure which the University's political environment dictated would be cheap and, in fact, inappropriate.

The academic task

A number of academic problems arose specifically because problem-based education is not the norm.

The method employed to develop the BInf programme and its constituent courses has been described in Abel *et al* (1985) and Ross *et al* (1985). As courses were built around a central question, such as 'How are problems of developing and evaluating information systems solved in a work environment organized into project teams?', the content of each had to be fashioned individually. Mostly, existing published material was scant help, not being organized around questions or problems. In some cases there was no relevant material published in either teaching or research literature.

The integration of material from different disciplines meant that most staff had to acquire new knowledge and skills. For example, the Problem Solving Workshop required both formal knowledge and skills in problem solving, design, interpersonal communication and organizational psychology. Most staff initially lacked some of these.

Organizational impediments

The organizational arrangements under which the academic task was carried out formed a series of impediments.

Housing the BInf inside another school produced a number of adverse outcomes. It was treated by some as second class because it did not have its own school. All formal communications outside the school were lengthened because they had to go through the dean, school administrator or relevant school committee. It was frequently ignored by central administrative procedures which assumed a one-school-one-degree programme.

The discrepancy in the 'cultures' of the BInf and its host school meant that additional time was often required to explain and justify proposals before they were allowed into the wider Griffith community. For example, bids for equipment funds and technical staff, modest by the standards of computer science departments, were regarded as wildly extravagant by the social scientists of the host school. Such bids would then be delayed, not because they were not justified but on the ground that they were unduly optimistic, the school never having received equipment funding on such a scale before!

Such examples were symptomatic of the root problem, that the BInf team lacked organizational and administrative autonomy. Though given separate budgets, it did not control them. The school did. BInf academic staff reported to the dean, while its administrative and technical staff reported to the school administrator. Its staffing policies were formulated by the school staff committee. Its course proposals were all reviewed by the school's review committees. In budgetary, staffing and academic matters the discrepancy in cultures manifested itself in chronic, often bitter, disagreements which seriously soured relations.

The programme's access to and influence in the University's senior decision-making processes was negligible because its leader was only a senior lecturer. In the early stages of design, a supportive dean mitigated the worst problems. His successor had a more bureaucratic view of how to manage BInf within the host school. This resulted in complete loss of access to power and incapacity to change the organizational structure.

Such organizational difficulties might have affected any new educational programme. However, they were felt particularly acutely because the BInf, being problem based, was innovative. It was not a routine development. Had it been as organizationally autonomous as other degrees at Griffith, it would have been able to resolve many issues more quickly.

Institutional impediments

The wider institutional environment of the university sector asserted itself in two ways. It served to limit the level of innovation permissible in the programme and it restricted the time staff could spend working on it.

The mechanism by which innovation was limited was the sequence of committees which reviewed and approved all course proposals. They would consider issues such as the consistency of courses with overall degree programme goals, volume and difficulty of academic content, and appropriateness of assessment. External review was desirable and proved valuable. However, courses were judged according to the institutionalized standards of conventional courses rather than ones appropriate to problem-based courses. Some courses were criticized for not including a strong enough core of conventional material. The very limited use of textbooks was seen as especially worrying. The value of projects set in commercial organizations was challenged. Would workshops that required students to resolve interpersonal problems be too stressful? How could group assessment be fair for groups that included freeriders?

Coming from outsiders such questions were legitimate, but coming from committees of other Griffith academics they demonstrated a deep-rooted respect for traditional academic values. For example, freeriders are only a problem if the principle of credit for individual merit alone is seen as paramount. Every deviation from traditional practices had to be set in its problem-based context and justified. Sometimes the same point might have to be argued at several committees in succession. In an institution publicly committed to problem-based education, the weight of the approval processes was energy sapping.

The allocation of staff time to the BInf was restricted through the prevailing staffing practices. For the purposes of securing tenure or promotion, the University's documented policy was to treat programme and course development as equivalent to research. Several staff were explicitly given this understanding in the process of their appointment. In practice, staff committees required evidence of successful research. This resulted in lecturers being distracted from the development of the BInf by the need to publish. To staff committed to the programme this was deeply galling given the University's official policy. It was particularly stressful for those still in the formative stages of their research. It demoralized some because they felt they were fighting an illicit practice. The contradictions of the University's policy and practice were made clear to the senior lecturer who was told that he could not expect promotion in the foreseeable future because he would be too occupied with the BInf to do sufficient research! He resigned.

Strategies for overcoming impediments

In general, the impediments discussed above worked in two ways. They either served to modify the programme as it was initially proposed, eg the insistence that a radical sociological perspective be included in the foundation programme, or they failed to change it but slowed progress, eg extensive and repeated queries about the experiential Problem Solving Workshop.

The BInf staff responded in a number of ways. Initially, they attempted to persuade the University on rational grounds that a new school should be created. The University, constrained to appear economically motivated, argued that schools were administratively too costly. The debate was a pantomime of oh-yes-they-are-oh-no-they're-not! The University won.

The next phase, roughly coinciding with the start of teaching, was to attempt to fashion an acceptable *modus vivendi* with the host school. For reasons of cultural and personal differences the detente achieved was only temporary. This reduced BInf staff to fighting each issue on its merits, a chronically debilitating strategy over a long period.

Eventually, as a result of the senior lecturer's resignation and other contingent changes it was agreed to appoint a professor. This gave the programme some status, and better access to senior management. Further structural changes in the University resulted in the BInf being incorporated in a new School of Computing and Information Technology. However, this was placed under the control of a new Division of Science and Technology with no increase in autonomy.

Conclusion

The problems described arose chiefly because of mixed messages. The objective of a cheap computing degree was inconsistent with the problem-based rhetoric employed by Griffith. The disparity between this rhetoric and the real agenda underlying academic development highlighted the difficulties that confront any genuine innovation. Comparable obstacles will be present in very different institutional settings. Separate conclusions are offered for academic design teams and for university authorities.

Clearly, it is essential that university authorities ensure that problem-based learning is consistent with its other objectives. Organizationally, strong support must be given. It is important to recognize the innovative nature of the problem-based approach and treat such developments flexibly. There must be scope for negotiation on all matters, otherwise existing procedures may pre-empt valuable alternatives.

The lesson for the academic team is that an understanding of organizational politics is a mixed blessing. It may uncover the 'possible', but also the costs. If the Blnf team had truly understood its situation, the line of least resistance would have been to emulate earlier developments at Griffith and design a more traditional programme, paying lip-service to the philosophy. The alternative was to fight for the academic objectives the team felt it had been employed to implement. Had staff understood the adversarial nature of this alternative, they might also have foreseen the costs to individuals. It is no mere coincidence that within two years of starting teaching, three of the first four academics had left, and within four-and-a-half years six of the first nine had departed. Subsequent rapid growth in the new division and its concomitant pressures soon ensured that only a small minority of more than 20 staff had any recollection or understanding of the holistic framework and problem orientation of the programme as conceived in its original design.

References

Abel, D, Bailes, P, Margetson, D, Oliver, I and Sauer, C (1984) An intellectual rationale for an undergraduate informatics programme, *Proceedings of Second Australian Computer Education Conference*, Sydney: Macquarie University, 283–289.

Abel, D, Margetson, D and Sauer, C (1985) Designing a problem-oriented degree in informatics, in Boud, D (ed) *Problem-based Learning in Education for the Professions*, Kensington: HERDSA, 81–94.

Barrows, H S (1986) A taxonomy of problem-based learning methods, *Medical Education*, 20, 481–486.

Ross, B, Abel, D, Margetson, D and Sauer, C (1985) Designing academic programmes with a problem orientation, in Boud, D (ed) *Problem-based Learning in Education for the Professions*, Kensington: HERDSA, 69–80.

Scott, W R (1987) The adolescence of institutional theory, *Administrative Science Quarterly*, 32, 493–511.

Topley, J and Willett, J (1976) The organisation of a new university, *The Journal of Educational Administration*, 14 (1), 54–69.

Part III
Design and Implementation

Our first edition saw the evolution of PBL as analogous with the early history of the church. In the 1970s a confident new philosophy emerged from several medical schools (McMaster, Maastricht, Beer Sheva). Word (that 'it works') and deed ('this is the way we do it') spread to and from other disciplines and countries in the 1980s, characterizing a decade of evangelism for PBL. And now it appears we are well into the decade of educational research and development, earnestly trying to assimilate PBL among existing educational theories and principles of learning. The biblical analogy continues, with more faculty making the change and experiencing the difference, while others want to see the evidence before adopting new methods. The decade of the 1990s is characterized by research efforts to explain how and why 'it works' – in general, and in specific contexts – using scientific language and methodology. It is also a period in which faculty are developing new models of practice-based learning in attempting to prepare new graduates for the changing roles of their respective professions. Health science institutions in particular are extending PBL principles to multiprofessional teamwork, and in community and workplace environments outside the comfort zone of campus classrooms, studios, doctors' offices, etc (Magzoub *et al*, in press; *Network*, 1996).

Part II reflected the dynamics of trying to change from a traditional approach – on different scales and within different contexts. Part III describes or provides an update on some of the research and development efforts at different institutions. Each chapter in this part reflects the new 'bonding' happening in their institution, triggered by the demanding nature of PBL. The renewed links between faculty and their students are no surprise to those who recognize the return to basics of 'good teaching' (Palmer, 1989). But the less predictable outcomes include mutual satisfaction in the complementary roles of practitioners and academics, educational support and teaching faculty, lecturers and tutors – as they become comfortable with a new team approach. As some have already discovered, dedication to improving the 'students' lot' can also produce benefits for faculty and the institution itself.

Peter MacDonald and his former colleagues at McMaster University have systematically addressed how to decide what is important to learn. The challenge to them is not just to list those diseases or illnesses which typify the burden of professional practice for medical graduates. Identifying factors which also denote their *educational* importance is more exacting and will result in a much more exciting curriculum for faculty and students alike. Nevertheless, while the McMaster medical curriculum is reportedly non-didactic (being almost exclusively based on case tutorials and patient experiences) the question remains as to whether this is an effective model for any other school or profession, given the wide variation in students' maturity, interest and confidence in their chosen vocation.

Issues relating to diversity of students are addressed in a new chapter. Imogen Taylor and Hilary Burgess at Bristol University describe the competing multi-roles and self-doubts of many mature-age social work students; but they do have a strong affinity for PBL – if it is implemented true to form – that requires an awareness of issues of difference and genuine interpersonal skills from tutors.

Engineering has a quite different approach to practice from medicine, and Don Woods indirectly takes up this challenge, reporting on the promotion of problem-solving activities for senior students in chemical engineering at the same university. Given severe logistic constraints, how can students themselves be trained (and trusted) to take charge of their own group process, problem solving and self-assessment? Intensive workshops seem to have worked well in fostering students' skills, self-confidence and self-reliance. The latter (which often includes *not* calling on faculty as 'expert' resources) would twinge the conscience of any self-respecting teacher. Students apparently do well on written exams and most are very satisfied with the programme.

How can teachers new to the idea of PBL be introduced to its particular methods and challenges? Shona Little found the same kind of workshops useful in helping New Zealand polytechnic teachers from a wide range of professional areas to realize the value and commitment of PBL. Her major challenge (similar to that described in Wilkerson and Hundert's chapter) is to facilitate tertiary teachers' understanding of the extent of role change required. The power of workshops seems to be self-evident: participants' actions speak louder than a facilitator's rhetoric.

One of the facts of life, in business as much as education, is that personal energies, creativity and liberties of the founders of an innovation must inevitably give way to more systematic, collaborative and routine operations. While this may seem intolerable for some advocates, its necessity is obvious: the new approach must become 'public property' to survive. From this broader base of experience will emerge new research helping us to refine PBL, as clearly seen in the respective chapters on Harvard Medical School's adoption of PBL. And some of the best innovations may not survive that challenge of assimilation, or must wait for more favourable conditions to develop further; meanwhile the portable features of their innovative model may transfer (with staff movements) to new locations.

PBL in nursing at the University of Western Sydney-Macarthur campus is one such story. Betty Andersen's (1993) leadership, well beyond her retirement from that nursing school, has influenced many aspects of academic nursing education and research in Australia. Greg Ryan has a new chapter, giving fresh insights into students' development of problem solving and self-directed learning in their very first semester. This work is based on his doctoral research which originated while he was a faculty member at Macarthur.

It is intriguing that PBL has flourished in the heart of one of the most esteemed research institutions: Harvard Medical School. Starting as a pilot project, the New Pathway for General Medical education recruited a small team of education specialists to work with faculty in carefully designing a new approach accommodating the School's unique requirements. When that pilot project upgraded to a whole-school venture in 1987 these specialists became part of a new Office of Educational Development, working with a much wider range of faculty and opinions (Maxwell and Wilkerson, 1990). We are fortunate to have their perspectives on different aspects of the educational process represented here.

Liz Armstrong elaborates on Harvard Medical School's 'hybrid' curriculum; Janet Hafler presents aspects of her research into what Harvard faculty and students seek in a 'good' case for tutorials; and LuAnn

Wilkerson and Ed Hundert reflect on what is essential for good tutoring and how best to achieve it. For many sceptics (not all from other institutions) Harvard's ongoing success story is paradoxical. Why has a strong research faculty become active in curriculum reform, especially this kind which downplays didactic methods? Why get excited about writing or tutoring clinical cases for learning about basic science? Why change staff attitudes and behaviour to students in class, particularly when both hold high expectations of each other?

We conclude this introduction by remarking that careful design and sensible implementation are hallmarks of any educational innovation. With PBL being so labour-intensive and foreign to many teachers, it has to be mutually satisfying for students *and* their teachers if this approach is to survive and subsequently lead to further improvement in higher education.

References

Andersen, B (1993) Clinical situations: an organizational basis and learning stimulus for nurse education. In P Bouhuijs, H Schmidt and H van Berkel (eds) *Problem-based learning as an educational strategy*. Maastricht: Network Publications.

Magzoub, M, Schmidt, H, Feletti, G and Nooman, Z (eds) (in press) *Handbook of Community Based Education: Theory and Practices*.

Maxwell, J A and Wilkerson, L (1990) A study of non-volunteer faculty in a problem-based curriculum, *Academic Medicine*, 65, 9, 513–514.

Network (1996) In retrospect: the 3rd international symposium on problem-based learning. Durban, South Africa, 21–25 September 1996. *Newsletter of the Network of Community-Oriented Institutions for Health Sciences*, 26, December, 12–15.

Palmer, P (1989) Good teaching. *Change*, January/February, 11–16.

Chapter 10

Selection of Health Problems for a Problem-based Curriculum

Peter J MacDonald

All educational institutions which train professionals must make decisions about what is 'important' enough to be in the curriculum. The curriculum of a medical school, almost by definition, outlines those aspects of health and disease which the faculty believes are educational priorities. In a problem-based learning environment, the health problems chosen for study define the basis of the curriculum; the way in which problems are studied (eg from the perspective of organ systems) defines the curricular emphasis. Given the immense variety of health problems which could be studied, educational planners need a method for choosing which problems must be included in the curriculum, and which other problems may be de-emphasized or left out entirely.

The first step in establishing educational priorities for medicine is to determine those factors of a health problem which are indices of its *educational* importance. The same health problem may have quite different indices of importance for other purposes, such as research. A widely used index of importance is the prevalence of the problem in the population under consideration. The University of Ottawa reported its attempts to base its medical curriculum mainly on an index of prevalence (Rosser and Beaulieu, 1984). The McMaster Priority Problems and Conditions Survey looked at prevalence, but also considered educational priorities (clinical logic, prototype value, urgency, treatability and interdisciplinary input) (Chong *et al*, 1984). In the context of quality assurance for health care of the elderly rather than of

Table 10.1 Priority illness conditions for medical education

ILLNESS CONDITIONS	PRIORITY HEALTH PROBLEM INDICES								SEVERITY SCORE C+Q+T	EFFECTIVENESS SCORE U+P+D+R	PRIORITY HEALTH PROBLEM WEIGHTING
	M	C	Q	T	U	P	D	R			
PRIORITY PROBLEMS											
COMMON PROBLEMS											
CARDIAC ARRHYTHMIAS	2	2	1	2	2	2	2	1	5	7	14
ISCHEMIC HEART DISEASE	2	2	1	2	2	2	2	1	5	7	14
BURNS	2	2	0	1	2	2	2	2	3	8	13
ASTHMA	2	1	1	2	2	2	2	1	4	7	13
ALCOHOL ABUSE	2	2	1	2	1	2	2	1	5	6	13
MALIGNANT NEOPLASM (SKIN)	2	2	1	2	1	2	2	1	5	6	13
MALIGNANT NEOPLASM	2	2	2	2	1	2	1	1	6	5	13
SEXUALLY TRANSMITTED DISEASES	2	0	0	2	2	2	2	2	2	8	12
. . .	.	.	.	.	.	.	.	.	.	.	.
ABDOMINAL PAIN NYD	2	0	0	2	1	0	1	1	2	3	7
MENOPAUSAL SYNDROME	2	1	0	2	0	1	1	0	3	2	7
ANXIETY	2	0	1	2	0	1	1	0	3	2	7
ACNE/SEBORRHEA	2	0	0	2	0	2	0	0	2	2	6
IRRITABLE COLON	2	0	1	2	0	0	0	1	3	1	6
MYALGIA/ARTHRALGIA NYD	2	0	0	1	0	0	0	2	1	2	5
ACUTE URI	2	0	0	1	0	2	0	0	1	2	5
CHRONIC RHINITIS	2	0	0	2	0	0	0	1	2	1	5

UNCOMMON PROBLEMS

SCHIZOPHRENIA
GLAUCOMA
VIRAL HEPATITIS

INFERTILITY
HYPERTROPHY OF TONSILS
SCOLIOSIS

RARE PROBLEMS

MALARIA
TYPHOID
MENINGITIS

NON-PRIORITY PROBLEMS

REYE'S SYNDROME
AIDS

PORPHYRIA
INFECTIOUS MONONUCLEOSIS

education, Fink *et al* (1987) used an expert consensus approach to choose seven conditions from an initial list of 42. Issues of prevalence decided the inclusion of a disease on the initial list, but the final list of seven conditions was chosen by applying indices of:

1. significant adverse effects on outcome,
2. the existence of beneficial interventions,
3. significant benefit if quality is improved, and
4. the feasibility of monitoring quality of care.

Similar concepts can be applied in the education of other professionals. For example, how does the Harvard Business School select the cases for its renowned case-study method?

My colleagues and I have described an approach to the selection of priority health problems using indices similar to those discussed above, but applied to actual Canadian health data (MacDonald *et al*, 1989). Our aim was to produce a list of priority health problems for use by medical curriculum planners at McMaster University. We used a number of indices in setting the priorities of disease and illness conditions: index M, the magnitude; indices C (case – fatality rate), Q (quality of life) and T (duration of the condition) which may collectively be called the 'severity' of the condition; and indices U (urgency), P (preventability), D (diagnosability) and R (treatability), which may collectively be called the 'effectiveness of intervention' scores. We collected existing health care data from a variety of sources, including the Canada Health Survey (national data) (1987), Ontario Ministry of Health data (provincial data), local hospitals (secondary and tertiary care level data), and eight local general practices (primary care level data). Using these data, we were able to construct a Priority Illnesses and Conditions (PIC) table, a portion of which is reproduced in Table 10.1.

The indices we used were taken primarily from the work of Tugwell *et al* (1985), who describe a method, the Measurement Iterative Loop, by which a health problem can be described in terms suitable for a priorization scheme. Originally proposed as 'a framework for the critical appraisal of need, benefits and costs of health interventions', the Measurement Iterative Loop (Figure 10.1) may also be used as a framework for the setting of educational priorities and as a tool for understanding the broader, population-based implications of a wide variety of diseases and adverse health conditions. Tugwell *et al* applied Loop analysis to the problems of hypertension and

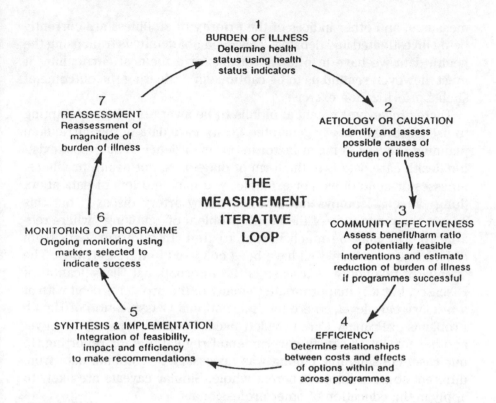

Figure 10.1 *The measurement iterative loop*

osteoarthritis in their original paper, while Pickering has used the
Loop as an educational model for health promotion and the role of the
physician in the problem of smoking cessation (Pickering *et al*, 1987).
Clearly, the schema outlined in Table 10.1 for judging the educational
importance of an illness or condition represents an ideal towards
which to strive, rather than a *fait accompli*. Indices of importance,
and the categories within the indices against which 'problems' or
'cases' are judged, will vary with time and between settings. What is
most important is actually to define and decide upon which indices are
most appropriate for a particular school and setting. In the medical
sphere, in developed countries at least, data on incidence, prevalence
and case-fatality rate are generally available and of reasonable quality.
However, data on quality of life following an illness, the accuracy and
predictive value of diagnostic tests under varying circumstances, the
efficacy of various preventive, therapeutic and rehabilitative

measures, and other indices of the priority of an illness are currently being investigated and debated. This need not detain us from using the health data we have in priority setting for a medical curriculum; it must, however, remind us to be cautious in evaluating the outcome of such a prioritization exercise.

There are several potential pitfalls to be aware of when attempting to use existing or newly generated health care data in the curriculum planning process. A major factor in our experience is that most existing health care data is in the form of diagnoses, not health problems, illnesses or conditions. For example, you may find lots of data about 'lung cancer', 'emphysema' and 'coronary artery disease', but this misses the magnitude of the health problem of 'smoking', where reliable figures may be much harder to find. In addition, data from dfflerent sources may well have been collected in different ways. The 'standard' taxonomy of disease is the International Classification of Diseases, but it is inappropriate to many of the problems dealt with at a primary care level, where the International Classification of Health Problems in Primary Care is widely used. Hospital data may be in yet another format to satisfy governmental regulations for reporting. In our case, considerable editing was necessary to combine data from different sources into a coherent whole. Similar caveats are likely to apply in the education of other professionals.

Common, severe problems for which effective interventions exist, such as ischemic heart disease, burns and asthma, are clearly high priorities for medical education when assessed either by a method dependent on analysis of health data (MacDonald *et al*, 1989) or by a consensus of clinical faculty (Chong *et al*, 1984). Similarly, conditions of lower prevalence and severity, for which interventions are of limited or questionable value, are considered to be of lower educational priority by both approaches. This second type of condition may well have a much higher *research* priority than an *educational* priority. It is also important to realize that we are speaking not only of 'curative' interventions, but also those interventions directed towards caring and rehabilitation. There is considerable evidence that physicians' interpersonal skills play an important part in the healing process in and of themselves. For example, the Headache Study Group (1986) found that the best outcomes after one year of follow-up were in patients who felt they had been given sufficient opportunity to tell the doctor all they wanted to say about their headaches on the initial visit. The diagnosis, type of investigation or treatment, or referral had no relationship to outcome. Thus, strong interpersonal skills are an 'effective intervention' in our sense for *all* illnesses, and the teaching and learning of these skills is vital in all medical curricula, problem based or otherwise.

When we compared the two approaches of analysis of health data and consensus of clinical faculty, we found some conditions which the faculty felt were priorities but which did not appear in the PIC table; among these conditions were spontaneous abortion, premenstrual syndrome and osteoporosis. Again, this illustrates the problems of using diagnostic data to plan a medical curriculum. Also of interest were health problems and conditions which one might believe should be educational priorities but which appeared neither in the PIC table nor in the faculty survey; such conditions might include deficient nutrition of the elderly, smoking and immobilization following accidents or surgery. Clearly, a combination of the two approaches is superior to either used alone; but the combination is far from infallible.

A combined approach to curriculum development using both expert consensus and analysis of existing data has been used at Chulalongkorn University in Bangkok, Thailand. This medical school already had two tracks – one for 'regular' physicians and one for those who would be practising in remote areas. Wishing to institute a curriculum which would be responsive to the health needs of the population in both rural and urban settings, curriculum planners began work on the Community-Targeted Problem-Based Curriculum (Sitthi-Amorn, personal communication, 1989). They studied Thai health data and, based on concepts of magnitude, severity and effectiveness of intervention, developed ten curricular 'blocks' for their six-year curriculum. The 'block titles' included such priorities as 'trauma' and 'infectious diseases'. Within each block priority health problems were chosen by a committee of content experts. This innovative approach was begun in 1989, and though analysis of its worth has not yet appeared, the concept is exciting.

It is also possible to survey medical students for their ideas concerning educational priorities. In January of 1987, the portion of the McMaster MD curriculum related to 'the life cycle' required students to seek out patients, preferably in community settings, and perform a history and physical examination. They then had to examine the patient's problem from the perspective of population health, and report to their tutorial group about their findings, conclusions and opinions on how medical care should change to improve the outcomes of patients with that particular condition. A series of modified essay questions based on the steps in the Measurement Iterative Loop guided the students' thinking in examining population perspectives of their patients' illnesses.

Before I describe what the students did, I should say a word about the medical students at McMaster. All students have at least a bachelor's degree; many have more advanced degrees. In addition, medical students at McMaster are chosen on the basis of demonstrated problem-solving skills, past history of community involvement, and other criteria in addition to the usual criteria of admission to medical school. Also, the curriculum unit in which this experiment occurred takes place in the 12 weeks just prior to the start of the clinical clerkship, the final year of medical school. Thus, these students were already seasoned adult learners when they were seeking out particular clinical problems which interested them. In a setting in which students have not had as much opportunity to develop their own self-directed learning skills, much more guidance from the faculty would be necessary to allow students to develop these skills in a progressive manner.

The health problems sought out by the students, while inevitably influenced by patient availability, still form an index of the educational priorities of the students themselves, since each student could choose which health problem he or she wished to study. When we analysed the data concerning the patients which the students had chosen to examine, we found that the correlation between the patients' diagnoses and the PIC table entries was 0.85 (the students were not aware of the PIC table). Thus it seems that the educational priorities of students correlated closelywith the priorities generated from analysis of health data. This information about medical students' own educational priorities is of considerable importance in a medical school which emphasizes self-directed learning.

In summary, the selection of priority problems on which to construct a problem-based curriculum requires input from a variety of sources. The faculty, naturally, have much to say about this, as they do in all professional schools. They are the content experts. The process which I have described differs in that problems selected for study must be shown to be priorities based on defined and clearly articulated criteria, however they may be defined in each institution. For example, the questions of the 'prototypicality' of diabetes vs hypothyroidism vs Cushing's syndrome when attempting to teach concepts of endocrine disorders is a proper matter for debate in the curriculum committee of a medical school. If you cannot afford the time to cover all three, which one(s) do you choose, and on what basis? Similarly, the curriculum committee of a business school might debate the relative priorities of the steel industry vs the dairy industry vs the toy industry to decide which is best to illustrate concepts of marketing.

In addition, the adult learners who are the consumers of PBL should be trusted to define their own educational priorities, and these should be taken into consideration. This does not mean that student preferences drive the problem selection process in a problem-based curriculum. Rather, it means that adult learners have some or all of the necessary characteristics to engage in self-directed learning and that this ability should be fostered by faculty. In a school where students have already obtained at least an undergraduate degree, this process is easier to implement than in a school where learners are accepted from the secondary education level. In the latter situation, much more initial guidance will be necessary for students to acquire self-directed learning skills. The product of this educational process should be a mature professional with a commitment to lifelong learning and the skills necessary to critique his or her performance, to know his or her strengths and weaknesses, and to take educational action to address areas of deficiency. It is the responsibility of faculty to foster the development of such individuals, both by providing graduated responsibility for self-directed learning as the students work through problems in the curriculum, and by modelling such skills themselves.

Finally, the use of existing or newly generated health care data will help to ensure that the problems selected for study are representative of real illnesses in real people, making medical education more responsive to the needs of individuals in the population served by graduates of the school. Similarly, educators in other professions may make use of existing data in their own fields to design the problems used for study in their own curricula. The major point here is that the problems chosen for inclusion in the curriculum should pass through a prioritization process to ensure that they are representative of the kinds of problem that graduates are likely to encounter. The prioritization schema includes indices of educational importance specific to the field of study; in medical education, the major indices are the magnitude and severity of the problem and the effectiveness of interventions.

References

Canada Health Survey (1987) Ottawa: Statistics Canada.
Chong, J P, Neufeld, V, Oates, M J *et al* (1984) The selection of priority prob-

lems and conditions: an innovative approach to curriculum design in medical education, *Proceedings of the Annual Conference on Research in Medical Education*, 23, 17–25.

Fink, A, Siu, A L, Brook, R H *et al* (1987) The Quality Assurance Panel: assuring the quality of health care for older persons: an expert panel's priorities, *Journal of the American Medical Association*, 258, 1905–1908.

Headache Study Group of the University of Western Ontario (1986) Predictors of outcome in headache patients presenting to family physicians – a one-year prospective study, *Headache Journal*, 26, 285–294.

MacDonald, P J, Chong, J P, Neufeld, V R *et al* (1989) Setting educational priorities for learning the concepts of population health, *Medical Education*, 23, 429–439.

Pickering, R J, Neufeld, V R and McIntyre, E L (1987) The Iterative Loop as an educational model for health promotion. Smoking and health: the role of the physician. Paper presented to the Kaiser Foundation by McMaster University Office of Health Sciences Education.

Rosser, W W and Beaulieu, M (1984) Institutional objectives for medical education that relates to the community, *Canadian Medical Association Journal*, 130, 683–689.

Tugwell, P, Bennett, K J, Sackett, D L and Haynes, R B (1985) The Measurement Iterative Loop: a framework for the critical appraisal of need, benefits and costs of health interventions, *Journal of Chronic Diseases*, 38, 339–361.

Chapter 11

Responding to 'Non-traditional' Students: An Enquiry and Action Approach

Imogen Taylor and Hilary Burgess

A rapidly growing literature addresses many dimensions of the philosophy, methodology and outcomes of courses using PBL. One aspect which has been neglected is the student experience of problem-based courses. It is important to begin to question whether PBL is particularly suited to some categories of students. Increasing clarity on this issue will contribute to our effectiveness as educators in designing and developing courses appropriate for the students we work with. In this chapter we open the debate by looking at the experience of 'non-traditional learners' with PBL. Non-traditional learners are those students who did not achieve a standard school-leaving qualification and enter higher education through a variety of routes, including access programmes and schemes which accredit prior learning.

For many years, attention has been given to broadening access to professional and higher education for students who have been educationally disadvantaged by virtue of class, race or gender. The focus has been on the entry stage, yet if the open door is not to lead to a revolving one (Woodley et al, 1987), non-traditional learners must have a positive experience of education. The focus of attention must now shift to include discussion about the accessibility of courses, and the 'transformation of higher education in such ways as to make it more attractive, relevant and open to all sections of the population' (Wright, 1991: 7).

Our experience with PBL implemented throughout a social work programme leads us to suggest that there are some elements of the

103

approach that make it particularly relevant for non-traditional learners. Our central thesis is that for these students PBL can mitigate the barriers to learning and the resulting sense of disjuncture, and can also enhance their sense of integration (Weil, 1986). In this chapter, after defining the diverse group of students who are the subjects for our discussion, we set the scene with a brief description of key features of the problem-based approach in question. We then explore the evidence which leads to our proposition. Finally, we discuss elements of the course which we suggest are central to structuring PBL for non-traditional learners.

Who are the non-traditional learners?

There is a noticeable absence of a developed discourse about non-traditional students. Terms such as 'drop-out', 'non-standard' and 'disadvantaged' all reflect the marginalization of students who are the focus of attention in this chapter. Whereas the term 'non-traditional' risks further marginalizing these students as it views them against the norm of the dominant majority who successfully complete their schooling and enter higher education using conventional routes, we hope the term also conveys the diversity of experience of the students we are concerned with here (Weil, 1986).

Evidence indicates that over-represented in the non-traditional group are working-class students, students from ethnic minorities and women in both of these categories. With respect to ethnicity, considerable advances have been made in the accessibility of higher education but there are significant differences between different ethnic minority groups, between institutions and between subjects (Modood, 1993). Class inequalities, however, have remained stable for the past three generations and 'it may even turn out on further evidence that ethnicity per se is not a barrier: only the asymmetric fit of race to class produces apparent inequality of access' (Halsey, 1993: 131). Disability is now being acknowledged as a further issue in equality of access to higher education (Barnes, 1991). There is also evidence that older students may be marginalized (Richardson, 1994). While inequalities in the access of women as a whole have diminished in recent years, there remains a problem in access for women who are also members of these other social groupings.

The above studies provide important data about entry to higher education. Yet, there have been remarkably few studies in the UK of the experience of non-traditional learners with higher education. One exception is a study of 'non-standard' students that concluded that of over-riding importance was an access-oriented culture and the willingness and competence of staff to respond to student need (Mills and Molloy, 1989). These findings are echoed in two other small studies (Rosen, 1993). Similar findings about 'retention' in the US (Berger, 1992) also focus on the importance of institutional support such as student advisers and study skills programmes to help students adapt to the requirements of the dominant system, rather than requiring the curriculum to become more accessible to a range of students.

It is our contention that whereas support is important, it is unrealistic in a context of continuing cutbacks and restraint to expect to increase or even sustain present levels of institutional support for students. Furthermore, continuing to focus on the need for support risks pathologizing an increasingly large group of students who can be assumed by virtue of reaching higher education via very circuitous routes to have been very resourceful. Our attention in this chapter is on harnessing such resourcefulness to a problem-based curriculum, building on the strengths which non-traditional students bring.

The context

In the late 1980s the model of PBL developed in medical education (Neufeld and Barrows, 1974) was adapted for the social work programme at Bristol University and in 1990 'enquiry and action learning' (EAL) was introduced. This name was chosen to emphasize the process of learning through discovery and action, and underlines the centrality of integrating theory and practice. EAL has been fully described elsewhere (Burgess, 1992). To contextualize discussion in this chapter, it is important for the reader to know that an EAL curriculum includes four central linked elements: a problem-based approach, learning in groups, strategies to encourage self-directed learning, and a balance between propositional, process and personal knowledge (Eraut, 1994).

Study themes are the focus for student activity and form the building blocks for the course which, with modularization from 1996, have been grouped into units or modules. Themes last for two to three weeks and are built around situations derived from social work practice. Each theme includes a central topic and a range of subsidiary or parallel issues. Each module has a supporting series of at most two lectures a week which address central theoretical issues.

The professional social work qualification, the Diploma in Social Work, is linked to a requirement for full-time (or equivalent) study for two years. This may be entered at the graduate or undergraduate level, and Bristol is unusual in that the course combines both categories of student. This provided an ideal opportunity to evaluate the experience of different groups of learners and in 1991, an indepth study of the experience of 12 non-traditional learners on the Bristol course was begun (Taylor, forthcoming). The research builds on an evaluation of EAL (Taylor, 1993) when initial findings indicated that the experience of non-traditional learners was an important area for further study. Students included in the sample all had very negative early experiences with education and left school at age 16 or earlier with minimal qualifications. Seven had since completed access courses with the objective of gaining entry to higher education. The sample was predominantly working class and included nine women, three of whom were from ethnic minority groups. The average age was 35.

Disjuncture and integration

In analysing the data, a framework of disjuncture and integration derived from an earlier study (Weil, 1989) was illuminating. Weil proposes that the experience of non-traditional learners is shaped by alternative values and experiences, and by an identity forged by differential access to opportunity (1988: 28). She defines disjuncture as arising from mutually interacting influences, the feeling of being at odds with oneself and involving issues of identity and how one's present experiences relate to the past. If disjuncture interacts with 'miseducation' then the overall identity of the learner is undermined. Weil found that adults experienced disjuncture in relation to dealing with multiple and conflicting roles, expectations of and initial encounter with the formal learning context, the ways in which social and power differences were experienced and managed, the kinds of knowledge allowed and disallowed, and the extent to which core aspects of identity felt threatened. In the following discussion we develop Weil's framework further by differentiating between external pressures over which educators have little direct control and course pressures which can be addressed through the curriculum.

Disjuncture can be anticipated and managed using a variety of strategies, resulting in learning and integration for the student. Of particular importance to integration is positive valuing, the appreciation and active use of different kinds of knowledge, the use of personal and social difference within the group, and making connections across interdisciplinary boundaries. As we hope to demonstrate in this chapter, it is our view that the implementation of PBL at Bristol actively supports strategies of this kind.

External pressures towards disjuncture

We only briefly touch on external pressures of role strain and student poverty here, because although they contributed significantly to the Bristol students' experience of disjuncture, they are not pressures which can be addressed through the curriculum itself. A Canadian study (Home, 1993) suggests multiple-role students now comprise the fastest growing group in universities. Particularly noticeable among Bristol students were the demands of caring responsibilities for children as well as older relatives. Role conflict may be further exacerbated by lack of familial support for entering higher education, an experience also reported in studies of ethnic minority students where family and community relationships are strained as students are perceived as joining an alien establishment (Rosen, 1993). These feelings can be reinforced by a sense of isolation when the large majority of students are from the dominant culture (Bird, 1996).

Lack of financial resources was also significant in students' experience of disjuncture. Full-time students felt they had no option but to sustain part-time employment which incvitably eroded study time and contributed to tensions in managing the demands of the course and external responsibilities. Pressures like as these must be addressed through structures such as part-time courses and the provision of adequate funding mechanisms.

Course pressures towards disjuncture

Similar to students in Weil's study (1989), the Bristol students experienced disjuncture particularly at the beginning of the course when the discontinuity between present and past experience was most acute. It is our proposition that discontinuity is almost inevitable and the crucial issue, as we shall see in the discussion of integrating factors, is how to manage it and avoid undermining the identity of the learner.

The students all shared negative early experiences with schooling and had left school identified as non-achievers and feeling inferior.

They entered higher education with feelings ranging from considerable trepidation to outright terror, described in a study of ethnic minority students as 'entering unknown territory and feeling their way blindfolded through what they understood to be a minefield, intended to explode their aspirations at the first chance' (Rosen, 1993: 182). Likewise, the Bristol students reported feeling they were in the wrong place and did not belong. Linked with this was a striking lack of preparation for the kind of course they were embarking on with the overwhelming preoccupation being doubts about their ability to succeed and fear of failure. This early research finding contributed to important course developments designed to alleviate this particular disjuncture (Taylor and Burgess, 1995).

Social and power differences are heightened for non-traditional learners simply by virtue of entering a traditional hierarchical establishment such as a university. The Bristol course emphasizes the importance of making explicit and critiquing social and power differences, both in relation to individual students and society as a whole. For students from disadvantaged groups, particularly those from ethnic minority groups, this was powerful as for some they began to speak freely for the first time, experience anger and understand some of the forces of oppression. This is an important step towards integration, yet it can also result in fracture and fragmentation.

The kinds of knowledge allowed and disallowed were important in the exploration of social and power differences. Students did not feel that all their experiences were allowed, either by other students or staff. This may not be surprising given the challenge for the group and the facilitator of containing the intense feelings which can be generated when different kinds of knowledge are confronted. This was particularly acute for example in acknowledging the depth of feelings about racism. When such knowledge is not allowed, it stirs up old feelings of being inferior and not being heard. This problem can be exacerbated by the dilemma for students of publicly revealing their uncertainties and tensions to staff, and risking being identified as problematic and failing.

The identity of non-traditional students was further challenged by a conflict between their language and the requirements of academic success. Students were required to change or adapt their spoken and written language to conform to that of the dominant group. On the Bristol course this was further compounded by a 'Use of English' policy which met requirements for professional competence.

It can be seen that whereas higher education appears to offer the

promise of fulfilment and improvement in life chances, opportunities for 'miseducation' (Weil, 1989) are inherent in the system,
threatening a non-traditional student's identity. In the next section we
go on to examine features of the curriculum which mitigate against
miseducation.

Integrating factors

The pressures towards disjuncture were mitigated in several important
ways by integrating factors. Key among these are positive valuing of
students, the appreciation of different kinds of knowledge students
bring, the emphasis on active learning, and learning across disciplinary boundaries.

The importance of positive valuing of non-traditional students is
identified elsewhere in the literature (Bird, 1996; Mills and Molloy,
1989; Rosen, 1993). Generally it is discussed only in relation to staff
valuing students. Weil extends this to valuing by the group:

> enabling teachers and groups can go a long way to counteract the impact
> of disjunction arising from forces that seem outside the bounds of one per-
> son's agency, and to create an oasis of integration in which the experience
> of other kinds of disjunction can be made sense of and more effectively
> managed. (Weil, 1989: 143)

Certainly for Bristol students, the positive valuing they experienced
from their peers in learning groups was central. The groups met three
times a week for a term and became a cohesive and supportive force
in the life of the students. First term groups in particular provided a
crucial base, thus playing an important integrating role in the students' experience.

Very much linked with positive valuing is appreciation of different
kinds of knowledge. Three aspects appeared significant in the Bristol
students' experience. The course places high value on integrating personal knowledge into an overall framework of professional knowledge
which views personal, process and propositional knowledge as equally
important (Eraut, 1994). This supported students to identify their pre-
course experiences as relevant, worthwhile and important to professional development, and contributed to their experience of being
positively valued. Second, valuing the pre-course experience of non-
traditional learners very significantly counterbalanced the value for
graduates of their prior academic training. Both graduates and non-
graduates became aware of the value of their particular kind of

pre-course experience and possibilities for reciprocity. Third, the emphasis on students learning from each other meant that they shared knowledge in ways they found accessible and over which they had control.

Another important integrating aspect was the emphasis on active learning. For this group of learners, much of their learning pre-course had been experiential and the switch to an abstract conceptualizing mode on entering higher education was too abrupt to be easily managed. The relatively few lectures were on the whole not favourably received; lecturers were accused of not using an accessible discourse, delivering the material too fast and not addressing the needs of the individual. In contrast, group learning activities were very positively received. Students reported enjoying the activities of searching out material from a range of sources and devising strategies for sharing the information obtained, using activities such as role plays or debates to extend their learning.

The students were also very positive about learning across disciplinary boundaries. They had the advantage of not having to unlearn a disciplinary approach to learning. Learning in relation to a problem or case study made sense and enabled the integration of personal, process and propositional knowledge. It also built on pre-course experiences of addressing problems and enhanced their motivation to learn. PBL appeared directly relevant to their objective of becoming professional social workers.

There are indications that these integrative aspects are particularly important for non-traditional women learners who account for a significant proportion of the Bristol students. Bristol women reported that the learning group afforded the opportunity to share struggles in learning with others (especially women), to confront crises of identity, to develop confidence and to link affective and cognitive learning. Similarly the emphasis on personal experience was felt to make the course accessible to women, for whom such an exploration was considered essential to learning. One student commented:

> I think EAL is in fact a feminine form of education, and as such allows feminine attributes to grow. As a woman my experience has been a valuable asset and I have found the course to be a creative experience.

Belenky *et al* (1988) in their research into women learning report similar findings:

> educators can help women develop their own authentic voices if they emphasise connection over separation, understanding and acceptance over assessment, and collaboration over debate; if they accord respect to

and allow time for knowledge that emerges from first hand experience; if instead of imposing their own expectations and arbitrary requirements, they encourage students to evolve their own patterns of work based on the problems they are pursuing (229).

In a professional education course where assessment is required, it is not possible to meet all these criteria. However, in the next section we identify some aspects of the problem-based curriculum which appear particularly enabling for non-traditional learners.

Structuring PBL for non-traditional learners

Despite the opportunities offered for non-traditional learners, PBL does not in itself offer a panacea. Key features which must be addressed in a problem-based approach to enable integration for these students include attention to curriculum content, assessment, the composition of learning groups, the skills of facilitation, and the availability of tutor support. These factors must be placed within the wider organizational context which clearly influences the experience and self-concept of non-traditional students. There is a considerable literature (see for example, Farish *et al*, 1995) on working towards equal opportunities in higher education, highlighting policies and procedures in areas such as admissions, assessment and the profile of staff, and all must be considered in a strategy to increase accessibility for non-traditional students. In social work at Bristol, some important equal opportunities work has been done, although the wider university context has been less developed in this respect.

Turning to the curriculum, attention must be paid to the content of the study outlines or problems used, to ensure that these reflect the concerns and needs of all sections of the population, and do not make implicit assumptions about 'normality'. If, for example, scenarios do not specify the ethnicity of individuals or families, the risk is that white Eurocentric assumptions are made. However, where racial origin is specified, there may still be difficulties. In a study theme on 'Offending behaviour', if the key character is African-Caribbean, this may collude with stereotypes about race and crime; but if the character is white, important issues about the treatment of people from ethnic minorities in the criminal justice system may not be addressed. Curriculum design must reflect diversity.

Assessment is an area of the curriculum which we have only just begun to develop, in part to address the integration of non-traditional students. Notably, assignments have a potential purpose beyond providing summative evidence. For example, preparing briefing papers or giving presentations may be particularly helpful for non-traditional learners, since they rely less on the use of academic writing than conventional assignments. There is evidence that written assignments with standard deadlines may also present particular problems for some disabled students, and we are beginning to explore introducing assignments which do not further disadvantage students.

Bristol students spend the majority of their time working in small groups. Groupwork theory identifies the importance of group composition and the risks for students already marginalized in society of being in a numerical minority in a group (Brown and Mistry, 1994). We have evolved a careful strategy for composing initial study groups taking into account aspects of the student profile, and using principles agreed with students. Students from ethnic minorities, who represent around 10 per cent of the student intake, are grouped so that they make up a significant proportion of a study group. Students are asked prior to admission whether they wish disclose to staff any physical or mental impairment and/or their sexual orientation, and whether they wish such factors to be taken into account in group formation. Consequently some gay and lesbian students, and some disabled students, are clustered to enable mutual support. Male students who are in a numerical minority are allocated proportionally to groups. Subsequent groups are formed largely according to student choice of elective work, with student needs and preferences as outlined above taken into account. Since students participate in a range of groups during the course they experience considerable variation in membership.

The group facilitator exercises considerable influence in relation to the experience of non-traditional students (Burgess and Taylor, 1995). First and foremost he or she has a responsibility to enable equal opportunity of participation by group members. This may include ensuring all students contribute their views at some point in each session, engaging with students at risk of being marginalized, and challenging discriminatory assumptions. Facilitating the expression of social and power differences and the sharing of different kinds of knowledge will inevitably generate the expression of intense feelings which the facilitator is important in containing (Taylor, forthcoming). Facilitation responsibilities must be shared with students and the facilitator acts both as a role model and an enabler of positive practice, demonstrating skills and values which are essential both to adult learning and to professional practice.

Empowerment practice occurs within a framework of power relations inside and outside the study group. It would be tempting to present the facilitation of study groups purely as an 'empowerment' model of groupwork (Mullender and Ward, 1991), but to do so would be to occlude the issues of power, authority and accountability inherent in the educational setting. For example, facilitators inevitably carry a variety of roles in the educational setting, including powerful gatekeeping roles of assessment. Preston-Shoot argues that if social workers are to promote empowerment and partnership within a practice framework which takes account of the power and authority structures, then,

> approaches must be found for tackling the structures of oppression, for identifying how power is defined, exercised and experienced; and for enabling people to acquire the confidence to take effective action to address that exclusion, isolation and powerlessness. (1992: 9)

Issues of power must be understood and addressed to support the learning of non-traditional students.

To manage these contradictions and tensions, facilitators must be clear with students about the power and authority they carry in different roles, the way in which they exercise power, and how it can be shared with students. In addition, facilitators must develop a critical appraisal of the educational institution's roles, tasks, functions and decision-making structures, and be willing to identify and challenge oppressive practices and policies. Crucially, staff must be clear about what is negotiable and non-negotiable. In relation to assessment, Heron (1988) formulates a continuum of models, with varying levels of student and staff control, and argues that the position of a course on this continuum may be less important than clarity about what is negotiable. While good practice in respect of these issues is clearly of relevance to all students, for 'non-traditional' learners a message is conveyed about a real commitment to disadvantage.

Finally, non-traditional students are more likely than others to have experienced oppression, their vulnerability is higher and they may have deep concerns about traditional expectations of learning relationships. A willingness on the part of tutors to listen to and help students make sense of their personal educational history, the new form of learning they are experiencing and their own reaction to it may be crucial. In a context of resource cuts, such time may be hard to find.

Conclusion

Our argument is that PBL enables non-traditional learners to integrate their learning and manage the impact of disjuncture inevitable in higher education as it is structured today. This proposition needs to be investigated in the context of different PBL courses. We recognize that there may be other powerful mitigating factors at work at Bristol such as a culture which is supportive to non-traditional students, and the location of the course in professional education which may in itself be favourable for PBL. It is also possible that PBL is an approach which suits a range of students, including those whose educational path has been a more traditional one.

In six years of operation EAL has attracted considerable interest in social work education both nationally and internationally, and has contributed to curriculum developments in other professional courses. In the assessment of teaching quality undertaken by the Higher Education Funding Council in 1994, social work at Bristol was one of a small minority of social work courses to be awarded the designation of 'excellent', representing a considerable public achievement for a PBL course.

References

Barnes, C (1991) *Disabled People in Britain and Discrimination: A Case for Anti-discrimination Legislation*, Calgary: Hurst.

Belenky, M, Clinchy, B, Goldberger, N and Tarule, J (1988) *Women's Ways of Knowing: The Development of Self, Voice and Mind*. New York: Basic Books.

Berger, R (1992) Student retention: a critical phase in the academic careers of minority baccalaureate students, *Journal of Social Work Education*, 28, 85–97.

Bird, J (1996) *Black Students in Higher Education: Rhetorics and Realities*. Buckingham: SRHE and Open University Press.

Brown, A and Mistry, T (1994) Groupwork with 'mixed membership' group; issues of race and gender, *Social Work with Groups*, 17, 5–23.

Burgess, H (1992) *Problem-Led Learning for Social Work: The Enquiry and Action Learning Approach*. London: Whiting and Birch.

Burgess, H and Taylor, I (1995) Facilitating enquiry and action groups for social work education, *Groupwork*, 8, 2, 117–135.

Eraut, M (1994) *Developing Professional Knowledge and Competence*. London: Falmer Press.

Farish, M, McPake, J, Powney, J and Weiner, G (1995) *Equal Opportunities in Colleges and Universities: Towards Better Practices*. Buckingham: SRHE and Open University Press.

Halsey, A H (1993) Trends in access and equity in higher education: Britain in international perspective, *Oxford Review of Education*, 19, 129–140.

Heron, J (1988) Assessment revisited, in D Boud (ed) *Developing Student Autonomy in Learning*, 2nd edn. London: Kogan Page, 77–90.

Home, A (1993) The juggling act: the multiple role woman in social work education, *Canadian Social Work Review*, 10, 2, 141–156.

Mills, A J and Molloy, S T (1989) Experiencing the experienced: the impact of non-standard entrants upon a programme of higher education, *Studies in Higher Education*, 14, 41–53.

Modood, T (1993) The number of ethnic minority students in British Higher Education: some grounds for optimism, *Oxford Review of Education*, 19, 167–182.

Mullender, A and Ward, D (1991) *Self Directed Groupwork: Users Take Action for Empowerment*. London: Whiting and Birch.

Neufeld, V R and Barrows, H S (1974) The McMaster Philosophy: an approach to medical education, *Journal of Medical Education*, 49, 1040–1050.

Preston-Shoot, M (1992) On empowerment, partnership and authority in groupwork practice: a training contribution, *Groupwork*, 5, 2, 5–30.

Richardson, J T E (1994) Mature students in higher education: a literature survey on approaches to studying, *Studies in Higher Education*, 19, 309–325.

Rosen, V (1993) Black students in higher education, in M Thorpe, R Edwards and A Hanson (eds) *Culture and Processes of Adult Learning*. London: Routledge, 178–193.

Taylor, I (1993) A case for social work evaluation of social work education, *British Journal of Social Work*, 23, 123–138.

Taylor, I (forthcoming) *Developing Learning for Professional Practice*. Buckingham: SRHE and Open University Press.

Taylor, I and Burgess, H (1995) Orientation to self-directed learning: paradox or paradigm? *Studies in Higher Education*, 20, 1, 87–98.

Weil, S (1986) Non-traditional learners within higher education institutions: discovery and disappointment, *Studies in Higher Education*, 11, 219–235.

Weil, S (1988) From a language of observation to a language of experience: studying the perspectives of diverse adults in higher education, *Journal of Access Studies*, 3, 17–43.

Weil, S (1989) Access: towards education or miseducation? Adults imagine the future, in O Fulton (ed) *Access and Institutional Change*. Buckingham: SRHE and Open University Press, 110–143.

Woodley, A, Wagner, L, Slowey, M, Hamilton, M and Fulton, O (1987) *Choosing to Learn: Adults in Higher Education*. Buckingham: SRHE and Open University Press.

Wright, P (1991) Access or accessibility? *Journal of Access Studies*, 6, 6–15.

Chapter 12

Preparing Tertiary Teachers for Problem-based Learning

Shona Little

How can tertiary teachers be helped to acquire the skills needed for effective implementation of problem based learning? What type of training module might best suit their needs? And what practical difficulties might teachers face when they implement PBL for the first time? These are some of the many questions I have addressed over the last eight years in my work as a teacher educator and professional developer of staff.

In the New Zealand tertiary education sector, teachers are generally recruited straight from business, industry, the professions, and the community. They are a hugely diverse group who represent not only a wide range of academic disciplines and practices, but also distinct professional and business 'cultures'. The module which was designed to train teachers in the implementation of PBL was an optional course for the Auckland Institute of Technology's Diploma in Adult and Tertiary Education. The teachers who selected this module as part of their training represented the full diversity of academic disciplines and subject areas. The module therefore had to address and encompass that diversity by meeting the individual needs of people whose experience and levels of education were very different, and it also had to accommodate the different value systems and perspectives which participants brought to their combined learning experience.

Course design

The aims of the module were to provide participants with:

□ an understanding of the process and practice of PBL;
□ an understanding of the philosophy and the main educational principles involved;
□ an opportunity to begin to develop their own problem-based course materials and to obtain peer feedback on these at the draft stage;
□ an opportunity to try out a short problem-based session with a peer group, and to gain peer feedback on both the facilitation and the structure of that session.

In achieving the module aims the following were the key processes and activities.

Problem-based sessions in which teachers participated as 'students' can be invaluable. These sessions provide not only models of the range of types of PBL, but also examples of content to be learned and assessed, a model and experience of group problem solving, and in-depth experiences of the PBL process. These experiences encouraged understanding at the 'feeling' and perceptual levels as well as the cognitive and metacognitive levels, and formed a framework for a realistic comparison with and analysis of their own teaching situations.

Meta-level discussion is a key means of generating skill transfer: it helps pull together isolated knowledge, skills and experience into an holistic in-depth understanding. The aspects of learning which are frequently automatic and hidden need to be made *overt* – visible, open to challenge, thoughtful, and applied to practice. This helps ground participants' reflection and analysis within the fullness and complexity of their own teaching situations.

Because problem-based experiences on their own are not always sufficient to create important attitudinal and perceptual changes, teachers need to identify the relationship between their current theories in use and their theories in action (Argyris and Schön, 1974) and realistically appraise their levels of skill as facilitators, curriculum developers and assessors.

Mindmapping. Most teachers have highly developed analytical skills. However, a surprising number have never thought about how any knowledge base might be structured; they have simply assumed that the structure is hierarchical. Mindmapping can swiftly undo this assumption, by showing the relational nature of knowledge, and by actually providing an experience of the way in which knowledge, its applications, and related thoughts and feelings are connected and interwoven. Mindmapping can be used very effectively to provide a summary of key aspects of a training programme. (Figure 12.1 provides an example of one group's end-of-module map of their ideas about the 'Basics for success' in PBL.)

Mindmapping has other benefits. After a mindmapping session, people often become more open to and tolerant of others' ideas and beliefs, and more appreciative of creativity and originality. This is important as problem solving requires both convergent and divergent thinking, and mindmapping is an extremely useful 'tool' for exploratory and generative thinking.

A problem-solving workshop. The aim of this workshop is to provide teachers with an opportunity to explore their thinking processes as well as their attitudes and feelings when problem solving. They are given five different kinds of puzzles or 'problems'. Working in pairs, in a non-competitive situation, they articulate and record (as far as possible) both their feelings and their thoughts from the moment they first glance at the puzzle through to the final outcome (Whimbey and Lochhead, 1991; Woods, 1984). This highlights the important attitudinal component of problem solving as well as clearly identifying some of the other barriers to problem solving; it also demonstrates a variety of approaches to problem-solving.

Provision of problem-solving strategies. These help teachers focus effectively and constructively on the task, remain focused, avoid or overcome interpersonal problems within the group, and monitor and evaluate their progress.

It can be both risky and unrealistic to expect groups, even groups of teachers, to either generate an effective problem-solving strategy themselves, or work systematically and constructively through a problem-solving process without a strategy to guide them. The introduction and initial use of a strategy requires careful facilitation. Teachers can (as readily as students) jump to conclusions and avoid clearly identifying their learning needs. If this happens, not only does important content not get mastered, but also the monitoring of progress and assessing of learning are likely to be less than adequate.

A positive climate for learning has been identified by many educationalists as a critical factor in effective learning. This is especially important when students are being encouraged to change, to take risks, and to become more autonomous, because it helps develop a

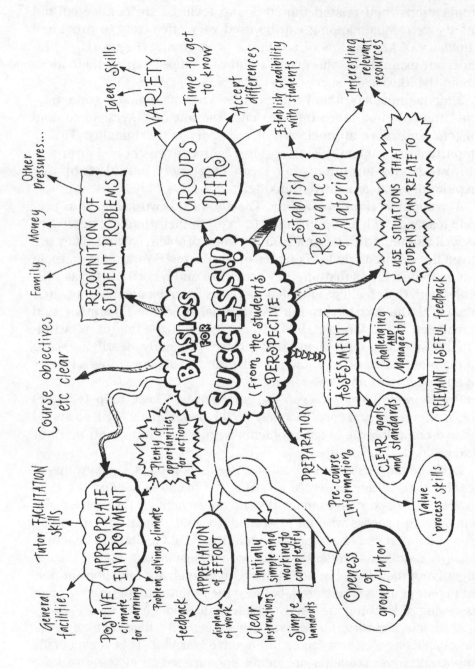

Figure 12.1 *An end-of-module map*

peer learning community (Heron, 1993) within which the individual student can gain both support and feedback.

It can be a delicate balancing act for a module leader to encourage much needed academic debate on the philosophy, theory and practice of PBL while at the same time avoiding the negativity which can result from an over-emphasis on critical analysis (at a time when people, who are used to being respected and to feeling both competent and confident, may be being challenged at levels of basic values and beliefs).

Difficulties with implementing PBL

The following list of difficulties is the result of many interviews and discussions with teachers and students involved in a variety of problem-based programmes over the last two years. I will comment on them in order of impact on the teachers.

Teachers' role change. By far the major difficulty in implementing PBL is the teachers' inability to understand thoroughly the extent of the role change they are going to have to make, and to see how this might affect the satisfaction they find in teaching and their feelings of being 'valued' as teachers. The path from lecturer to facilitator is often an uneasy one. Those who have taught competently and efficiently using lecturing techniques, and who prize that competence and efficiency, can find the change especially hard to adjust to. Such teachers usually value themselves as subject 'experts' and for these people the reality of implementing PBL can sometimes prove too much to accept.

Some teachers do not fully understand the complexity of the facilitation process (though they may well be fully committed to and understand the philosophy of PBL). They expect their students to move straight from teacher-directed to student directed learning, and blame the students when the latter are resistant, become confused or fail. As Woods (1985) has pointed out, the skills of PBL often require direct instruction and careful modelling – they don't 'just happen' as a result of the students participating in problem-based experiences.

Candy (1988) describes the error of mistaking the ends for the means – of making no distinction between the characteristics of an ideal product and the characteristics of the process that is supposed to lead to such a product. Heron (1993) has written of the adult learner's need to be 'led' into autonomy.

Students' role conflict. The second major difficulty also involves role conflict, this time for the students. Although they may have been helped to see the relevance and the benefits of PBL, the reality can sometimes be too much in conflict with their habits and expectations of learning. This is especially true of recent school-leavers who, unless introduced carefully and gradually to the process, and given the opportunity to acquire successful learning skills early in the course, can actively resist the new approach. It is also true of competitive students and those used to gaining very high marks in traditional exams.

These students are sometimes unable to identify what is wrong – they only know that they feel confused, disoriented and resentful. They blame the teachers, the course, or PBL itself.

Reactions of colleagues who are not using PBL. The third major area of difficulty concerns the possible negative reactions of colleagues. This is especially important for individuals or small groups who decide to use the PBL technique when the rest of the faculty retains traditional lecturing methods with the same students. Reactions experienced can be: lack of support, downright hostility, or patronizing behaviour.

Sometimes students take to PBL with tremendous enthusiasm and energy. They improve their thinking, their problem-solving and their learning skills, and they transfer these new skills to other subjects. They no longer sit passively accepting what they are told. They become much more aware of the quality of the teaching and assessing being demonstrated by other lecturers and are likely to challenge (often in a mature and articulate manner) anything they regard as less than competent. For other teachers this, understandably, can be threatening or intolerable.

Keeping the team together. This can be difficult but is vital for any group implementing PBL. Serious differences can easily emerge in interpretation of the philosophy as well as the practical realities. Teachers need to be aware of these possibilities and develop strategies for supporting each other and uniting the group.

Factors basic to the success of PBL

An action research project with teachers beginning to implement PBL, showed the following to be some of the most important factors in success.

□ *A commitment* to the philosophy of this type of learning. That is, the commitment that enables a tutor to overcome difficulties, believe in and achieve success.

□ *An understanding of the philosophy* in terms of assumptions about learning, and the changes in the role of the tutor and the student.

□ *A realistic acceptance of this role change* together with an understanding that the former 'rewards' of teaching may change.

□ *The ability to model process skills* (ie, the skills of critical thinking, problem solving and learning to learn).

□ *Assessments which mirror the 'real world' context* and which engage students in demonstrating the complex capabilities and competencies of that profession.

□ *Frequent opportunities for students to gain feedback.*

□ *An acceptance that students will need time* to change their assumptions and expectations about learning and to develop and practice new skills.

□ *Institutional support*, preferably at departmental, faculty and senior management levels.

□ *A pragmatic and realistic approach*. It seems that tutors who are successful tend to take a pragmatic approach. Their starting points in planning and in course development are usually the everyday realities and the constraints within which they have to work. They use the theory to provide insight into that reality. They do not attempt to impose the theory onto that reality. They adapt others' theories and models in order to maximize the effectiveness of their planned programmes.

Conclusion

Successful implementation of PBL does not come easily. All our strengths and skills as teachers will be required. Our behaviour and beliefs will be challenged. Complex difficulties may arise, and we will need the ability to explore options and generate creative solutions in cooperative contexts. Commitment, determination and team work are essential, and above all we need self-knowledge and considerable understanding of the learning process.

References

Argyris, C and Schön, D (1974) *Theory in Practice: Increasing Professional Effectiveness*. San Francisco, CA: Jossey-Bass.
Candy, P (1988) On the attainment of subject matter autonomy. In D Boud (ed) *Developing Student Autonomy in Learning*. London: Kogan Page.
Heron, J (1993) *Group Facilitation: Theories and Models for Practice*. London: Kogan Page.
Whimbey, A and Lochhead, J (1991) *Problem Solving and Comprehension*. New Jersey: Lawrence Erlbaum Associates.
Woods, D (1984) *A Strategy for Problem Solving*. Toronto: McMaster University.
Woods, D (1985) Problem-based learning and problem solving. In D Boud (ed) *Problem Based Learning in Education for the Professions*. Sydney: HERDSA.

Chapter 13

Ensuring that Students Develop an Adequate, and Well-structured, Knowledge Base

Greg Ryan

The findings of recent meta-analyses of studies which have compared the knowledge performance of students in PBL with students in more traditional courses indicate that PBL students may not be developing adequate knowledge structures (cf. Albanese and Mitchell, 1993; Berkson, 1993; Norman and Schmidt, 1992; Vernon and Blake, 1993). Although it is acknowledged that the issue needs substantially more study, this is nevertheless a disturbing preliminary conclusion. Why should this happen when, at least on the face of it, PBL can represent so well in practice what most of educational theory and research tells us *should* be happening in our classrooms?

This chapter explores the ways in which 'closed loop' or 'reiterative' PBL (Barrows, 1986) can promote, through its application of sound educational principles, the development by students of an adequate and well-structured knowledge base. Results are also reported of a recent extensive and in-depth study which confirms the overall positive effect of PBL on student learning, but which also identifies a number of important course-related factors which, if not adequately addressed, can undermine this effect.

In the published studies there is considerable variation in the ways in which PBL is implemented, but often with insufficient detail about how this implementation occurred. While not implying a need for conformity, there nevertheless should be more careful consideration given to the likelihood of success of some of these methods. Barrows' (1986) taxonomy provides a ranking of the likelihood with which a range of PBL methods will achieve each of the primary objectives of PBL: the structuring of knowledge within the context of professional practice; development of effective reasoning and self-directed learning abilities; and increased motivation for learning. The rankings range from the least likely – the lecture-based case (in which 'the teacher presents ... students with information ... and then a case or two, usually vignettes, to demonstrate the relevance of the information' [1986: 483]) – to the most likely: 'closed loop' or 'reiterative' PBL. The latter method is the focus of discussion in this chapter.

Reiterative PBL and the notion of 'constructivism'

In this form of PBL the following stages typically occur:

- ☐ The problem is encountered first in the learning process, before any preparation or formal study has necessarily occurred.
- ☐ The problem is presented to students in the same way that it would present itself in reality.
- ☐ Students work with the problem in a manner which permits their ability to reason and apply knowledge to be challenged and evaluated, in a manner that is appropriate to the current level of learning.
- ☐ Needed areas of learning are identified as the problem is explored and used as a guide to individualized study.
- ☐ The skills and knowledge acquired by this study are applied back to the problem, to evaluate the effectiveness of learning and to reinforce learning (the reiterative loop).
- ☐ The learning that has occurred in work with the problem and in individualized study is summarized and integrated into the students' existing knowledge and skills. (Barrows, 1986; Barrows and Tamblyn, 1980)

The theoretical framework which best encapsulates the beliefs about knowledge and learning which underlay this approach to PBL is that of *constructivism*. As an educational theory attributed to Jerome Bruner, constructivism maintains that 'learning is an active process in which learners construct new ideas or concepts based upon their current/past knowledge' (Kearsley, 1996: Constructivist Theory). Cognitive structures are utilized (and in the process, changed) to provide personal meaning and organization to experiences.

As an epistemological position, constructivism is based on a view of knowledge that differs from that of logical positivism, which holds that knowledge exists 'out there' as objective truth. The 'subjectivism' of a constructivist viewpoint is also often contrasted with that of 'objectivism', in which 'the world is completely and correctly structured in terms of entities, properties and relations ... (and) experience plays no role in the structuring of the world; meaning is something that exists in the world quite aside from experience' (Duffy and Jonassen, 1991: 7–8). Accordingly, data from this objective world are

> passed through mental structures by cognitive mechanisms in an analo-
> gous way that a message flows through a telephone wire. The process of
> learning becomes one of mapping this external knowledge into some form
> of internal representation that more or less approximates the external
> 'objects'. (Knuth and Cunningham, 1993: 164)

Constructivists, on the other hand, acknowledge that we experience a 'real' world, but argue that meaning is imposed by us, rather than existing in the world independently of us. This meaning is 'rooted in, and *indexed* by, experience' (Duffy and Jonassen, 1991: 8) – that is, understanding is embedded in the experience of the individual (Brown *et al*, 1989; Honebein *et al*, 1993). By acknowledging the existence of a 'real' world beyond the individual knower, constructivists avoid the charge of the metaphysical position of solipsism 'or the claim that there is no reality outside the self, and that all human perception and experience exists only in the mind' (Candy, 1991: 263).

A particular concern expressed about adopting a constructivist viewpoint is that if truth is a subjective and relative construct, where does this leave, for example, established scientific knowledge? A constructivist, as we have seen, would not deny the existence of this knowledge. In arriving at 'personal meaning' a student should look critically at the evidence and eventually commit to an idea. This does not mean blind acceptance; and the progress of science itself is marked by milestones in paradigm-change, when individuals have challenged conventional scientific wisdom.

Educational principles which arise out of constructivism and which are applied in reiterative PBL

There are a number of implications for teaching which arise out of such a constructivist view of knowledge. One of the most succinct summaries is provided by Koschmann *et al* (1994) in a set of six principles of effective learning and instruction. These principles capture well the essence of what reiterative PBL is trying to achieve:

The Principle of Multiplicity

This principle reflects the idea that no two people will see the world in exactly the same way; that few issues in the world have a single 'correct' resolution; and that 'positions are something we commit ourselves to, not something we adopt because... an authority figure decrees that we must' (Knuth and Cunningham, 1993: 169–70). The principle of multiplicity emphasizes the importance of dialogue with other individuals through collaborative learning, and is reflected in the focus on small group learning which is seen in so many applications of PBL.

Also emphasized is the idea that construction of knowledge of concepts is best achieved through multiple and varied applications of the concept. For example, Honebein *et al* (1993: 97) point to the 'long standing prescription for instruction that numerous examples of a concept should be provided for study and practice'. As Koschmann *et al* also point out, 'aspects of richness in concepts and cases will be missed with single representations, and the resultant simplification may prove misleading' (1994: 233). This is clearly of importance for the development of knowledge in PBL courses. The real-life cases around which problem packages are constructed must represent both the breadth (reflected in the range of cases chosen) and the depth (reflected in the number of different cases which show the applications of the same concepts) of professional practice.

The Principle of Activeness

'Learning is an active process requiring mental construction on the part of the learner; instruction should foster cognitive initiative and effort after meaning' (Koschmann *et al*, 1994: 233). It is about active engagement with the task, whether working individually or collaboratively with others. The emphasis in reiterative PBL on students posing their own questions and seeking the respective answers is an application of this principle.

The Principle of Accommodation and Adaptation

Accommodation and adaptation are terms which are usually associated with the epistemological theory of Piaget, who, in Glasersfeld's (1989:125) opinion, was 'the most prolific constructivist in our century'. The terms are used within the framework of Piaget's theory of 'schemes' which are cognitive constructions, based on experience, consisting of three parts: recognition of a certain situation; association of a specific activity with that kind of item; and the expectation of a certain result. The learning theory which emerges from his work is summarized in the following way:

> cognitive change and learning take place when a scheme, instead of producing the expected result, leads to perturbation ... (which) ... in turn leads to accommodation that establishes a new equilibrium. (Glasersfeld,1989:128)

The construction of knowledge, undertaken by the student, involves connecting current experience with past learning, and establishing connections amongst concepts. Processes such as these contribute to building the abstract conceptions and generalizations referred to by Kolb (1984) in his experiential learning cycle and are essential components of the establishment of personal meaning in what is learned. Adult learning theory also emphasizes the importance of building on the learner's prior understanding, and the importance of experience to the learning process (cf. Brookfield, 1986).

As Boud *et al* (1985) observe, just having an experience does not necessarily mean that learning has occurred. The important factor which can turn raw experience into learning is the process of reflection. Critical reflection (Brookfield, 1986) helps students to develop awareness of their own thinking; and includes self-questioning activities such as 'How did we go about our (self-directed learning)?' 'Were we successful?' 'Are there alternative actions we should have taken?' and 'Against what standards/expectations did we measure our success?' Schön (1987) refers to this process as 'reflection-on-action'. Skilled performers of these 'metacognitive' functions are able to plan their activity, monitor the success or failure of their own activities, and alter behaviour in accordance with the monitoring activity (Royer *et al*, 1993: 204).

The process of reflection is a key element in Engel's outline of PBL tutorial process in Chapter 2. The tutor assumes a pivotal role in this process, and in so doing is provided with opportunities to monitor the quality of the students' understanding of concepts and issues. Constant challenge, used in a supportive way, of the level of metacognitive awareness, combined with integrated application of knowledge, skills and attitudes to professional situations has the capacity to encourage 'deep' rather than 'surface' approaches to learning (Biggs, 1991; Ramsden, 1992).

The Principle of Authenticity

The Cognition and Technology Group at Vanderbilt (1993) uses the term 'anchored instruction' – anchoring or situating instruction in meaningful (that is, in reference to the environment in which the learning will ultimately be used) problem-solving contexts. For an activity to be authentic, Honebein *et al* (1993) also suggest that the activity requires learners to have ownership of their learning and performance; and that it exists as both a global (defining the entire task) and local (defining the sub-tasks) entity. The use of actual cases as the basis of the problem packages used in reiterative PBL is an application of this principle.

The Principle of Articulation

Opportunity should be provided for students to explain to others their newly acquired knowledge, including both content (declarative) and process (procedural) elements. This usually requires that they summarize and present their findings in ways which foster understanding by their colleagues, another key aspect of problem-based tutorial process outlined earlier by Engel in Chapter 2. Thus the outcomes of self-directed learning are shared in order to develop collective understanding. Adequate time should be allocated for this to occur, and should be included in the calculation of overall student hours per week; rather than, as is often the case in more traditional courses, self-directed learning being relegated almost entirely to 'homework'.

The Principle of Termlessness

'Learning of rich material is termless; instruction should instil a sense of tentativeness with regard to knowing, a realisation that understanding of complex material is never completed, only enriched, and a lifelong commitment to advancing one's knowledge' (Koschmann *et al*, 1994: 238).

The emphasis in PBL on self-direction in learning actively promotes the application of this principle. As students 'discover' and construct personal meanings about the issues which they are researching, opportunity is provided for them to develop the 'competencies necessary to be efficient and effective in lifelong learning' (Koschmann *et al*, 1994: 247). This principle aligns closely with that of 'multiplicity', where acknowledging different perspectives can highlight the 'uncertainty' of knowledge and the multiple interpretations of existing information which are possible. Experience of this nature aims at moving the student away from, in Perry's (1970) terms, dualistic 'right/wrong' beliefs about knowledge towards a relativist position involving considered, personal commitment.

Course-related factors which can undermine the potential of reiterative PBL

To this point, I have outlined some of the ways in which reiterative PBL, with the use of small group activity, has the potential to greatly enhance students' development of adequate and well-structured knowledge, through application of sound educational principles. One of the factors which sets this form of PBL apart is its emphasis on tutorial process. The tutor retains an active role in the process – as a facilitator and coach of student learning and, as I will argue later, acting at times as a resource person.

But if this form of PBL offers such potential, why then are we seeing the kind of results reported in the meta-analyses referred to earlier? While these studies provide considerable insights into the problem, a recent intensive case study of PBL tutorial process (Ryan, in press) sheds a clearer light on some of the factors which can interfere with this process.

The study, using both quantitative and qualitative research methods, looked at the experiences of 120 students and their six tutors throughout the first semester of a three-year undergraduate degree course in nursing. The course was well established (it originated in 1984), and implemented totally integrated, reiterative, small-group PBL; and provided, in its overall structure and organization, an opportunity to apply the educational principles outlined earlier.

The course gave considerable emphasis to the importance of tutorial process, with problem-based tutorials accounting for approximately 60 per cent of total student 'contact' (or 'class') time. Tutorials were conducted in a similar manner to that outlined by Engel in Chapter 2, with the reiterative element providing considerable opportunity for tutors to monitor the quality of student learning. 'Resource sessions', which included more traditional approaches such as lectures and laboratories, were designed to help students to further explore the concepts and issues which arose out of the problem packages being explored during tutorials, and during self-directed learning.

The study's findings were consistent with a number of those of Albanese and Mitchell (1993), namely well-developed study behaviours by students: studying for understanding, and assuming considerable control over their learning; positive views about the learning environment, particularly the emphasis on self-directed learning; high levels of satisfaction with PBL, from both students and teachers; and enjoyment of small-group interactions.

In terms of the objectives of PBL outlined earlier, there was also clear evidence of increased motivation for learning, and well-developed problem-solving ability which transferred successfully out into the students' clinical practice in a hospital setting. By the end of semester, the students were also demonstrating highly developed self-directed learning ability – successfully monitoring and self-correcting their construction and use of knowledge.

However, from tutorial observations, from interviews conducted with both the students and the tutors, and from the results of an individual (as opposed to group) problem-solving exercise, it was evident that at times there was not a sufficiently deep understanding by students of knowledge issues. Several reasons for these findings were evident: excessive workload, lack of time to explore issues in adequate depth and non-availability of resources. (These factors, of course, are not unique to PBL courses.) There was clearly a problem with the *number* of concepts and issues which students were required to explore in any one problem package. Time constraints often meant that important 'core' concepts were either overlooked, or received only cursory attention – a danger also noted in Albanese and Mitchell's (1993) findings.

Data from tutor interviews indicated that the primary focus of the first semester was to develop in students a process of inquiry, particularly the use of a particular problem-solving heuristic; and discussion of process during tutorials was often at the expense of in-depth discussion of the knowledge issues. It was pointed out by the tutors that during subsequent semesters, when the 'process' was much more automatic, more time would be devoted to discussion of learning issues. These findings highlight the difficulties that teachers face when seeking a satisfactory balance between content and process, and indicate that if this balance tips continually in favour of process, problems may start to emerge with the quality of students' knowledge.

From their point of view, the students were critical of the role which the tutors had adopted – that is, to consistently reflect knowledge questions back to the student for exploration as self-directed learning. (The tutors had, over several years, established their role as a 'facilitator' of student self-directed learning.) It can be argued that this is a necessary strategy, particularly when the overt aim is to have students assume responsibility for learning. But it is of little benefit to the student at the time if

(i)   they are already feeling pressured by a heavy workload of learning issues;

(ii) there is insufficient time in which to adequately explore the issues; and

(iii) there are inadequate library resources.

As well as the issue of availability of resources, there again is the question of balance between the expectation that students will find the information for themselves, and the tutor acting as a resource person. Even within relatively highly supportive learning environments such as this, when both the curriculum and the tutors provide a high level of structure and direction in the early weeks of the course, it can be difficult to get the balance 'right'.

Albanese and Mitchell (1993), in their conclusions about teacher directiveness in PBL tutorials, canvass a number of models and ideas about how such a balance can be achieved. The areas of agreement lie in what Brookfield (1987) would refer to as 'critically responsive teaching' – that is, the kind of 'micro' decisions that are made by the teacher in response to a particular classroom situation, and takes into account both the identified needs of the student in relation to their immediate learning goals, and the broader course-related goals; as well as tutor-related factors such as the ability to answer knowledge-related questions. The result can be a gradual progression toward independence for the students, with the tutor perhaps being more directive and 'telling' initially, but becoming increasingly more 'participatory' or 'delegative' (Albanese and Mitchell, 1993: 74) as the course proceeds.

Thus in these courses there may be times when the tutor needs to act as a resource person. For example, there may be a particular issue which is blocking progress with the problem and, being 'critically responsive', the tutor may decide that it is better in this instance to provide some brief information, together with an indication of where and how further detail will later need to be found. Or, there may be occasions when the students have developed misconceptions about material explored – for example, during self-directed learning – and the tutor intervenes to 'correct' these misconceptions. This latter point raises the issue of tutor expertise – how 'expert' should the tutor be in the content areas represented by the particular problem package? In Chapter 2 Engel suggests that it is not necessary for the tutor to be an expert in the topics being explored by the students in the early stages of the course. Albanese and Mitchell in their conclusions about this issue acknowledge both the advantages and the disadvantages of using either expert or non-expert tutors. While expert tutors tend to be more directive, 'they appear to better enable students to identify relevant learning issues and correct gaps in knowledge and errors in processing' (1993: 75). On the other hand, while non-expert tutors may be 'more facilitative of student-centred, self-directed learning, it could be at the expense of perpetuating misconceptions arising during self-directed learning' (1993: 75). The latter was the finding, at times, in the Ryan (in press) study.

Concluding Remarks

Reiterative PBL holds much promise for high quality outcomes in student learning. In particular, this chapter has outlined how the processes involved in implementing this form of PBL can ensure that students develop an adequate and well-structured knowledge base. It is one of the most evident examples of the application of sound educational principles such as those outlined earlier. But we need to ensure that our courses ultimately deliver what the approach can offer. If such a goal is to be achieved by students, workload must be realistic, adequate time needs to be provided for successful self-directed learning to occur, and sufficient resources must be available. Students can be very innovative when it comes to finding appropriate resources for themselves, but they need time to do this. In addition, care is needed in striking the 'right' balance between content and process, and between the tutor's roles as promoter of self-directed learning and resource person.

References

Albanese, M A and Mitchell, S (1993) Problem based learning: a review of literature on its outcomes and implementation issues, *Academic Medicine*, 68, 1, 52–81.

Barrows, H S (1986) A taxonomy of problem based learning methods, *Medical Education*, 20, 6, 481–486.

Barrows, H S and Tamblyn, R W (1980) *Problem-Based Learning: An Approach to Medical Education*. New York: Springer.

Berkson, L (1993) Problem-based learning: have the expectations been met? *Academic Medicine*, 68, 10, October Supplement, S79–S88.

Biggs, J (1991) Teaching: design for learning. In B Ross (ed), *Research and Development in Higher Education, Vol. 13*. Canberra: HERDSA (Higher Education Research and Development Society).

Boud, D, Keogh, R and Walker, D (1985) Promoting reflection in learning: a model. In D Boud, R Keogh and D Walker (eds) *Reflection: Turning Experience Into Learning*. London: Kogan Page.

Brookfield, S D (1986) *Understanding and Facilitating Adult Learning: A Comprehensive Analysis of Principles and Effective Practices*. San Francisco, CA: Jossey-Bass.

Brookfield, S D (1987) *Developing Critical Thinkers: Challenging Adults to Explore Alternative Ways of Thinking and Acting*. San Francisco, CA: Jossey-Bass.

Brown, J S, Collins, A and Duguid, P (1989) Situated cognition and the culture of learning, *Educational Researcher*, 18, 1, 32–42.

Candy, P (1991) *Self Direction for Life Long Learning: A Comprehensive Guide to Theory and Practice*. San Francisco, CA: Jossey-Bass.

Cognition and Technology Group at Vanderbilt (1993) Designing learning environments that support thinking. In T M Duffy, J Lowyck and D H Jonassen (eds) *Designing Environments for Constructive Learning*. Berlin: Springer-Verlag.

Duffy, T M and Jonassen, D H (1991) Constructivism: new implications for instructional technology? *Educational Technology*, May, 7–12.

Glasersfeld, E von (1989) Cognition, construction of knowledge, and teaching, *Synthese*, 80, 121–140.

Honebein, P C, Duffy, T M and Fishman, B J (1993) Constructivism and the design of learning environments: context and authentic activities for learning. In T M Duffy, J Lowyck and D H Jonassen (eds), *Designing Environments for Constructive Learning*. Berlin: Springer-Verlag.

Kearsley, G (1996) *Explorations in Learning and Instruction: The Theory into Practice Database*. Washington, DC: http://www.gwu.edu/~tip/

Knuth, R A and Cunningham, D J (1993) Tools for constructivism. In T M Duffy, J Lowyck and D H Jonassen (eds) *Designing Environments for Constructive Learning*. Berlin: Springer-Verlag.

Kolb, D (1984) *Experiential Learning: Experience as the Source of Learning and Development*. Englewood Cliffs, NJ: Prentice-Hall.

Koschmann, T D, Myers, A C, Feltovich, P J and Barrows, H S (1994) Using technology to assist in realising effective learning and instruction: a principled approach to the use of computers in collaborative learning. *The Journal of the Learning Sciences*, 3, 3, 227–264.

Norman, G R and Schmidt, H G (1992) The psychological basis of problem-based learning: a review of the evidence, *Academic Medicine*, 67, 9, 557–565.

Perry, W (1970) *Forms of Intellectual and Ethical Development in the College Years*. New York: Holt, Rinehart and Winston.

Ramsden, P (1992) *Learning to Teach in Higher Education*. London: Routledge.

Royer, J M, Cisero, C A and Carlo, M S (1993) Techniques and procedures for assessing cognitive skills, *Review of Educational Research*, 63, 2, 201–243.

Ryan, G L (in press) The development of problem solving and self directed learning ability in problem based learning. Doctoral Thesis. Faculty of Education, The University of Sydney.

Schön, D (1990) *Educating the Reflective Practitioner*. San Francisco, CA: Jossey-Bass.

Vernon, D T and Blake, R L (1993) Does problem based learning work? A meta-analysis of evaluative research. *Academic Medicine*, 68, 7, 550–562.

Chapter 14

A Hybrid Model of Problem-based Learning

Elizabeth G Armstrong

If we observe the process which we call instruction, we see two parties con-jointly engaged – the learner and the teacher. The object of both is the same, but their relations to the work to be done are different ... [The] essential part, the appropriation and assimilation of knowledge by the mind, can be performed by no one but the learner ... [from which] ... it follows that he is in fact his own teacher, and ... that learning is self teaching ... The Teacher's part then in the process of instruction is that of a guide, director, or superintendent of the operations by which the pupil teaches himself. (Joseph Payne, 1883)

General principles

As the opening citation – from Joseph Payne, first Professor of the Science and Art of Education at the College of Preceptors in London – demonstrates, the idea that adult learners teach themselves is scarcely revolutionary. By incorporating this idea as its first principle, and augmenting it with an acknowledgement of the range of adult learning styles born of modern cognitive psychology, the New Pathway curriculum at the Harvard Medical School displays what might be considered its most characteristic quality: hybridization. The New Pathway aims to innovate without sacrificing the best of the old, to stimulate individual initiative without inefficiency, and to balance the latest developments in medical science with the age-old values of healing. In every sense, our goals and implementation of those goals are hybrids – with, we hope, the strength and adaptability that hybrids usually display.

More specifically, our new curriculum challenges the assumptions of the predominant lecture-based model of medical training that crystallized and became standard during the first eight decades of the 20th century: two years of 'pure science' and laboratory work followed by two clinical years. The New Pathway incorporates our assumptions that passive attendance at basic science lectures will not guarantee learning for every student; memorization of increasingly large numbers of facts will not necessarily provide the accessible knowledge base required for clinical practice or research; and, finally, that presenting discrete bodies of information in totally separated courses during the first two years of medical school will not prepare every student to apply and integrate that information in solving clinical problems in the second two years of training. The New Pathway at the Harvard Medical School is a broad-based attempt to create a four-year pedagogical structure within an organization that supports students to equip themselves with the skills, knowledge, and sensitivities they will need in a swiftly evolving professional environment (Tosteson, 1990).

These three pedagogical objectives for the new curriculum – knowledge, skills and sensitivity – have dominated faculty planning discussions from the beginning of the design process. By knowledge, we mean a broad, deep and flexible familiarity with the intellectual materials of the profession. By skills, we mean competencies that will require renewal over a lifetime of learning; and by sensitivity, we mean ethical awareness and openness to the world of the patient. It was to promote these broad goals that we implemented the framework for the first pilot track in September 1985. And it is these goals that support the continuing evaluation and evolution of our curriculum.

Application of principles

Throughout the planning and implementation process, faculty members met in committees to clarify goals, design programmes, and provide 'feedback' and suggestions for improvement. From an institutional context that includes a range of diverse opinions, the planning group reached consensus on the pilot programmes. As its intellectual base they endorsed and implemented the concept of problem-based learning along with the teaching strategies that support this philosophy. Tutorials in which small groups of students, each led by a tutor, approach general medical education by reading, studying and discussing 'real life' medical cases were to become the primary launching pad for problem-based learning. The rationale for teaching by the discussion of paper cases is that students who discover for themselves the basic science concepts of a given set of symptoms or a diagnosis not only enjoy the process but retain the information. At Harvard, where our goal is to preserve excellence in general medical education and accommodate a wide range of adult learning styles, the cases assume a key integrative role in the new interdisciplinary courses.

To accommodate a variety of learning styles, there was strong sentiment for the retention of lectures, labs and conferences along with the implementation of small discussion tutorials. Replacing all lectures with discussion groups or tutorials would merely substitute one lopsided system for another. Extensive debate resulted in the realization that the scope, frequency and format of lectures and laboratory sessions could be effectively altered to dovetail with active problem-based discussions. Our hybrid curriculum, therefore, incorporates a range of carefully planned teaching strategies. The planning committee's objective became the integration of all these pedagogical elements around a core of student-directed learning.

Overall planning: an integrated approach

A Core Faculty Planning Group designed the framework and goals for the first two years of basic science study with a set of interdisciplinary blocks (Figure 14.1). Each block includes small group case discussions (tutorials) led by instructors called tutors. Tutorial time varies from block to block. In the human body block tutorials meet for one hour a day five times per week; in the human nervous system and behaviour block, and most of the other blocks, they meet for three one-and-a-half- or two-hour sessions each week. For each block, there is a smaller faculty planning unit called a Curriculum Design Group comprised of scientists and clinicians from each represented discipline and a curriculum coordinator providing expertise in education. The members of these groups continually re-evaluate, redesign and re-implement each block guided by the Masters of the five Academic Societies who share responsibility for the oversight of the curriculum and integration of content across the four years. The curriculum

Sep	Oct	Nov	Dec	Jan	Feb	Mar	Apr	May	Jun	Jul

Year I

The Human Body [8 WEEKS]
- Anatomy
- Histology
- Radiology

Chemistry & Biology of the Cell [7 WEEKS]
- Biochemistry
- Cell Biology

Integrated Human Physiology [5 WEEKS]
- Integration of Human Organ Systems

Pharmacology [4 WEEKS]

Genetics Embryology Reproduction [6 WEEKS]
- Molecular Genetics
- Morphogenesis
- Early Development
- Reproduction

Immunology, Microbiology & Infectious Diseases [9 WEEKS]
- Immunology
- Microbiology
- Infectious Diseases

Patient/Doctor I — Tutorial and Clinical Sessions (34 sessions — 2 hrs/wk)

Core Courses — Social Medicine and Biostatistics/Epidemiology (Required, 2 hrs/wk, students select term)

Year II

Human Nervous System & Behavior [8 WEEKS]
- Neuropathophysiology
- Neuroanatomy
- Neurology · Psychiatry
- Neurophysiology

Pathology [3 WEEKS]

Human Systems (Pathophysiology)

Module I [11 WEEKS]
- Dermatology · Respiratory
- Cardiovascular · Hematology

Module II [14 WEEKS]
- GastroIntestinal · Musculoskeletal
- Renal / Endocrine / Reproduction

Patient/Doctor II — Introduction to Clinical Medicine (4 hrs/wk, Sep-Feb; 1 day/wk, Feb-Mar; 2 days/wk, Apr-May)

Psychopathology (3 hrs/wk Sep - Dec) — Preventive Medicine and Nutrition (2 hrs/wk Jan - Apr)

Figure 14.1 *Outline of courses in years one and two*

design groups are charged with establishing the goals of the course, integrating its disciplines, identifying the level of content appropriate to a general medical curriculum, and matching that content to the most effective pedagogy (see the model schedule of a prototypical week, Figure 14.2).

	Monday	Tuesday	Wednesday	Thursday	Friday
	LECTURE	LECTURE	LECTURE	LECTURE	LECTURE
Morning	Tutorial	Lab	Tutorial	Lab	Tutorial
Afternoon		Selective	Patient/ Doctor		

☐ *Lecture 8.30–9.30am*

Figure 14.2 *Prototypical weeks – years one and two*

Most Curriculum Design Groups for individual blocks begin by pairing the course goals with a series of increasingly complex written cases, usually one per week. The cases are the primary vehicles for the students' tutorial discussions and self-directed study (Glick and Armstrong, 1996). As a supplement to the cases that organize each unit, regular lectures, labs, conferences and computer-aided instruction sessions offer a variety of perspectives on the major instructional theme of each week.

The curriculum coordinator plays an active role in facilitating the preparation and review of cases and all support materials for the block. The coordinator acts as an educational consultant to the planning group and is sometimes referred to as the producer of the block. The primary responsibility for facilitating communication among numerous faculty and guiding the planning and implementation of the course rests with the coordinator.

A two and a half year patient/doctor course promotes conceptual and practical integration. It is offered one afternoon per week in the first and third year concurrently with the human biology blocks and the third year clerkships. In the second year, it increases in time from one afternoon, to one day, and finally to two days per week during the last two months, allowing students to expand progressively their physical examination skills. Committed to the importance of the development of sensitivity as a new curriculum goal, planners soon realized that emphasis on the knowledge and skill components of the basic sciences might overwhelm this area in the human biology component. While not precluding any discussion of psychosocial issues in the small discussion groups of the basic science blocks, the planners designed a longitudinal course in which social science issues would be explored in the context of learning to care for patients. In the patient-doctor course, behavioural, ethical, fiscal and attitudinal aspects of the patient-doctor relationship are explored as students master the basic skills of history taking and physical examination.

During the first two years, the patient/doctor course is designed to dovetail with the content of the human biology courses and encourage students to assimilate what they are learning into a coherent whole. For example, while the students are engaged in learning the physiology of male and female reproduction in the genetics, embryology and reproduction block they are also learning to take sexual histories from their patient in the patient/doctor course. During the third year, the patient/doctor tutorials revisit many themes of the first two years at a level more appropriate for students immersed in the clinical care of patients, such as ethical and medical financing issues. They also offer the opportunity to share clinical experiences in the tutorial setting.

Lectures

One of the goals of the new curriculum was to increase active learning and decrease students' experience of the sort of passive learning that occurs in lectures. Accordingly, the number of lectures was reduced below that of the traditional curriculum, and the remaining lectures were focused to emphasize key concepts, build a framework of ideas and relate to the case of the week. Lectures are used to present material that is new or more conceptually difficult and, therefore, less likely to be readily assimilated from the readings or tutorial study. In addition, lecturers are asked to make their presentations interactive – to permit interruptions and take more questions.

Our hybrid model differs from the traditional first- and second-year medical curriculum in having fewer contact hours and lectures per week (see Figure 14.2) and in balancing case discussions with lectures and other pedagogical modes (Feletti and Armstrong, 1989). Within the existing weekly schedule, lectures are presented as a multidisciplinary series whose theme relates to the teaching objectives of the particular week. Lecture material is also integrated with labs and discipline-based conferences. All the approaches combine to prepare students to grasp and apply what they are learning.

To maximize continuity and focus – and avoid the 'cameo appearance' syndrome that plagues many institutions with large and diverse faculties – lecturers are requested to provide a minimum of three related presentations. Ideally, in this structure, lecturers have the time and opportunity to construct conceptual frameworks within which students may assimilate their new understandings as these emerge from tutorial discussions and independent studies.

The pervasive goal of interdigitating content and teaching modes requires a high level of communication and preparation, for faculty and students alike. Each course director generally offers guidance to faculty members who are asked to lecture, and each lecturer has an opportunity to see how his or her presentation fits into the overview and relates to the case and labs of the week. To promote coherence, lecturers receive copies of the case(s) to which their lectures must correspond and they are requested to submit one- or two-page lecture outlines which, when reviewed and accepted, are published in student guides and distributed before the lectures. These outlines specify learning objectives and list one or two key references. Students report that these outlines enable them to prepare for lectures, organize their independent studies and learn actively during lectures. As a result of preparation and careful curricular integration, it is also common for students to bring up unresolved questions from tutorial discussion or independent study in the lecture hall. This approach has permitted lectures in the new curriculum to promote far more active learning than in the past.

Tutorial discussions and cases: the key to student learning and faculty development

The range of cases developed for the curriculum makes Harvard's course materials somewhat unusual in the community of problem-based medical learning. Our cases tell a story about a patient that is revealed through a set of progressively distributed pages. Generally the student begins the first tutorial with only a brief introduction to the patient that includes a description of the presenting symptoms. After the learning agenda is established in the tutorial, the tutor distributes the subsequent case parts. The agenda is used by the students to direct their self-study. Frequently they will decide to establish tasks related to agenda items that can be divided among the tutorial members, and report on their progress at the next meeting.

In one block – Genetics, Embryology and Reproduction – the diagnosis is presented in Part I of some cases, while in other blocks it is always withheld until much later in each case sequence. Presenting the name of the genetic disease on the first page of the case effectively prevents students from hypothesizing about a diagnosis, but it also drives them to focus their learning agenda quickly on the molecular biology that underlies the disease whose name they have been given. To date, faculty and students seem quite satisfied with the learning that takes place in this block, but further research will be necessary to determine the effects of this pedagogical variation in case development.

All our paper cases include learning objectives, which we present either in behavioural terms or in the format of study questions that encourage students to evaluate their own progress. Tutors distribute the objectives or questions only after students have had the opportunity to create and follow their own learning agendas. Students may use these objectives to guide their studies and self-assessment – or not.

Each case includes a list of available audio-visual resources and suggested readings from course textbooks and/or collections of journal articles. Faculty resources (experts) who may be consulted are also listed in each case. In some teaching blocks, cases are supplemented with prepared packets of articles for which copyright clearance is obtained. In addition to these materials, a wide range of multimedia resources including DXplain (Barnett *et al*, 1987) are available. These supplement the paper cases in two ways: they offer students the chance to explore the significance of different clinical manifestations described in a paper case by presenting parallel examples, and they portray other patient cases with related symptoms.

Tutors receive a written tutor guide or teaching note for each case. These guides detail the key features of the case and may include suggestions for pacing the case through the allotted tutorial time. Some provide a brief update on related research or clinical practice. Often, tutor guides are organized around information related to key concepts that underlie each objective or study question in the case. The guides provide an invaluable standard body of basic knowledge, which tutors – who range from generalists to specialists – find extremely useful as a point of reference. In addition, weekly tutor meetings provide tutors with a forum in which to review the tutorial process, discuss content issues related to the case under study, and prepare for the case of the following week. The preparation for the forthcoming case may include a presentation from the case author or an expert on the content and objectives of the case. These meetings throughout each course support our faculty development efforts and enhance a collegial network among tutors.

Continued challenges of the 'paper case'

As our curriculum and experience with written cases evolve, we find ourselves challenged to increase the variety and range of our cases and make them come alive for students. While our cases are rooted in actual patient scenarios, frequently drawn from medical records, we continue to examine ways to make the patients seem real in an effort to blend cognitive and affective learning modes for students. Working at all times within the constraints of preserving patients' confidentiality (or obtaining their written permission), we have created addenda to cases including: epilogues, photographs, videotaped interviews, letters from medical records, X-rays, ultrasounds, and relevant lab data. Courses have World Wide Web home pages that include reference to additional computerized resources and easier access to some expert faculty. Occasionally the actual patient in the case is able to visit the class and be interviewed or take part in a clinic presentation.

A further challenge in our use of paper cases is adaptation of the method and materials for use in different time-frames and with groups of different sizes. Conference and lab leaders are also examining opportunities to use problem-based learning techniques and employ cases. Some of the blocks employ mini-cases of one to three paragraphs to link lab groups' work with real patient encounters. Other blocks use a series of short cases, presented to groups of 40 students at the end of a week, to highlight and review key concepts.

Clinical curriculum keeping pace with health care delivery

Substantial recent changes to the last two clinical years provide additional time in ambulatory settings and a longitudinal primary care experience promoting a generalist perspective. One month has been added to each of the surgery and the medicine clerkships, specifically designed for outpatient teaching. A twelve month, one afternoon per week, primary care clerkship gives each student the opportunity to have a continuous experience with a primary care preceptor and patients in one practice. To complement these more decentralized teaching activities in disparate sites, a Clinical Commons course offered one afternoon per week, in conjunction with the Patient Doctor 3 course, addresses clinical problem-solving in central sessions at the medical school.

A one month course offering a return to the basic sciences is also required during the third and fourth years. Students may choose from among 20 Biomedical Sciences (ABS) courses ranging in topic from the Biology of Solid Tumor Progression to Epidemiologic Approaches to Major Clinical Problems. Each ABS course examines basic science concepts in the context of clinical medicine, taking advantage of the students' increased clinical sophistication (see Figure 14.3).

Some benefits of the new curriculum

Christensen (1987) described several benefits of case method teaching for both students and faculty at the Harvard Business School. He highlighted students' opportunities to discover in their own ways and build unique personal frameworks for the knowledge base they acquire. For faculty, case teaching and development provide opportunities for intellectual stimulation and pedagogical risk-taking. Faculty who shift from lecturing to case method teaching often report new learning and a refreshing sense of adventure. Christensen went on to note that, for some faculty members, case development rekindles research interests and faculty and students all benefit from the general culture of change that results.

> The case method is supportive of a culture that places high value on review and innovation. Too often, faculties teach change – but practice the status quo. Individual course and overall curriculum reviews often depend on the personal initiative of an instructor or the work of faculty committees. But

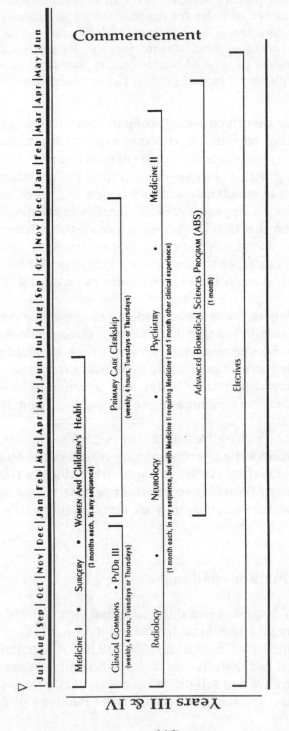

Figure 14.3 *Outline of courses in years three and four*

147

when faculty must prepare teaching cases, their continuing contact with the world of practice provides the institution with an external force for change. Suggestions that a familiar framework be reviewed or new concepts developed are often received more sympathetically when they derive from the impersonal demand of practice rather than from colleagues or departments, with their personal agendas. The case method encourages an adaptive culture.

What Christensen described about problem-based learning in a business school setting appears to be transferable to a medical school. Many of our faculty members appear to enjoy all aspects of their tutoring from training with colleagues to working with students. Tutor training sessions, in which case authors review their own cases, also provide faculty with opportunities for professional development. Some tutors report that insights gained in these settings have provided the stimulus for changes in their practice or research. In addition, the marketing of our cases to other institutions may increase collaborative ventures and contribute significantly to advances in medical education.

In a formal study of the first two student cohorts in the curriculum, Moore *et al* (1994) showed that there were no measurable differences in biomedical knowledge acquisition between these students and those in the traditional curriculum. The New Pathways students were consistently and often significantly better able to relate to patients and they perceived their curriculum as more challenging, stimulating, difficult and relevant.

Our hybrid problem-based learning curriculum may benefit our own institution by virtue of the interdisciplinary nature of the blocks. New research is stimulated by involving a network of faculty from varied fields in a full range of teaching modalities integrated into a single curriculum. As faculty are learning to work together in teams so too are our students.

Conclusions, further challenges

Kaufman (1985) suggested that the conceptual idea of problem-based learning can only take root in an institution if a broad representation of the faculty samples it. The Harvard Medical School curriculum shift has accomplished just that. By creating a hybrid curriculum that promotes active learning and self-direction *in concert with* a variety of other teaching modes, we have tapped large numbers of faculty as tutors, lecturers, lab leaders, conference leaders and clinical clerkship instructors. While this chapter has focused more on the first two years of our programme, we are committed to enhancing our support for innovations in the clinical years through expanded faculty development programmes and a regular curriculum meeting to review the educational experience of years three and four. Teaching has become the responsibility of many faculty members in disparate areas as they work towards common goals – not only in interdisciplinary content areas, but also in a shared commitment to helping students succeed as self-directed adult learners.

Having now developed our own network of faculty to write paper cases and design and implement a new curriculum that supports self-directed learning in a variety of teaching modes, we acknowledge the ongoing need to adapt to changing times. As curriculum designers and implementers, we must conduct the same sort of continuing self-assessment that we expect of our students. Our perpetual question must be, 'How well does our curriculum support learning?' A good curriculum is never finished.

As students, faculty and society change, new technologies in teaching will emerge. Discovering new content and new processes in the next decade and beyond will require us to apply all the problem-solving skills that we expect our students to acquire. For those of us who design, implement and evaluate curricula, each new iteration is a case in problem-based learning for us to study. This continuous improvement process – begun through the efforts of the team that launched the New Pathway – is already under way.

References

Barnett, G O, Cimino, J J, Hupp, J A and Hoffer, E P (1987) DXplain: an evolving diagnostic decision-support system, *Journal of the American Medical Association*, 258, 67–74.

Christensen, C R (1987) *Teaching and the Case Method*, Boston: Harvard Business School Publishing.

Feletti, G and Armstrong, E G (1989) Problem-based education at Harvard Medical School: a short report on the New Pathway to General Medical Education, *MEDUCS*, 2 (2), 36–39.

Glick, T and Armstrong, E (1996) Crafting cases for problem based learning: experience in a neuroscience course, *Medical Education*, 30, 1, 24–30.

Kaufman, A (ed) (1985) *Implementing Problem-Based Medical Education*, New York: Springer.

Moore, G T, Block, S D, Style, C B and Mitchell, R (1994) The influence of the New Pathway curriculum on Harvard Medical students, *Academic Medicine*, 69, 983–989.

Payne, J (1883) *Lectures on the Science and Art of Education*, Boston: Willard Small.

Tosteson, D C (1990) New Pathways in General Medical Education, *New England Journal of Medicine*, 322 (4), 234–238.

Chapter 15

Case Writing: Case Writers' Perspectives

Janet P Hafler

Curricula which advocate PBL generally use case studies in some form (paper cases, simulations or real patients, etc) with the intention of stimulating classroom discussion within a problem-solving framework. While real patients and cases have always provided the framework for teaching in medicine in the clinical years (Cabot, 1906), the practice of writing cases for the basic science courses within a problem-based curriculum is relatively new (Barrows, 1984).

In 1985, Harvard Medical School (HMS) launched the New Pathway curriculum in general medical education as a pilot project involving 24 students. Two years later the New Pathway approach was expanded to include an entire class of 160 students and it continues in that mode today (with about 170 students). The HMS problem-based curriculum includes various teaching and learning strategies but the small group tutorial is central to the curriculum. Paper cases used in the tutorials not only generate discussion but also stimulate the learning of basic science within a clinical situation. Through self-directed study, students solve problems and explore the psycho-social dimensions of issues found within the cases.

This chapter describes the development of one type of paper case. The original work is based on interview data from earlier dissertation research (Hafler, 1989) which covered a sample of 22 case writers at HMS in the academic year 1987/88. The sample represented half the total number of authors who had developed one or more basic science cases for the human biology tutorials. Nine of the 22 case writers interviewed were members of course planning committees; ten had tutored; six of the 22 had both tutored and served on curriculum planning committees; and nine were case authors only. Their perspectives on case writing and how their cases were written and developed remain relevant today, some ten years later. From those origins, the HMS case collection now numbers about 225 documents.

Definitions of a case used in the human biology courses: perceptions from case writers

Cases can be written in a variety of formats (Barrows and Tamblyn, 1977; Waterman and Cooley, 1985), from one-paragraph vignettes to 20-page presentations. The basic science cases generated by the original sample of writers were generally about five pages long. The patient's story unfolds as the case is distributed over the course of three or four tutorial sessions, which last from one to two hours each. Every case written in this format had the following components: title, author, case narrative, objectives (written as behavioural objectives or questions), resources (ranging from expert resource faculty to audiovisual materials, texts and/or articles and computer materials) and a tutor guide – a summary not distributed to the students that covers the writer's perception of the important issues in the case.

Cases were typically written about a patient and the problem which brought the patient to the physician. One writer described it simply as, 'A case is a story about a patient', while another elaborated: 'A case consists of a description of a patient and a situation, followed by a series of extensions of the experience … into specific aspects of what was initially presented and what evolves.'

Pre-writing: the planning phase

Each course was planned by a Curriculum Design Group, composed of faculty from each discipline within the course, and an education specialist referred to as a curriculum coordinator. Collaboratively, they decided on the topics for the course, defined the overall course objectives and selected the case writers, but did not choose the actual patient cases. The case authors themselves determined the case content – based on the goals of the course and not for 'esoteric content' or some relationship to a common medical problem.

Some authors were invited to write a case because a member of the committee might have been familiar with an author's personal experience which bore promise of a case situation appropriate for the course; others were asked based on their expertise in a field. For example one writer, a basic scientist and expert in insulin metabolism, was asked to develop a case about a patient with diabetes mellitus and to include physiological and biochemical concepts that related to this disease. Knowing that cases are used to teach basic science within a clinical (ie, patient-focused) context, the case writer sought advice from both a biochemist and a clinician as he developed his material. Frequently a basic scientist and a clinician co-authored a case. Most case writers were experts in the field related to the main topic in the case. The small number of authors who may not have been considered experts generally wrote from personal experience and sought and received assistance from experts.

Case writers who had tutored said that their tutorial experience gave them a better understanding of the student's perspective, of how cases are used and of the relationship between the length of the case and the amount of time in the tutorial. One such author found that his tutorial experience enabled him to answer questions that he would pose to himself, specifically:

> What is a reasonable amount of material for an hour's discussion? [What] will generate a substantial study agenda? [What] is reasonable to cope with in one day, because we meet each day?

Another said, 'Writing as a tutor is really important. I can tell you what content will work.' And, according to two others:

> I don't understand how you can dissociate the teaching from the writing. It's very hard for me to imagine how you can write cases without tutoring, not knowing exactly first-hand what you are supposed to do.
>
> Tutoring affects case writing because it is very hard to put yourself at the level of the students. To be very bright and incisive, but not to have a common base of knowledge, is hard for any case writer to re-create. That is the hardest thing about tutoring and case writing.

While the experience of having been a tutor seems to have helped faculty understand how cases are used, those case writers who had not tutored availed themselves of Curriculum Design Group members who met with them, described case usage and elaborated on course objectives. In fact, before any writer actually settled upon a case, a member of the Curriculum Design Group would have briefed them about the course; about possible case topics and goals; and about the students, the number of tutorials and the amount of time allotted for each tutorial.

Writing cases was optional, but whether writers were tutors or were involved in planning the course, they found the experience to be a very enjoyable and creative aspect of their work, different from their daily responsibilities. Authors described writing a case as being similar to creating a short story. 'I love sitting quietly at midnight to write', one said, and another noted, 'It was easy because I didn't have to make anything up. I just wrote it. The facts were in my head and after a few double-checks with the records [the case] was written.'

Case writers offered a variety of reasons for agreeing to develop a case, but they all said that students' education was of concern and interest to them, as was knowing the importance of applying theory to practice PBL. Some mentioned that they wanted to contribute to a more active method of learning than they had experienced in medical school. One writer stated: 'The job of cases is to take this opportunity to clarify the relevance of basic science to what these students want to do.'

The authors all said they needed the freedom to write the case according to a broad goal that the Curriculum Design Group identified, rather than to a list of specific objectives. They said the broad approach encouraged them to be creative and facilitated the writing process while specific objectives limited their range. One author who early on had been given a suggested list of objectives went back to the committee and asked for the freedom to write his case without reference to the list. He was unable to even begin, he said, because not all objectives were related to the real case scenario he had chosen. Working from just a broad goal, he then proceeded to write, allowing the case to unfold as it happened in real life.

Writing the case

The case writers said that one issue they struggled with was the challenge of selecting appropriate information for the students – of choosing from the range of complex data available in real cases. The general consensus was that cases should have one central topic or theme, similar to a mystery story, rather than multiple threads.

> I'm trying now to decide what to pack into this case and what to leave out. So I left out a lot of past medical history because it was all distracting and not relevant to my objectives. I know we want to stick to the thyroid part

of this case, because that was my objective. So, I definitely see how I am going to trim it down.

Another writer discussed the pitfalls of these attempts 'to trim it down':

> We say the head, eyes, ears, nose and throat were negative, the chest was normal. We inundate the reader's sensorium with too much data that is irrelevant. I will grant you this: you take the risk that the information you left out may be relevant to someone else. It is an editorial assumption on my part, but anything irrelevant to the point I want to make, I leave out.

Yet at times authors do include irrelevant data in a case – with a particular goal in mind. 'Red herrings' are commonly written in for advanced students, but seldom for first-year students. Students new to PBL, case authors discovered, had first to work on prioritizing a list of topics to study within the main topic of the case. The students' ability to differentiate and prioritize among topics seemed to be an important consideration for writers as they made decisions about what to include and exclude in cases. Leading students off on a tangent risks confusion.

On the other hand, most real cases do naturally include red herrings, and so a case writer's decision to include or exclude them is always worth further investigation, depending on the goals of the course and how tutorials are taught. Red herrings aside, writers who had tutored said that often a wide range of topics emerges as a case is discussed in tutorial, many of which are only indirectly related to the main theme of the case. However narrowly focused an author seeks to make a case or to keep it to a single theme, discussion often branches out in unexpected directions.

Another relevant issue to authors was that of deciding where the data for a case come from. The key questions case writers asked themselves were: should I write a case with only real data? Or from my memory of a real situation? Or from a hypothetical set of facts? Many writers said they could effectively and easily write real cases without any altered data, just from a recollection of their experiences. One writer said: 'I take ideas from my experiences and probably look at a few charts just to be sure the data is accurate.'

In fact, among the authors surveyed, all cases were from actual situations. When authors used medical charts, permission and confidentiality were felt to be critical. As one writer said, 'One sacred responsibility of the physician is to preserve the confidentiality of the patient in case writing.'

If cases are read, critiqued and edited by others before the final draft, content selection is often influenced by those who participate in the readings. One author noted:

> Now I've got a case, I think I'm tailoring; I think I've got the kind of case we [the Curriculum Design Group] want. This is a good time to get help. A psychiatrist was there. She wanted a long involved mental status evaluation of the patient. She said the case was missing a detailed mental status exam. I thought that would be distracting because it really would get too far off track. There's so much going on in any given case.

Generally, as they finished their work, case writers produced a brief tutor guide describing the key points in the case as they saw them. The authors who had tutored said that such a guide had been extremely helpful to them. Often the guide was an author's final involvement with a case, unless revisions were suggested after the case was used.

A general overview of the case writing process is indicated in Figure 15.1. It involves the following steps: development and planning, writing the case, case review, case use and, finally, evaluation of the cases after their use by the students. The writers were generally involved in case selection, content selection and writing the case and not all the steps outlined in Figure 15.1.

After finishing a case the authors said they would reflect on whether they had produced a 'good' case – and all had similar definitions for the characteristics of 'good' cases. The best ones, they all said, were those they had written from personal and professional experiences because they were familiar with the patient and they could select content based on their expertise. As one writer said, a good case 'rests on someone's assessment that they condense the material for presentation. In the story there are bits and pieces that require me to make a decision.'

Real cases seemed to stimulate more interest than hypothetical cases. One author said, 'I think when people know it is a real case their interest is greater than if it were a hypothetical case.' Another two writers said, 'Good cases give them a sense it is real', and 'I try and make my cases as true as possible, believing firmly that cases work best when they are not concocted.'

Most of the writers said that they preferred real situations over hypothetical ones because they were 'more powerful teaching cases'. The following statement represented most of the writers: 'If you start trying to clean up cases and get rid of inconsistencies and errors in management you strip them of their teaching power.'

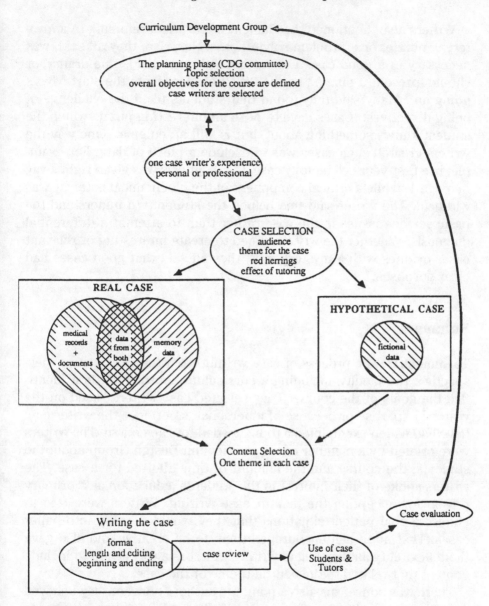

Figure 15.1 *Case development and writing*

Good cases also needed to be well organized, interesting and accurate. For example, one writer said, 'A good case grabs their interest', and 'I think a good case, in general, has some emotional content, some little shtick to it.'

Writers also mentioned the element of surprise, referring to a mystery, a puzzle, or a problem-solving case. Surprise, they all said, was necessary in a good case. Cases, they said, needed 'some drama' or should 'present a puzzle', so that 'it's not clear from the start what's going on'. Many said they found that students liked the challenge of being detectives: 'Cases have to pose an interesting puzzle which the student knows something about, but is still an enigma.' One way the writers created such cases was to exclude a piece of data. For example, in a first-year cell biology case, the diagnosis was given right away on page 1, while a critical component of the biochemical pathway was withheld. The writer said this helped the students to understand the basic science issues in the case rather than to attempt a differential diagnosis. Whether the writers aimed to create interesting or relevant cases or ones with a mystery in it, they all said that good cases had clear purposes.

Summary

To summarize the process of case writing from the case writers' perspective: the faculty, including a curriculum coordinator, first identified the goals of the course. They selected case writers based on the writers' expertise or because of a personal experience the writer may have had which exemplified a topic needed for the course. The writers were briefed by a member of the Curriculum Design Group about the students, the course and the amount of time allotted for a case. The writers spoke of their interest in the students' education as a primary reason for accepting the task of case writing. Writers were free to choose actual patient situations that they would develop into paper cases. That approach encouraged them to be creative and also gave them flexibility as they began writing. Authors always tried to include content that related to the central theme of the case.

There was consensus also among the authors on what they believed were the characteristics of a good case. They all said that good cases were written from professional and personal experiences, developed from either real situations or written to reflect a real situation. This gave a case relevance and thus made for a powerful teaching tool. Good cases contained a puzzle which helped the students develop problem-solving skills.

Once written and submitted, a case would be reviewed by one or more members of the Curriculum Design Group. At that point, changes, if necessary, were made and the case was then included for use in the curriculum. Curriculum Design Groups continue to review and edit old and new cases and, where appropriate, original writers are sought and consulted if significant changes are to be made.

Writing cases has proven an effective way for faculty to be involved with both faculty and curricular development and has become a recognized scholastic endeavour to be cited in one's portfolio in the HMS teacher-clinician track for promotion (Lovejoy, 1995). Additionally, faculty generally find case writing to be a personally creative and rewarding aspect of their involvement in teaching.

Case writing and usage has been and continues to be an integral part of the HMS New Pathway curriculum. How those first cases were written and developed and how the authors saw their roles remain surprisingly current and relevant today.

References

Barrows, H S (1984) A specific problem-based, self-directed learning method designed to teach medical problem-solving skills, and enhance knowledge retention and recall. In H G Schmidt and M D DeVolder, M D (eds) *Tutorials in Problem-based Learning*. The Netherlands: Van Gorcum & Company.

Barrows, H S and Tamblyn, R M (1977) The Portable Patient Problem Pack: a problem-based learning unit, *Journal of Medical Education*, 52, 1002–1004.

Cabot, R C (1906) *Case Teaching in Medicine*. Boston: Heath and Company.

Hafler, J P (1989) Case Writing in Medical Education: A Study at Harvard Medical School. Dissertation, Graduate School of Education, Harvard University.

Lovejoy, F H (1995) A Promotion Ladder for Teachers at Harvard Medical School: Experience and Challenges, *Academic Medicine*, 70, 1079–1086.

Waterman, R E and Cooley, B (1985) Curriculum: problems to stimulate learning. In A Kaufman (ed) *Implementing Problem-based Medical Education*. New York: Springer.

Chapter 16

Becoming a Problem-based Tutor: Increasing Self-awareness Through Faculty Development

LuAnn Wilkerson and **Edward M Hundert**

In 1985, Harvard Medical School took the bold step of beginning the New Pathway, a problem-based curricular track for a small group of incoming students. In this pilot project, the traditional lecture-oriented basic science courses were replaced with interdisciplinary, problem-based blocks with a major commitment of time in each to small group tutorial being focused around clinical cases. For many faculty members, the tutorial approach was a new and unfamiliar one.

During the early years of the New Pathway, t˘˘˘˘chool relied heavily on a core of faculty volunteers who participated because they found the problem-based perspective compatible with their views of learning and wanted to work with like-minded colleagues (Wilkerson and Maxwell, 1988). Faculty development was a simple matter of providing workshops on tutoring skills. However, when the pilot curriculum was expanded to include the entire entering class of medical school students in the autumn of 1987, we were faced with the need to involve teachers who had never thought much about learning nor worried about facilitating student interaction. In fact, some thought facilitation was educational jargon meaning keep quiet while students talk!

This chapter is the story of what we have learned over the last few years about the skills needed by problem-based tutors and how to assist faculty members in re-framing their views of the educational process – an essential first step in tutor training. The chapter begins with the stories of three tutors to illustrate common tutorial dilemmas and provide a framework for the discussion that follows. Next, we consider the multiple roles that the teacher plays in a problem-based learning group, a challenge that requires a heightened sense of awareness of self in relation to others. In the final section of this chapter, we examine ways in which faculty members can be encouraged and assisted to increase self-awareness by working with colleagues and educational consultants in exploring and responding to tutorial dynamics – a problem-based approach to problem-based faculty development.

Three case studies

The following stories are about three different tutors and the struggles they faced in adopting new teaching roles within the problem-based tutorial. In what ways might the teacher redefine relationships and roles in order to be more effective?

Case 1

The student group has become increasingly annoyed with their tutor, Dr A, because nothing ever seems to get accomplished in the tutorial. Two students use up most of the time quibbling about subtle differences in the way they view fairly unimportant aspects of the material. The tutor and most of the group are unaware that these two students are currently engaged in a conflict over the leadership of one of the social activities in the school. The group finishes the course angry that they got 'stuck with a tutor who did not focus the group on the material'. The tutor, who had only barely been convinced to try teaching in this format, becomes sure that problem-based learning is a hoax and refuses to be a tutor the following year.

Case 2

In a pharmacology tutorial, two students are arguing enthusiastically over the definition of tolerance in a case of possible drug abuse in a young man with cancer, with one student assuming a psychological definition and the other, a biological definition. Susan, a female student in the group, proclaims, 'As physicians, we will have to be very aware that pain has both a biological and a psychological component. The perspective of the patient is extremely important.' Almost before the words are out of her mouth, Dr B responds, 'Let's take a closer look at the biological aspects of pain and tolerance.' Susan turns quickly towards the tutor and gives him a puzzled glance. He notices her glance, but does not know how to interpret it. The discussion quickly picks up speed again, this time focusing on the biological components of pain.

Case 3

The tutor, Dr C, is a junior faculty member who feels insecure about the content of the course, having been a student of most of her fellow faculty members only a few years before. One of her main interests is family dynamics. Despite spending a great deal of time reading for each tutorial session, she discovers that it is more fun to talk about group process than the actual course content. The students, although they consider it an 'okay' tutorial and like Dr C quite a bit, also find that they look forward to tutorial more as a group therapy session or an 'escape from professional school' than as a time to learn.

A redefinition of relationships

Teachers who are considering a shift to a problem-based mode of teaching are faced with the need to re-examine many of the relationships that may have characterized their teaching in the past. First, there is the relationship between the teacher and the students' learning. Our behaviour in typical lecture-oriented classes suggests that we hold certain beliefs about how learning occurs (Cook, 1989). Whether consciously or not, most of us teach in ways that suggest that we equate telling with learning and view the teacher as the ultimate source of knowledge.

'If I don't cover it in this course, they will never get it.'

'I told them about organelles in lecture last week and this week it's like they never even heard of them.'

'This generation of kids just cannot follow directions.'

Rather than seeing themselves as the central players in the dissemination of knowledge, problem-based teachers stimulate and guide the students as they make sense of information and experience. Serving as a coach rather than a player, the problem-based teacher is responsible for designing appropriate activities, observing learners at work, and guiding their progress through questioning and feedback. A success-ful problem-based teacher must learn to trust the learners to do the work of learning. Given the range of topics that any one case can stim-ulate, tutors cannot be the ultimate authority on every topic under dis-cussion. In fact, since case discussion turns control of topical selection over to the students, even the expert will be frequently outside his or her 'comfort zone'.

Second, aspiring problem-based teachers may need to redefine their relationship to the content to be learned. Rather than seeking to cover everything themselves, they need to ask what do students need to cover? What are the critical learning objectives that should be dis-cussed? How do their objectives relate to material encountered by stu-dents in previous courses or life experiences? Realizing that a rich network of connections among ideas facilitates understanding and remembering (Glaser, 1984), problem-based teachers use their exper-tise to assist learners in making connections among ideas.

Third, problem-based teachers experience new relationships with students. In a teacher-centred classroom, a strict hierarchy of exper-tise is maintained. There is an authority who knows and novices who listen respectfully from a distance and 'speak only when spoken to'. In problem-based learning, teachers become partners in the learning process. Through interacting with students around the identification and resolution of problems, teachers come to know students as indi-viduals with differing needs and abilities. They come to care that every student achieves to full capacity. As the problem-based teacher loosens control of the content and process of learning, students learn to ask questions and provide extended explanations for one another, often in ways that were unanticipated by the teacher. The teacher, too, becomes a learner.

Fourth, when teachers replace lecture with problem-based discus-sion, students experience a new relationship to one another. No longer is discussion a matter of student response to a teacher question. When working with problem material, students become actively engaged with one another in building understanding, a process that has been compared to that required to raise a barn (McCormick and Kahn, 1986). They become a team responsible for accomplishing shared goals, one that is characterized by cooperation rather than competi-tion. As a member of the group, the teacher shares in the work and the play, attentive to the needs of both individuals within the group and the health of the group itself and mutually responsible for fostering a cooperative spirit in the class room (Johnson *et al*, 1984).

Fifth, although problem-based teaching requires a certain amount of skill in setting learning goals, selecting and designing problems, asking thought-provoking questions and managing individual participation, the greatest challenge for the problem-based teacher is to develop an increased level of professional and personal awareness of self in relation to others. Donald Schön has described this awareness as the ability to reflect on one's actions and asserts that it is the hallmark of professional practice (Schön, 1987).

The best problem-based teachers in our experience demonstrate an ability to follow carefully the flow of a discussion and to intervene at just the right moment and in just the right way to maximize learning and facilitate group process. They are sensitive to the emotional and cognitive expressions of students and skilled in responding in what Schön (1987) calls the 'indeterminate zones of practice', those unique situations in which the rote application of previous knowledge or skills is not enough. They are aware of the multiplicity of roles that they are playing in the life and work of a group and thrive on the challenge. Finally, they make themselves vulnerable, admitting when they do not know and modelling the process of self-directed learning.

The challenge of multiple roles

Teachers have always had to struggle with multiple, sometimes conflicting, roles. Two of these roles are almost always present, no matter what the educational format: the role of information disseminator and that of evaluator. The problem-based tutor quickly discovers just how many other roles are implicit in the relationship between 'teacher' and 'student'. We have found a few of these to be especially relevant to the issues of faculty development, especially with regard to our theme or self-awareness.

The parent

Students often bring to their relationship with tutors all the feelings and conflicts that attend their own family situations. As soon as an authority enforces some basic rules of behaviour and perhaps even has some (real or imagined) expectations, some students immediately take up positions as trouble-maker, instigator, mediator or angel. In the problem-based tutorial, some of these familiar roles can be heightened by the presence of 'sibling rivalries' as in Case 1, and especially by the explicit acknowledgement that the tutor does not have all the answers.

Although most students have conflicting feelings about authority, the only thing worse is when that authority is not the omnipotent being he or she has been feared (or hoped) to be. Teachers used to teaching in a setting where they could collude with the class to continue the myth that they have all the answers may feel as uncomfortable as the students with this type of environment where the responsibility for learning is shared.

The professional consultant

When discussing paper cases in a tutorial, it is not unusual for the case suddenly to come alive in the form of one of the student's family members, friends or indeed one of the students in the group. Often, a student will (publicly in the tutorial or privately afterwards) confide that the case under study has some special personal relevance and may ask for a consultation on personal problems or professional dilemmas. In the medical school context, this often amounts to a medical consultation about whether the student or some family member might have the diagnosis under study.

While the consultant role may also arise in more traditional settings, the problem-based tutorial makes for more intimacy, and tutors quickly feel the full weight of 'getting to know the students better'. Whether it is a medical consultation for distressing symptoms, a business consultation for some risky new venture or academic consultation about specific career options, confidentiality issues and group conflicts can quickly emerge, especially if the student has a serious illness, is involved in some potentially dangerous or unethical enterprise, or the level of emotion in the tutorial is more than the group can handle. Tutors new to problem-based learning may get more than they bargained for!

The confidant

Students naturally confide in those teachers whom they get to know better, and here again the small tutorial group gives rise to potential educational strengths as well as problems. Periodic individual feedback sessions with students become a chance to do some supportive listening, and perhaps even to give some advice concerning everything from study schedules to love life, financial problems or career directions. Of course, tutors less open to hearing about such matters will hear about them less. But the relationship of adult learner to adult teacher makes for a lower threshold to enter into this type of confidant role than the more traditional relationship of child novice to adult expert.

Conflicts can arise with this new view of the teacher-learner relationship and may get played out in a very concrete way around the issue of students' using their teachers' first names, rather than the more traditional 'Dr Jones' or 'Professor Smith'. We have seen some teachers who have found it shocking and others who have found it refreshing, some who were initially shocked, but then warmed to it; others who absolutely could not tolerate it.

And, of course, the confidant role can cut both ways. Indeed, most personal disclosures invite a counter-disclosure, and tutors often open up more about themselves than they ever would in a lecture hall. In the small tutorial group, it is not at all unusual for the tutor to invite the group to his or her home for dinner – another symbol of how faculty also might reveal more about themselves. Some faculty feel that such personal disclosure is a show of respect for the students as fellow adults; others feel that students show disrespect by wanting to 'get to know the teacher more as a person'.

The learner

An important aspect of problem-based learning that is perhaps the most different from the traditional lecture format is that attention is drawn to the faculty member's not having all the answers. Almost any well-written case opens up an infinite array of possibilities, and even if the case falls squarely in the tutor's field of expertise, it does not take long for someone to enquire about the legal issues that might impinge on the question under study, or about the ethical or biochemical issues raised by a particular medical case that otherwise was right in the tutor's specialty.

Faculty members have differing levels of comfort with uttering the words 'I don't know' – especially in front of students! While students uniformly praise tutors for adopting an attitude of learning along with them, some faculty members feel they will lose the respect of the students if the students realize their knowledge of the field is not complete. In courses covering interdisciplinary topics, it is virtually impossible to find faculty members who are truly expert in all aspects of the course content, and in such cases it becomes especially important to find and to develop teachers who feel comfortable about their own learner role in the problem-based tutorial.

The mediator

In the problem-based tutorial, the tutor is often called upon to mediate in conflicts between students. Cases 1 and 2 both demonstrate this dynamic. The conflicts may relate to simple differences of opinion as to content matters, differences in values, different life experiences, feelings of competition, or preference about how best to use tutorial time. Creation and maintenance of a safe learning environment is a prerequisite to the accomplishment of any other learning objective. Success in the mediator role is essential when conflicts between students begin to interfere with attention to the content of the course.

Role-related issues can make or break a faculty member's continued involvement in a problem-based curriculum, and faculty development programmes cannot ignore these fundamental aspects of tutoring. Success in balancing multiple roles requires a certain degree of sensitivity on the part of the tutor to the dynamics of the group. The three troubled tutors introduced earlier in the chapter illustrate the difficulties that arise from this lack of awareness.

In Case 1, Dr A was unaware of the tension in his group. In Case 2, Dr B not only took some of the responsibility for learning away from the students by directing them only to the biological side of the debate about pain and tolerance: he also missed a cue from a student who felt personally slighted by his redirection of the discussion. Here, the group tension could have been put to good educational use in driving them to delve deeper into both sides of this important debate. The tutor's inattention to the group dynamic not only missed this opportunity, it also left one student feeling hurt and left the group with the unfortunate (and dangerous) message that this complex topic is much more straightforward than is actually the case.

At the other extreme, Case 3 demonstrates that attention to group process is only one part (a 'necessary but sufficient condition') of success in the educational mission of the tutorial. For reasons concerning her own level of self-confidence in the tutor role, Dr C did not realize that the importance of attention to group process comes from the contribution this makes to the learning of the students – both in terms of building their knowledge base and shaping their attitudes towards the subject and the process of learning itself.

Again, the tutor needs to recognize and respond to role and process issues, not to be a good group therapist, but to be a good teacher. Problem-based learning makes it possible for cases to 'come alive' and connect with more aspects of students' own lives and past experiences than could ever be possible in a lecture. It is a process that includes the tutor's noticing how students are reacting to aspects of the case and then drawing out those features of the case that connect most with this unique mix of individual students. And in order to achieve this process in its fullest potential, all the roles, task structures and personalities that make up the tutorial – along with the tutor's own comfort level and ability to recognize all the subtle phenomena mentioned thus far – must be managed and negotiated in all their complexity.

Problem-based faculty development

Becoming a problem-based teacher requires both a desire to change, and an increased awareness of self and others. In addition, the effective tutor needs to possess a broad set of specific teaching skills to use in responding to learner needs. Faculty development is that set of resources and activities that the individual uses in accomplishing these changes. Although individual teachers can seek out such resources on their own, an institution committed to the initiation of problem-based curricula has a responsibility to provide support for these activities (Bok, 1989). In a recent pilot study of university teachers and the improvement of teaching, Blackburn, at the National Center for Research to Improve Postsecondary Teaching and Learning, found that a number of institutional features influence faculty members' willingness to experiment with their teaching: administrative support of teaching, help and time to think about alternatives, flexibility in scheduling, and availability of money for instructional resources.

Faculty development activities can be used to stimulate interest in problem-based learning, to challenge teachers to enhance their awareness and redefine relationships, and to assist teachers in developing basic skills in leading a student-directed tutorial. Effective faculty development programmes (Benor and Mahler, 1989) draw on the same principles that guide problem-based learning:

- ☐ Teachers work together to solve real problems.
- ☐ Teachers direct their own learning.
- ☐ There are opportunities for teachers to collaborate in teaching one another.

□ Previous experience is explored in the process of learning.
□ The leader is a coach, observing and giving feedback.

At Harvard Medical School, the faculty development programme consists of multiple opportunities for faculty members to learn from one another about problem-based learning. For example, as our first recruitment effort, we invited all interested faculty members to a dinner at which an experienced tutorial group and its tutor demonstrated the tutorial process and answered questions about the why and how of the approach. One hundred faculty members indicated an interest in attending, a response so overwhelming that we had to hold the dinner on two separate nights!

Current faculty development activities include institutional conferences, course-specific workshops, opportunities for individual feedback based on direct observation of tutorials, and formal and informal student evaluations of teaching. In each of these activities, faculty members are encouraged to examine their own assumptions about learning, to reflect on the events of their tutorial groups, and to use one another as resources in resolving tutorial problems. New tutors continue to report that two activities are particularly influential in their development as problem-based tutors. First, participating as a learner in a tutorial with a skilled tutor is an essential feature of every new tutor workshop. By participating as learners, the faculty members experience the power of problem-based learning and the excitement of learner-directed collaboration first hand. Second, most new tutors appreciate the opportunity of being observed while interacting with their tutorial groups, often commenting on how much fun it is to talk about teaching and learning with another person and how much they have learned about themselves that they can use not just in tutorial but in relationships with colleagues and families! Experienced tutors convene each summer to explore the complexities of the tutorial process in a day-long conference focused on dilemmas that they have encountered in their own tutoring.

Through the support of faculty development activities, the institution signals a commitment to problem-based learning and underlines the importance of excellence in teaching. One final institutional commitment is essential to the process of course and curricular reform – the design of a reward system in which excellence in teaching and educationally relevant scholarship (eg problem-based cases, computer programs, textbooks and research on one's teaching) are valued as means of professional advancement. In the same year that Harvard's

Dean, Daniel C Tosteson, formed the initial problem-based curricular design groups, he appointed a committee of faculty to consider faculty development and evaluation. Five years later, the work of this committee resulted in a new set of criteria for promotion and tenure that recognizes contributions to the educational goals of the medical school.

The teacher clinician ladder provides opportunities for academic advancement for those full-time faculty members who demonstrate excellence not only in teaching and clinical work but also in educational leadership and scholarship. Recognition of these activities and the physicians who perform them is a key element in the success of curricular reform at Harvard Medical School and in medical education in general. This ladder is designed to reward the currently unrewarded teacher clinician and to encourage a new emphasis on national leadership in teaching and medical education.

There were several basic principles that formed the basis for the teacher clinician ladder:

1. The new criteria are as rigorous as those of other full-time ladders and mirror the quality and standards associated with each level of academic appointment.
2. A reward system is a powerful way to change behaviour in a desired direction; thus, the new ladder encourages and rewards previously under-emphasized academic contributions as well as previously encouraged but unrewarded contributions.
3. Appointments and promotions are based on reliable criteria; letters attesting to excellence in teaching are a necessary component of such criteria but do not substitute for a systematic assessment of teaching contributions.
4. To the greatest extent possible, criteria for promotion need to be valid. Thus, the new track carefully defines what activities are to be recognized as criteria for appointment and promotion and ensures face validity and content validity.

The teacher clinician ladder has become an established part of the culture at Harvard Medical School since the first academic appointments were made in 1989. Up until October 1996, there have been 97 appointments made on the teacher clinician ladder with 44 assistant professors, 37 associate professors and 16 professors (Lovejoy and Clark, 1995).

In this chapter we have not delineated specific teaching skills needed by the problem-based tutor, but focused instead on the need for teachers to develop a greater awareness of themselves, of learners, and of the relationships that characterize their interactions. Once more aware of the multitudinous feature of the learning process, the problem-based tutor will need a broad range of specific teaching skills to select responses that will maximize learning. The reader is referred to articles by Barrows (1988), Wilkerson (1995; 1996) and Schmidt and Moust (1995) for a description of more specific teaching skills useful to the problem-based tutor.

These questions of the tutor's own self-awareness and psychological sensitivity cannot be emphasized enough as ingredients in the mix that makes for a good learning environment – and so also as a central issue in faculty development. Faculty members need some insight into what they expect to attain from tutoring before they can improve their ability to function in that role. A tutor who seeks to satisfy a narcissistic need to show how much more he or she knows than the students is unlikely ever to be effective in the problem-based tutorial. Faculty development can only have real meaning in such a case if the tutor comes to embrace new goals, such as helping students learn how to learn on their own. Similarly, a tutor who identifies too strongly with the students, like Dr C during her first year as a faculty member, can be helped to develop a stronger identity as an 'expert', even if that expertise will not be 'transferred' to the students through the traditional format of lecturing on the subject.

The real challenge of faculty development is the wide variety of backgrounds that tutors possess in the subtleties of individual and group psychology. Some people are psychologically aware by temperament; some are not. Some people value self-awareness, some do not. These facts of life apply to professional school faculty as much as they apply to any other group of individuals. It is no small task to try to help a tutor see the value of attending to group process if that tutor has never done so before. Ultimately, the experience of seeing its beneficial effects is the best tool for developing tutor self-awareness. Making explicit some of the implicit roles discussed above can also jar faculty members out of a simpler world where their primary educational task was the presentation of course content.

Acknowledgement

This work was supported in part by the Kaiser Family Foundation.

References

Barrows, H S (1988) *The Tutorial Process*, Springfield, Illinois: Southern Illinois University School of Medicine.

Benor, D E and Mahler, S (1989) Training medical teachers: rationale and outcome, in Schmidt, H G *et al* (eds) *New Directions for Medical Education*, New York: Springer-Verlag.

Bok, D (1989) Needed: a new way to train doctors, in Schmidt, H G *et al* (eds) *New Directions for Medical Education*, New York: Springer-Verlag.

Cook, R I (1989) Learning theories implicit in medical school lectures, *Journal of the American Medical Association*, 261, 2244–2245.

Glaser, R (1984) Education and thinking: the role of knowledge, *American Psychologist*, 39,93–104.

Johnson, D W, Johnson, R T, Holubec, E J and Roy, P (1984) *Circles of Learning: Cooperation in the Classroom*, Alexandria, VA: Association for Supervision and Curriculum Development.

Lovejoy, F H, Jr and Clark, M B (1995) A promotion ladder for teachers at Harvard Medical School: experience and challenges, *Academic Medicine*, 70, 1079–1086.

McCormick, D and Kahn, M (1986) *Barn Raising: Collaborative Group Process in Seminars*, Harvard Business School Publication 8–386–025.

Schmidt, H G and Moust, J H C (1995) What makes a tutor effective? a structural-equation modeling approach to learning in problem-based curricula, *Academic Medicine*, 70, 708–714.

Schön, D A (1987) *Educating the Reflective Practitioner*, San Francisco: Jossey-Bass.

Wilkerson, L (1995) Skills for the problem-based tutor: student and faculty perspectives, *Instructional Science*, 22, 303–315.

Wilkerson, L (1996) Tutors and small groups in problem-based learning. In L Wilkerson and W Gisjelaers, W (eds) *Bringing Problem-Based Learning to Higher Education: Theory and Practice*. New Directions for Teaching and Learning No. 68, San Francisco, CA: Jossey-Bass.

Wilkerson, L and Maxwell, J A (1988) A qualitative study of initial faculty tutors in a problem-based curriculum, *Journal of Medical Education*, 63, 892–899.

Chapter 17

Issues in Implementation in an Otherwise Conventional Programme

Donald R Woods

For years I was an avid observer and student of the McMaster Medical School's innovative problem-based approach to teaching and learning using the process of a self-directed, small group or 'tutorial' approach. The more I discovered about PBL from my colleagues across campus, the more I realized the challenge to implementing their approach in my traditional, lecture based course in a conventional chemical engineering programme. This chapter summarizes the context, the major hurdles and how we overcame them, the resulting problem-based activity, and comments about other issues that might affect the implementation.

The context

Twenty years ago our chemical engineering department decided to add explicitly to the development of our students' problem-solving and interpersonal skills and to improve their ability to learn on their own. Such 'process' skills were not being developed, as we had hoped, by the traditional lecture-tutorial-project courses in our four-year curriculum. To develop the problem-solving and interpersonal skills, we created 80 additional hours of workshops on these process skills, and added embedding activities to develop students' confidence to apply the skills in the context of chemical engineering (Woods, 1989a and b; Woods *et al*, 1984; 1988; 1997). We selected the McMaster Medical

School model of problem-based tutorial to empower our students with self-directed learning ability. Chemical engineering students experience the problem-based approach in two project courses: a sophomore communication skill course and a senior design project. However, a formalized small-group, self-directed process has not been used. Thus, the problem-solving skill development was structured so that we could exploit the Medical School approach for a five-week problem-based tutorial activity to learn subject knowledge and to develop skill in self-directed learning. However, the Medical School context is different from the context where this learning activity would occur. Traditionally, I lecture, whereas, in the Medical School problem-based tutorial programme, the faculty facilitate discussion about what individuals have learned. I work in a three-three-three system based on three hours of lecture per week, three hours of homework per week and three hours in the final exam system, whereas in medicine they have blocks of time, take a 'systems' approach and have peer and tutor continual assessment with no final formal three-hour exam.

Our students (age 18 to 23) have been accepted into the chemical engineering programme based on their academic marks, whereas admission into the Medical School is based on academic marks, interviews, an essay, references and a simulated tutorial (where the students' abilities to solve problems and work effectively in a group are assessed). Our class sizes are 20 to 45, whereas they have a faculty facilitator/tutor for groups of five. My students have experienced 13 years of traditional lectures, tutorials and laboratories, whereas students in the Medical School enter the programme knowing that the learning will be problem-based in small group tutorials. The students I work with have five concurrent courses, whereas in the McMaster Medical School the students have only one theme to consider at a time.

The focus for this chapter is on how we adapted the Medical School problem-based tutorial approach to our context. I could not change the admission criteria, the staff to student ratio, nor the number of concurrent courses.

Overcoming the first major issues in implementation

Our department took a three-stage approach to address three major issues in implementation in this context, namely:

1. to increase students' confidence and skill in group process, problem-solving and self-assessment;

2. to train them in stress management and ways of coping with the dis-equilibrium they will experience when such a different approach is taken; and
3. to devise ways of providing the tutor-facilitator role for small groups when we had one faculty person available for a class of 20 to 45 students.

We addressed the first two issues by implementing the 80 hours of workshops described above. Thus, students part-way through their senior year had everything in place for problem-based tutorials to be effective. However, to focus on the process skill of self-directed learning (SDL) we shifted the small group activity from 'discussion' to 'teach each other via mini-lecture with discussion'. To help to clarify for the reader this small but significant shift we refer to this as problem-based, self-directed learning (PB-SDL).

For the third issue of staff/student ratio, we chose to empower the students to take over most of the tutor-facilitator role and to evolve options for providing the 'expert' input as needed. We would rely on the previous explicit training on being an effective chairperson/facilitator to address this issue. The PB-SDL activity should give as much emphasis to learning the 'process of self-directed learning in a small group' as to learning the chemical engineering 'content'. Thus, the students receive explicit training and feedback about PB-SDL.

PB-SDL small group activity

The PB-SDL workshop starts by pre-testing students' ability to use this approach effectively, gives some learning objectives, and introduces the grieving model (Woods, 1994) to help students adjust to the activities ahead. Throughout the five-week period, each student continually received feedback from peers about the group process and about their effectiveness as participants in the learning process. At the end of the five weeks they received a post-test about the process, and submitted summary critiques of their personal growth in PB-SDL.

For the 'content', we selected engineering economics. The students were given a series of four problem statements that posed all the key issues to be addressed. We had already constructed an 'expert's' set of objectives. The students were asked to create their own objectives and problems and to validate them with ours (Woods, 1995a). Thus, the students made their own decisions about what, when and how to learn. They took charge completely and monitored their own progress.

Groups of five were given five and a half weeks to learn both the process and the content. Typically the groups would meet early in the week to identify issues, set goals and agree on resource utilization. Later in the week, they would reconvene and teach each other the content. For the past five years we have added a third meeting in which the students pose test questions to each other (Woods, 1993; Woods, 1995a). For each meeting, one student was appointed chairperson. Usually the meetings were held in the 'lecture' time so that I would be available as a resource person.

This approach has been used for ten years. It has exceeded both my expectations and those of the students. They become confident using this approach to learn on their own. They can acquire the 'process'. The evidence is provided by their self, peer and faculty assessments that are part of this whole programme (Woods *et al*, 1988). Anecdotal comments include: 'I found that the idea of SDL is great. I strongly recommend that it be introduced earlier in the curriculum. Why not year 2?' Based on such comments, we now offer one PB-SDL experience in the junior year.

For the 'content', students report that they learn more and study harder than if they had been exposed to lectures. Although we were confident of our students' ability to self-assess (Woods *et al*, 1988), we continued to require a formal, three-hour written final exam set by the instructor. We wanted to compare the effectiveness of this approach with the norms of performance from the three-three-three approach, and we needed to convince faculty outside our Department that academic standards were being maintained. On the three-hour written examinations, the overall average is as high if not higher on 20 to 30 min. problems (deemed by the instructor to be of equivalent difficulty) compared to the performance of previous students who received the three-three-three based learning.

Issues affecting implementation

To sum up, the main issues (and our experience) were:

□ To prepare the students with the required skills. The 80-hour explicit workshop-style training was sufficient and effective. Over the past four years, we have adapted about 14 hours of workshops for the key process skills. Options for astutely using these are available (Woods, 1995b).

☐ That the students must be willing to take charge of their own learning and to cope positively with the attitudinal shifts that occur when they experience change. Our approach, based on the grieving model, Perry's attitudinal scale (Perry, 1974) and Taylor's model (Taylor, 1986), has been effective.

☐ Empowering the students to be their own facilitators, through such activities as a 15-hour workshop on chairperson skills, worked well. But how might we supply the expertise a faculty tutor brings? The use of one expert teaching assistant per group failed because the students did not draw on their expertise. Currently, the tutor/teacher must validate the learning objectives of each group before it can proceed further. Other issues relating to implementation include preparing the teachers, selecting the case problems and the resources, choosing the size and members of the student groups and coping with problems of attendance and participation (Woods, 1994; 1995a and b; Woods *et al*, 1996).

Selecting and preparing teachers to operate in PBL courses

This is not a trivial task. Faculty must be willing to take the risk. They will have to give up the sense of 'control' that one is familiar with in a lecture setting.

I had trouble with this the first year that I tried the PB-SDL approach. I felt that the students would not learn the material as effectively. In addition, no one requested information from me as a resource. The students, on the other hand, reported that they studied harder, enjoyed it more, and learned more. They performed well on the written exams. This was an anxious and eye-opening experience for me. I would expect that others might have some of these feelings. Skill at facilitation and a willingness to empower the students with the excitement of learning are important attributes for the faculty.

Student attendance and participation

All has not been positive. Some students reported a 'lack of morale and dedication to self-directed learning in our group; many meetings had to be rescheduled because people were unprepared or did not show up.' Empowerment brings student accountability. To help monitor progress, and to make individuals accountable, we have devised a range of feedback and journal-writing activities that seem to be effective (Woods, 1995a and b; Woods *et al*, 1996). Nevertheless, lack of attendance continues to be a challenge. We establish the rules of conduct that require any absences from the group to be negotiated among the peers. If such conduct is not followed, then the group asks the instructor to notify the student that he or she receives no credit for the unit being learned. Each year about two such letters are sent. Usually the student elects to negotiate to be reinstated.

Choosing and formulating the problem; preparing the resources

Neither of these was difficult. The problem was formulated from 'content' objectives that I hoped to achieve in the ten hours of 'lecture' material. Creating the resources for 'independent' learning included preparing an annotated list of resources, creating two short videotapes and supplying copies of the transparencies and lecture notes. These were put in the resource centre of the library.

Creating the student groups

I used the same, randomly selected groups of five for the whole activity so that norms of behaviour and trust could develop. This random selection has worked very well.

The size of the group seems to be important. The students' views are that three did not provide enough people to share the load of teaching; seven was too large. Five seems ideal.

Summary

We prepare our students for a PB-SDL five-week activity through 80 hours of workshops on problem-solving and group skills. We focus on developing both the skill at the 'process' of PB-SDL and learning the 'content' in the context of chemical engineering economics. Our planning strategies were reasonably successful although we provided more resources than they needed, and we did not anticipate that attendance and attitude toward PB-SDL would be the problem it was. The resources were more than adequate. The main surprises were the enthusiasm and degree of learning that the students showed, and that they chose to draw on the expertise of each other rather than on the faculty.

The key problem with implementation was to get the students to take charge of their own learning, and to devise a scheme to promote participation. For the faculty, the main problem was to convince them to become a resource as needed and that students could learn the material on their own.

PB-SDL has been enthusiastically received by both the instructor in the course and the students. The challenge is to extend this to other courses.

Acknowledgments

I am pleased to acknowledge the help of Vic Neufeld, Donna Mitchell, Geoff Norman, Elizabeth Brain and Chris Woodward, McMaster Medical School.

References

Perry, W G, Jr (1974) *Intellectual and Ethical Development in the College Years: a scheme.* New York: Holt, Rinehart and Winston.

Taylor, M (1986) Learning for self-direction in the classroom: the pattern of a transition process, *Studies in Higher Education*, 11, 1, 55–72.

Woods, D R (1989a) *MPS Unit A: The MPS Program.* Internal Report, McMaster University, Hamilton, Ontario.

Woods, D R (1989b) *Being an Effective Chairperson. MPS Unit 29.* Internal Report, McMaster University, Hamilton, Ontario.

Woods, D R (1993) *The MPS SDL program.* Videotape, Chemical Engineering Department, McMaster University, Hamilton, Ontario.

Woods, D R (1994) *Problem-based Learning: how to gain the most from PBL.* Waterdown, Ontario: Woods; distributed by McMaster University Bookstore, Hamilton, Ontario.

Woods, D R (1995a) *Problem-based Learning: helping your students gain the most from PBL.* Waterdown, Ontario: Woods. Available on the WWW: http:\\chemeng.mcmaster.ca

Woods, D R (1995b) *Problem-based Learning: resources to gain the most from PBL.* Waterdown, Ontario: Woods. Available on the WWW: http:\\chemeng.mcmaster.ca

Woods, D R, Crowe, C M, Taylor, P A and Wood, P E (1984) The MPS Program for Explicitly developing Problem-solving Skill. *1984 ASEE Conference Proceedings*, Washington DC: American Society for Engineering Education, 1021–1035.

Woods, D R, Duncan-Hewitt, W, Hall, F, Eyles, C and Hrymak, A N (1996)

Tutored versus tutorless groups in problem-based learning, *American Journal of Pharmaceutical Education*, 60, 231–238.

Woods, D R, Hrymak, A N, Marshall, R R, Wood, P E, Crowe, C M, Hoffman, T W, Wright, J D, Taylor, P T, Woodhouse, K A and Bouchard, C G K (1997) Developing problem solving skills: the McMaster Problem Solving Program. *Journal of Engineering Education* 86, 2, 75–91.

Woods, D R, Marshall, R R and Hrymak, A N (1988) Self assessment in the context of the McMaster Problem-solving Program, *Assessment and Evaluation in Higher Education*, 13, 2, 107–127.

Part IV
Examples From Different Professions

Chapters in this part provide examples of PBL in a variety of contexts, most of which are on a smaller scale than the school-wide programmes discussed elsewhere. In including these examples, we hope to stimulate discussion about implementation in circumstances less favourable than those which prevail in schools where major adoption occurred. It is certainly possible to introduce significant elements of PBL without major wholesale change to a degree programme. Whether it is desirable to do so depends on local circumstances. Individual teachers in higher education have greater opportunity for innovation within their own courses than most ever realize. The authors represented here have seized that opportunity and demonstrated what can be done. Some have involved colleagues, others not. They all report positive student responses though.

Why has there only been partial adoption in some cases? It may be the constraints of colleagues not wishing to change their practices, the constraints of resources for development, or the limitations of time available for the teacher. On other occasions the approach might not be widely understood or, if understood, not desired as a new approach. In such circumstances it is tempting for the teacher to introduce a partial version of PBL or to implement the approach in one aspect of the curriculum. This can work well, but it can also place intolerable strains on students and on colleagues. However, a problem-based sequence can be fitted into a lecture-based course – if carefully designed. Lectures can form part, albeit a small one in terms of total contact hours, of a problem-based curriculum as witnessed at the Harvard Medical

School and the Architecture School at Newcastle. The most important consideration in making PBL work alongside other approaches is a commitment to the holistic design of courses. Students experience the totality of a course whereas teachers are normally only directly aware of that part in which they are immediately involved.

As well as providing illustrations in different subject areas, authors in this part address a number of issues. Peter Cawley and Jan Lovie-Kitchen address how a problem-based course can be incorporated alongside parallel conventional classes. Natalie Bolzan and Karen Heycox describe how one part of a course, say the first year, can be changed to provide a problem-based foundation for that which follows. How a problem-based segment can provide an interface between a lecture-based course and professional and industrial practice is illustrated separately by authors Peter Cawley, and John Usher and colleagues. Keith Winsor describes how an existing course focusing on preparation for professional practice can incorporate a problem-based approach. Debra Creedy and Christine Alavi in a new chapter on PBL in nursing education reflect on how PBL fits the demands of their discipline and can operate in an integrated curriculum.

In the first edition we drew attention to the paucity of examples from areas other than the health sciences. While that has changed and there are many examples available elsewhere, there is no doubt that by far the largest number of illustrations that have been well-documented and systematically evaluated come from the health sciences. See, however, the major example of economics and business at Maastricht, by Alan Gilbert and Stephen Foster, and also of architecture at Newcastle, updated by Barry Maitland. In part this is a function of the recent origins of PBL and the culture of university departments in these professions where there has been a long-standing tradition of research into teaching and learning. However, it is interesting to speculate on whether some of the features of PBL emphasized by Barrows (1986), for example, are particularly suited to professional fields in which problems are bounded by individual bodies and exist within relatively discrete communities. When we wrote in 1991 that there were very few examples in fields other than the health sciences, where an all-encompassing professions' problem-based approach had been adopted, we had our doubts about whether PBL could translate on a major scale to other fields.

Those doubts have receded, only to be replaced by a consciousness that the adoption of problem-based approaches in other disciplines will lead to approaches which are quite dissimilar to those found, for example, in medicine. Indeed, the second wave of problem-based innovation in medicine has a different flavour to the first.

The features which we believe will need to underpin new developments in other professions are:

- [ ] the centrality of 'real' problems or problematic situations which might not be labelled as 'problems' as starting points for learning. Without this feature developments could hardly be termed problem-based;
- [ ] an emphasis on viewing professional education and the preparation of professionals as an holistic enterprise. This view exists, however, in considerable tension with notions of modularization and multiple pathways through degrees which are currently popular for general education;
- [ ] a well-developed view about the nature of professional practice in any given area. If it is not possible to envisage what practitioners will do once they graduate, it is difficult to devise meaningful simulations of practice which participants will appreciate;
- [ ] a learning-centred conception of the curriculum in which decisions about content and process are made primarily on the basis of the consequences for student learning;
- [ ] a commitment to progressive refinement of programmes. A problem-based curriculum involves complex forms of cooperation among a wide variety of personnel and unless there is a deep and systematic commitment to processes of improvement, the course will unravel no matter which desirable features were incorporated into the original design.

Reference

Barrows, H (1986) A taxonomy of problem-based learning methods, *Medical Education*, 20, 481–486.

Chapter 18

A Problem-based Module in Mechanical Engineering

Peter Cawley

Introduction

The course described in this chapter is a final-year option on vibration in an honours mechanical engineering degree programme. I had previously taught the subject for several years as a conventional lecture course and, although the student response to the course was satisfactory, I was concerned that there was too much emphasis on technical theory and too little stress on the application of the material to real engineering problems. It was noticeable that in the examination, the students tended to avoid questions requiring the type of diagnostic and problem-solving skills which are essential to engineering practice.

I therefore decided to convert the course to a problem-based format and to broaden the original aim of merely transmitting technical content to include developing the professional skills of using this material to solve real problems, and of communicating the solutions effectively. The major aims of the new course are to:

1. develop the students' skills of modelling, analysing and proposing practical solutions to vibration problems in engineering;
2. develop the students' skill of criticizing proposed solutions to problems;
3. develop students' appreciation of how systems vibrate;
4. introduce several standard methods of analysis;

185

5. develop the students' independent study skills;
6. develop the students' oral and written presentation skills.

The detailed objectives arising from these aims are given in Cawley (1989).

Since the course was to fit into the existing final-year course structure, it had to be designed to fit into the standard timetable of 30 possible contact hours over 20 weeks, with one class every week and a second class in alternate weeks. Two staff are allocated to each course, the workload being more or less equally shared between them. It was important to ensure that, after the course design had been completed, there was no significant increase in staff loading. Similarly, since the students would be taking other courses in the normal way, it was essential to ensure that there was no overall increase in student workload, and that there were no clashes with submission deadlines in other subjects. Fortunately, there were precedents for final-year courses being assessed by assignments during the year rather than by examination, so there was no requirement to have a conventional final examination.

Course outline

The course is centred on six problems which are typical of those which practising engineers would be likely to meet in the early stages of their careers in design, development or trouble-shooting departments in industry. The selection of appropriate problems is a major factor in determining the success of the course; it is essential that the students perceive them to be similar to those which industrial engineers meet, but it is also important to ensure that a reasonable solution can be obtained in a relatively short time. Ideas for problems have often come from short consultancy jobs which I or my colleagues have done. An example of one of the problems is given in Figure 18.1.

The problems cover all the technical material of the course and are also the vehicle for attitude and skill development. The need to solve them is designed to provide the motivation for the students to study the technical content of the course, and the students' solutions to the problems form a major part of the course assessment.

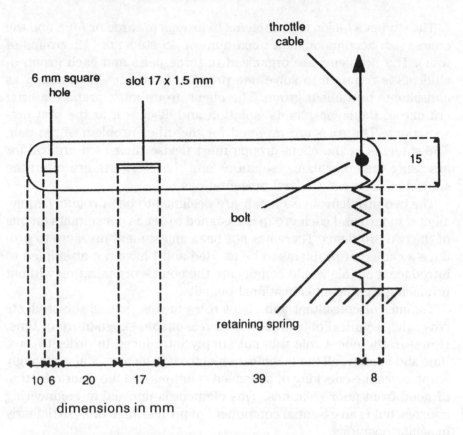

dimensions in mm

The throttle lever on a fuel injection pump is stamped out of 2 mm thick steel sheet as shown in the diagram. The volume of fuel injected is varied by the rotation of a solid steel spindle which has a squared end and shoulder. The square hole at the left-hand end of the lever fits on the spindle and the lever is held in place by a nut and washer. The lever is actuated via a Bowden cable which is secured to a bolt at the right-hand end of the lever and the cable is directed to the accelerator pedal via a rubber bush in a bracket 100 mm from the lever. The bolt weighs 5 g and the cable weighs 50 g/metre. The throttle cable acts against a soft retaining spring of stiffness 100 N/m and mass 5 g. The slot in the lever enables it to be fitted to another pump; it is not used here.

In its original application, the pump ran at a maximum speed of 3,000 rev/min and ran satisfactorily. Later, however, it was redesigned to run up to 6,000 rev/min and fatigue failures of the lever at the point of attachment to the shaft occurred. You have been called in by the development department to sort out why the failures are occurring and to propose a solution. You are to prepare a written report and give an oral presentation on your proposals.

Figure 18.1 *Example problem*

The students tackle the problems in groups of three or four, and the course can accommodate a maximum of 48 students (12 groups of four). The problems are organized in three pairs and each group of students is required to solve one problem from each pair, acting as consultants to a client group. The client group must prepare a brief critique of their consultants' solution and discuss it at the oral presentations. The roles are reversed for the other problem of the pair. The students in the client groups must devise their own criteria for assessing the consultants' solutions and these criteria are often the subject of debate at the oral presentations.

The two problems in each pair are designed to be of roughly equivalent standard and each group is assigned to act as consultants on one of the two problems. There has not been any student pressure to produce a choice of problems to be tackled and I have not attempted to introduce it as this would complicate the course organization without producing significant educational benefits.

The mix of consultant and client roles means that all the students cover the technical objectives with a reasonable expenditure of time. However, the client role was not simply introduced in order to save time and to allow all the technical objectives to be met; it also strongly emphasizes the checking of proposed solutions and the discrimination of good from poor solutions. This element is unusual in engineering courses, but is an essential component of professional life, particularly in senior positions.

There are three phases of the course, each lasting six or seven weeks, during which the students deal with one pair of problems, each phase ending with oral presentations. These take the form of a meeting lasting one hour between two groups, one of which plays the consultant role on the first problem of a pair and the client role on the second problem, the roles being reversed for the second group. By using two tutors, two meetings each involving two student groups can be held in a one-hour session, so 12 student groups can be accommodated in three timetabled sessions.

Each group of students has one compulsory tutorial lasting 20 minutes while it is tackling each of the first two pairs of problems. These tutorials are designed to check that the students have appreciated the requirements of the course, that they have adapted their learning style to the requirements of a non-conventional course, and that they have thought about what will constitute a satisfactory solution to the problems. Apart from these brief tutorials, the groups do not have any formal contact with the tutors before the oral presentations, so most of their work is done independently of the staff.

There are no compulsory tutorials during the third pair of problems. However, students are free to seek the advice of tutors during the timetabled periods which are not used for formal activity, or at other times. This shifting of emphasis, away from the compulsory tutorials of the first two phases of the course, to an open system in the third phase, is designed to encourage the students to take more responsibility for their own learning.

Apart from the tutorials, the only formal input to the students comes in four short lecture/demonstrations which are primarily designed to illustrate the way in which systems vibrate. Students are also provided with a bibliography of around 20 textbooks and with some printed notes which were produced when the course was lectured in the conventional way. No new support material has been written for the problem-based course.

Assessment

The assessed elements of the course are consultant reports on three problems, client reports on three problems, oral presentations of these reports and one solution to an example on a particular topic (receptance analysis) which experience has shown that students find difficult. The reports are prepared by the groups and the example is solved by each individual student. There is also a one-hour 'test of understanding' at the end of the course. This was introduced in the light of experience in the first year the course ran when several students complained that 'passengers' in groups were not being detected. The test is designed to check the students' grasp of the basic principles of the subject, rather than the analytical details which are the basis of many exams, a typical question being of the form, 'A junior member of your department suggests that the problem may be solved by ... Is this likely to be feasible?'

Thirty per cent of the total marks on the course are allocated to the 'test of understanding' and the individual solution to the assessed example is worth 4 per cent, the remaining marks being allocated to the written and oral presentations. More weight is given to the later problems, partly because these problems are more demanding, but also because the earlier problems are designed to be formative (giving students practice at tackling problems and enabling them to learn from tutors' comments) rather than purely summative (assessing the

				mean score		
				86/87 (N=21, 88%)	87/88 (N=37, 86%)	88/89 (N=34, 69%)
1. Have you found the course interesting?	very	5 4 3 2 1	not at all	4.6	4.5	4.6
2. Have you enjoyed the course?	very much	5 4 3 2 1	not at all	4.5	4.1	4.3
3. Did you find that focusing the course on real engineering problems made the course seem more relevant to your interests?	very much	5 4 3 2 1	not at all	4.5	4.4	4.7
4. Did working in groups mean that you learned from each other?	very much	5 4 3 2 1	not at all	4.0	3.5	4.1
5. Have you understood the technical material of the course better than if it had been lectured in the conventional way?	much better	5 4 3 2 1	much worse	3.9	3.9	4.1
6. Do you think you have learned as much technical material as you would on a conventional lecture course?	much more	5 4 3 2 1	much less	3.2	3.2	3.8
7. Considering the material you have learned, do you think you have learned it more thoroughly than you would on a conventional course?	much better	5 4 3 2 1	much worse	4.1	3.9	4.3
8. Has this course taken more or less time than other conventional lecture courses? (In your assessment of the time taken by other courses. you should include the time you will spend on revising for the exams.)	much more	5 4 3 2 1	much less	3.2	4.2	4.4

Figure 18.2 *Extracts from course evaluation*

extent of the students' attainment), and it is hoped that the students will learn from these. A full breakdown of the weighting given to each element of the assessment is given in Cawley (1989).

Reaction to the course

The problem-based course was run for the first time in 1986/87. As expected, since the format was unfamiliar to the students, only 24 students chose to take it, giving eight groups of three students. In 1987/88, the number of students rose to 43 and in 1988/89 the course was over-subscribed, 49 students opting to take it. Fortunately, it was possible to accommodate them all because a third member of staff was interested in learning about the new teaching method. In this year, the course ran with 14 groups of three or four students.

At the end of the course, the students are asked to complete a comprehensive evaluation questionnaire with a set of questions requiring numerical gradings, and others requesting comments on each aspect of the course. The responses to the numerically graded questions are shown in Figure 18.2. Several of the questions involve comparisons with a hypothetical conventionally taught course. While this form of question is not entirely satisfactory, the students are in a good position to make those comparisons since they take conventional courses in related subjects. The response rate in 1988/89 was lower than that in previous years because of difficulties with the timetabling of the evaluation session.

The students clearly enjoy the course and feel that they learn as much technical material as they would on a conventional course. The 1986/87 questionnaire returns indicated that the student time input was similar to that on conventional courses. However, I suspected that the time spent was somewhat greater than their estimates, since students could frequently be heard discussing the problems in the coffee room, an almost unknown occurrence on conventional courses, and this valuable peer learning may not have appeared in their estimates.

The 1987/88 and 1988/89 returns indicated that the students felt that the course was much more time-consuming than a conventional course. This change did not seem to be due to the introduction of the test, as the students confirmed that they had not felt it necessary to spend a significant amount of time on revision for it. It may be that several other courses have increased the proportion of coursework in their assessment, which made the students' perception of the workload higher. This is borne out by comments from several staff that students were spending less time on their project work than in previous years. In response to several courses changing in this way, it may be necessary to restructure the final-year timetable.

I find that teaching the course in this way is much more enjoyable than lecturing, not least because the students clearly enjoy it and their skills visibly develop as the year progresses. I find that the discussions with the students at tutorials are more productive and generally at a higher level than those on conventional courses, probably because the students are well motivated and have dealt with many of the basic issues by themselves. The oral presentation sessions turn into important learning forums; on many occasions a consultant group will make an incorrect statement which is seized on by the clients, or failing this, by the tutor, and in the ensuing debate the issue is clarified. Subsequent conversations with students suggest that their retention of points raised in this way is very high.

Two other staff have been involved in this course and together with two other similar courses, 10 staff from a department of 45 have now helped with tutoring problem-based courses. Thus far, the staff have been volunteers and the only training has been by observation of tutorials and oral presentations which I or others have been running. More attention would have to be given to staff training if the department was to introduce a larger element of this style of teaching.

One source of concern about the course is that the final marks tend to show a very small spread, whereas in tutorial discussions it is clear that some students' grasp of the subject is much better than others'. The small spread is explained by the preponderance of group assessments; in practice, even at the oral presentations, it is difficult to assign significantly different marks to different members of a group. The 'test of understanding' does increase the spread somewhat, but since it only accounts for 30 per cent of the overall mark, its effect is limited.

My impression is that the students cover slightly less material than they would on a conventional course, largely because the topics which they deal with as clients are not covered in as much detail as I had originally hoped. However, the material which is relevant to the problems which the students tackle as consultants is generally dealt with in more depth than would be achieved on a conventional course. Also, since the course develops principles which are introduced in the second year, these frequently arise in discussion and are reinforced more thoroughly than was achieved when the third-year course was lectured in the conventional way. Since the style of the assessment changed along with the move to the problem-based format, no quantitative data are available on the comparative performances of students taking the conventional and problem-based versions of the course.

Conclusions

The experience of running a problem-based option within a conventional degree course has demonstrated that it is feasible to mount courses of this type alongside standard lecture courses. A gradual introduction of the approach in this way is much more likely to be successful in existing institutions than an attempt to convert a whole degree course without first gaining experience of the method. However, for such an innovation to be successful it is essential that it is carefully planned and that the workload on both students and staff is monitored closely.

The success of this initial experiment has now led to two other courses in the department converting to the problem-based approach and also to the institution of a full review of the degree course which may lead to a further shift towards this method.

Reference

Cawley, P (1989) The introduction of a problem-based option into a conventional engineering degree course, *Studies in Higher Education*, 14, 83–95.

Chapter 19

Use of an Issue-based Approach in Social Work Education

Natalie Bolzan and **Karen Heycox**

The School of Social Work at the University of New South Wales (UNSW) introduced PBL in 1983. In the early 1990s the name was changed to 'issue-based learning' to more appropriately reflect its placement in a social work course. It was felt that naming as 'problems' issues such as those associated with ageing and immigration unnecessarily pathologized them. Furthermore, presenting situations as problems implies there is a solution whereas social work is about exploring a range of perspectives and acknowledging the diverse responses which may be appropriate. 'For social work students to start out with the notion that complex social and individual issues are problems to be solved is in itself problematic' (English *et al*, 1994: 279). It is important for social work education to emphasize the need to engage consumers and others in this process rather than imply that social workers solve problems (Humphreys and Heycox, 1992: 5).

The issue-based approach to learning is seen as appropriate for social work education because of the breadth of the profession, the various intervention types used by the profession, and social work's integration of values alongside knowledge and skills. Social work educators at the University of Sydney, for example, believe that it is increasingly important that students have the capacity to transfer knowledge and skills across different contexts and levels of intervention, from interpersonal to societal.

Context

The issue-based approach is currently employed in the first year of a four-year social work degree at the University of New South Wales. The objectives of the first-year programme are broadly: to introduce social work students to the scope and range of social work practice; to present a number of social work intervention methods (casework, groupwork, community work, research, policy); to commence the process of questioning one's own knowledge and value base; to develop the ability of students to work collaboratively in groups; and to take some responsibility for their own learning, utilizing and sharing the knowledge they already have, while also identifying the gaps in their current understanding and developing future learning goals.

In the first year four distinct scenarios are presented and worked through. Currently these are: an older woman living in the community; refugees living in Australia; two young people with mental illness; and the discrimination of people with a developmental disability. The situations are chosen to meet the following objectives: relevance to current social work practice; development of specific social work skills; and representation of the broad base of the social work profession.

Structure

Each of the four scenarios runs for seven weeks and is structured each week as two small group tutorials placed either side of a large group lecture/presentation. These lectures/presentations enable practitioners and consumers involved with each scenario to provide the large group with a context based on first-hand experience. They also serve to identify the dimensions of the issue and various contributions of social work, both direct and indirect.

Each scenario is introduced at a tutorial through trigger material (video, newspaper clippings, documents, case history, etc) and supplemented with a specific book of readings. The content to be covered is set for each tutorial, but each group is able to explore these topics in a flexible way. An additional reading list enables students to pursue further readings. Students are required to undertake a relevant agency visit in at least two of the four scenarios where they explore the agency's role and the role of social work in that agency.

Each situation is reviewed at its completion for relevance of the material, contribution to learning, and functioning of the group as it facilitates student learning.

Process

One tutor is allocated to a tutorial group for a minimum of one semester (14 weeks). The importance given to process as well as content means the tutor's style is central in our application of the issue-based approach. Tutors (social workers) are expected to be active participants who draw on their own experience throughout the tutorial and are able to respond appropriately to the particular dynamics of the group with discussions, exercises, role plays and other input. This role is varied and includes that of facilitator, resource person, group processor, role model, support person, devil's advocate, administrator and ultimately assessor.

During tutorials the tutor facilitates discussion around several key issues. The discussion results from the student's own knowledge based on their life experience and formal education (Vinson *et al*, 1986). This form of self-disclosure not only provides information for other students but also facilitates the group process. This aspect of the issue-based approach is given much attention, as the group is an important medium for learning. For this reason each tutorial group spends some time in 'getting to know you' exercises and in group process reviews. As the group develops trust and cohesion the members gain confidence in pursuing different aspects of the topics presented.

The tutorial teaching team meets regularly to share their ideas on group process, innovative exercises, course content and varied formative assessments. This has become a source of support, particularly for those tutors new to the course.

Assessment

The formative assessments, administered at the end of each scenario, test and consolidate the knowledge and skill development that have taken place around each issue. This often takes the form of a practice-based situation which demands some form of professional response from the student, eg, a letter, a presentation, a submission or a report.

A bi-yearly summative assessment is also administered. These summative assessments are in the form of an exam which focuses on the skill, knowledge and values covered in the previous two scenarios.

Example of how this approach is applied

One of the four scenarios used in the first-year programme is concerned with the experiences of refugees in Australia. Table 19.1 outlines the content and process by which this issue is addressed. It demonstrates the integrated nature of this approach and exemplifies the ways in which knowledge, skills and values are combined and applied to a social work situation. The assessment further reinforces this integration by requiring students to write a report to another worker on the needs of one particular refugee community.

Table 19.1 *The content and process for addressing 'The experiences of refugees in Australia'*

	Tutorial	Lecture/Presentation	Tutorial
1st Week Readings: Learning Units 1 and 2 3, 4 and 5 Objectives	Who are refugees? Which issues are highlighted? What do we know of refugees? *Hope and Survival Game* *Handout 1: Defining Refugees*	Guest lecturer from Community Health Centre speaking on: 'Personal experiences of the never ending journey'	Australia's immigration history/policy? Issues, attitudes, policies, programs? What do social workers need to know? How do we find out? Multiculturalism? Personal/institutional racism *Video: Admission Impossible* *Handout 2: Racial prejudice*
2nd Week Learning Units 6 and 7	Resettlement needs? Barriers to meeting needs? Empathy skills with refugees Indicators of trauma and stress?	Guest lecturer from School of Social Work 'Differences and similarities between migrant and refugee communities'	Needs of children and young people? Social work responses to these needs? Meaning of community? Community assessment *Video: Make a little difference* *Video: A promise to keep* *Handout 3: Getting to know the community*

3rd Week Learning Units 9 and 10	What happens when different values meet? *Simulation: A Visit to Albatross Handout 4: Ten Assumptions of cultural bias*	Guest lecturer from STARTTS (Torture and Trauma Service) 'Issues of torture and trauma'	Overcoming communication barriers? Using interpreters *Role play Handout 5 Video: Counselling with interpreters*
4th Week Learning Units 11, 12, 13 and 14	What is community work? Social work with refugees? *Video: 'Tightrope juggling trick' Handout 6: A Community Work Job Description*	Guest lecturer from the Adult Migrant Education Service 'The language experience'	The community work process *Role Play Video: 'Where's the fight?'*
		Students visit Refugee Agencies	
5th Week Learning Unit 15	Report on visits to Refugee Agencies	Guest lecturer: Ethno-specific community services worker 'Resettlement issues for Vietnamese youth: working with a community group'	Processes of community meetings Effects of values and beliefs in meetings *Class exercise Handout 7: Meeting scenario*
6th Week Objectives	Writing skills *Handout 8: Getting Ideas/exercise*	Guest lecturer on 'Community education'	Review and group evaluation

Advantages of this approach

This approach has received positive feedback from various sources including workers in the field who come into contact with students via the lecture presentations and subsequent field education subjects. The advantages have been seen in students who are better informed early on about their chosen profession and are able to make career choices based on this information (Smith, 1985: 109); are able to critically evaluate career choices; can begin to question their own value base with reference to its impact on their practice; have more confidence about what knowledge and skills they bring to the course; acquire basic social work skills at an early stage of their course; practise the application of knowledge and skills *in situ*; and meet potential supervisors for later field subjects.

To maintain the accuracy of the information used, the course coordinator liaises closely with practitioners, policy makers and administrators. This has the added advantage of keeping educators in touch with the field. Practitioners from the field thereby have an opportunity to contribute to the content of the course and provide feedback on the performance of students. The flexibility of this approach enables new situations to be devised in line with current developments in the health/welfare field, for example the exploration of a rights-based approach for people with a developmental disability. It should be noted that part of Sydney University's implementation of an issue-based approach includes the establishment of 'partnerships' between university and field agencies. Partnerships involve an exchange of resources, knowledge and experience, evidenced in teaching and research activities as well as field visits in relation to a particular scenario of the issues-based approach (Davis *et al*, 1996).

The form the issue-based approach taken at UNSW is very much tied to the profession of social work. Some of the influences of this professional context have meant that small-group teaching is used as both the method of instruction and as an example for the discussion of small-group behaviour, with specific times being set aside to analyse the group's performance (English *et al*, 1994: 289; Smith, 1985: 115). Furthermore, attention is focused on students' own world views and life experiences in recognition of the use of self in social work as well as an ongoing emphasis on a range of intervention, both direct and indirect.

Issues for the issue-based approach

Despite the many advantages of this approach there are certain resource and structural constraints which need to be addressed or at least taken into consideration. Our application of the issue-based approach is resource-intensive. The updating of materials and the arranging of agency visits across a range of issues have proven to be demanding tasks requiring constant field liaison. Further, ongoing development of formative assessments and the bi-yearly summative assessments have been a drain on resources. This is exacerbated by funding cuts in the tertiary sector which have implications for tutorial sizes and consequently small-group teaching.

The unique structure of an issue-based approach requires a high level of commitment by both educators and the host institution. The introduction of such an approach into an already established course (such as at UNSW) is limited by the degree to which other subjects can accommodate the demands of this approach. On the other hand the development of a new degree is an ideal point at which to implement an issue-based approach more globally. The University of Newcastle's social work course is an example of a whole course being informed by an issue-based approach (English *et al*,1994).

Furthermore the preparedness of students to engage in this style of learning may be influenced by a variety of factors. Some of these identified by us include the life experience and maturity of students; a student's willingness to explore the breadth of social work beyond their particular practice preference; the placement of this material in the course in terms of the student's level of competence and their openness to different learning styles; the actual learning to be undertaken in this course, eg, abstract or concrete; as well as the difficulties inherent in trying to cover the breadth of the social work profession in enough depth to prepare the beginning practitioner.

Current developments

Recently, other social work schools, both well-established and new, have introduced an issue-based approach to the curriculum. Sydney University is an example of the former. They have argued that to meet the accelerating demand for more highly specialized material in social work, 'compartmentalized subject structure and traditional pedagogical practices are no longer able to meet these demands and produce coherent professional education' (University of Sydney, 1996: 4). They have introduced this approach into the professional third and fourth years of a four-year degree. The context-based modules 'demand that students acquire both specific knowledge and skills in relation to Theories, Values and Research in social policy and social work' (University of Sydney, 1996: 8). As in the UNSW course, the units are sequenced to achieve greater depth. Within the recently established social work course at the University of Western Sydney individual subjects have been developed based on this approach and the Department there is considering its degree in light of the contribution this approach may make more broadly.

The University of Newcastle introduced its new social work degree based totally on this approach. It has a strong focus on values, which is not designed to compel students to conform to some ideal notion of a 'professional' nor is it closed-ended. In this university's course information handout it is stated that the examination of values should be seen as open-ended, challenging and designed to help each student understand their own values, to explore the range of value positions in social work and in related fields, and prepare them for dealing with value issues in practice. This course is now in its fifth year and appears to be well regarded by the community in which it is based. The contribution of the issue-based approach to social work education could not be assessed until the first cohort graduated from a full social work degree course informed by this approach. This has now occurred and therefore it seems timely to evaluate this contribution to social work education.

Conclusions

The problem-based approach when applied to social work education evolved into the 'issue-based approach' to learning. This occurred in recognition of social work's particular value framework and the complexity of social work practice. Significantly this approach appears to some degree in all social work courses in the state of New South Wales. Its contribution to social work education appears to be increasing as more academics and practitioners become familiar with the approach and realize its value in integrating knowledge, skills and values in a way that builds competencies in the beginning social work practitioner.

Acknowledgement

Table 19.1 is adapted from the materials developed by Carmel Flaskas, Jan Breckenridge and Christine Gibson for the module 'Far from home: social work with refugees' used in the School of Social Work, University of New South Wales.

References

Davis A, George, J and Napier, L (1996) Hidden partners: inviting change in the social work curriculum. In D J McDonald and L R Cleave (eds) *Partnerships That Work? Proceedings of the Asia Pacific Regional Social Services Conference*, Christchurch, New Zealand 1995, 93–97.

English B, Gaha, J and Gibbons, J (1994) Preparing social workers for an uncertain future. In S E Chen, R M Cowdroy, A J Kingsland and M J Ostwald (eds) *Reflections on Problem Based Learning*. Sydney: Australian Problem Based Learning Network, 279–296.

Humphreys, C and Heycox, K (1992) Keeping issue-based learning relevant: 9 years on, *Probe: Newsletter of the Problem Based Learning Network*, 5 April.

Smith, B (1985) Problem based learning: the social work experience. In D Boud (ed) *Problem-Based Learning in Education for the Professions*. Sydney: Higher Education Research and Development Society of Australasia, 109–119.

University of Sydney (1996) 1996 Full Program Proposal, University of Sydney: Department of Social Work, Social Policy and Sociology, June.

Vinson, T, Leu, L, Smith, B and Yamey, N (1986) A problem solving approach to social work education, *Australian Social Work*, 39, 3, 3–8.

Chapter 20

Problem-based Learning in Optometry

Jan Lovie-Kitchin

Giving the same lectures year after year was boring! My decision in 1986 to use a problem-based approach in teaching final-year optometry students was not initially based on fine educational motives, but because I wanted a change. Also I felt that by their fourth year at University, students would probably enjoy a change too. Fortunately there were sound educational reasons, which are covered elsewhere in this book, for adopting the problem-based approach.

Optometry is a profession in which clinical problem solving, in an atmosphere of an ever-changing and expanding knowledge base, is the foundation of everyday practice (Scheiman *et al*, 1989). This is no more true than in the management of patients with visual impairment due to eye disease. Clinical practice in this optometric specialty requires the optometrist to be flexible and to adapt to the differing needs of individual patients in order to manage or solve their problems. The 'solutions' may require prescription of optical devices, referral to other rehabilitation professionals or information to be obtained from any of a number of different sources.

Because of the wide variation in the nature of, and solutions to, the visual problems of visually impaired patients, the need to know facts, while important, seemed less crucial than the ability to solve problems (Gibbs, 1982). The specialized subject, vision rehabilitation, relies on the clinical knowledge learned in previous years, but is separate from other subjects in final year (which are taught in traditional lecture format). Therefore, I felt that the teaching of this subject would be well-suited to the problem-based approach. The bases for my use of the approach are as follows:

- Real life problems are used to stimulate students to determine what they need to learn.
- Learning is directed to finding answers.
- Learning is multidisciplinary.
- Underlying processes are as important as 'solving' the problem. (After Staples, 1985.)

To cover the basic principles of vision rehabilitation in the 16 hours of contact time over 14 weeks, three patient cases are 'managed'. These are an elderly house-bound patient, a child in the education system and a working adult. A fourth case, which serves as part of the assessment, is varied each year, but has included a tertiary student and country housewife.

At the first session I explain the problem-based learning process to the class and set a few rules. One of the most important requirements is that students participate in the small-group discussions. I therefore expect attendance at every session, completion of the weekly exercises set by their own group and a log of all activities related to the course.

The class is divided into six groups of five or six students. In the past, students have chosen their own groups, which sometimes has resulted in small cliques evolving. Rarely in life are we able to choose the people we work with, so I assign students to groups; part of the learning process is to deal with any disagreements which may arise within the group.

The process

1. Trigger

The trigger is a brief but broad statement of the patient's problem, given in the way a patient would present it at an initial consultation. The trigger can be presented in a number of different formats: videotape, audiotape, role play, slides, written description, computer simulation or a real person with visual impairment. (Case notes give too much information without the students covering the background to how that information was gathered.) For the first case I show two minutes from a videotaped interview with an elderly low vision patient, Eileen, who describes her feelings at the loss of her central vision. For variation, the students 'interview' a real 'patient' as their second case. Background information, which is common to the management of most low vision patients, is given in brief written summaries for the other cases.

2. Problem

From the trigger, the students, first individually then in their small groups, identify all the possible problems and implications of the vision loss for the patient, for example, difficulties reading mail, recognising friends in the street, etc (see Figure 20.1). For the first case, I follow this with a class discussion to ensure they have thought as widely as possible and to indicate that they are on the right track.

3. Need to know

Following broad discussion on the information they need to know for the management of the patient, the students then set more specific questions for each pair in their group to research before the next session. To answer these learning questions, students may have to consult the course manual, textbooks or journals, draw on and modify their previous clinical knowledge, or contact rehabilitation services for visually impaired people. Summaries of their findings are handed in to me prior to the next session. I give feedback on the answers, copy the summaries for the other members of their group and hand these back the next day.

4. Solve or manage

This process is repeated over the following weeks until an assessment and rehabilitation plan is developed for the patient. The first case usually takes five to six weeks, but the next cases are completed more quickly because the assessment methods have been covered. Each group compiles a flow chart of their management of the patient and these are presented by a spokesperson to the whole class (Figure 20.1). The presentation of each group's management plan indicates to the students that there are a number of alternative solutions to patients' problems, that none are right or wrong and that they must accept a degree of uncertainty in their management of some patients.

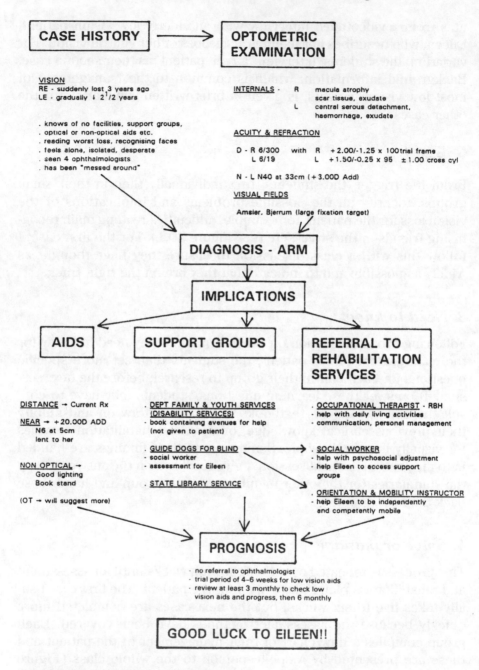

Figure 20.1 *The case of 'Eileen'*

Assessment of the subject, vision rehabilitation, includes a mid-semester examination in the form of a patient management problem, a rehabilitation plan for the fourth case and a case report on a real patient whom the student has managed in the QUT Vision Rehabilitation Centre.

Students' evaluation of problem-based learning

To evaluate the effectiveness of the problem-based approach, students complete a short written questionnaire which investigates:

- □ the extent to which objectives were attained;
- □ the usefulness of resource materials;
- □ the difficulties of the tasks involved; and
- □ the students' perception of problem-based learning compared with traditional teaching methods.

Table 20.1 *Students' assessment of problem-based learning compared to traditional teaching methods*

| | Per cent agree | | | | |
	1990 (n=24)	1991 (n=30)	1992 (n=30)	1995 (n=27)	1996 (n=29)
Requires more organized study	61.9	66.6	63.3	70.4	70.0
Too time-consuming	33.3	23.3	36.7	44.4	58.6
Too demanding	4.8	13.3	17.9	29.6	35.7
More related to clinical situations	100.0	100.0	100.0	92.6	93.1
Helps more with understanding	100.0	86.7	83.3	84.6	62.1
More enjoyable	80.9	96.7	65.5	77.8	65.5

It is clear that the majority of students are satisfied with the problem-based approach, especially its clinical relevance (see Table 20.1). On the question of organized study, about two-thirds of the students obviously have required a change in study habits to cope with the different structure of the course. The proportion of students who feel that more time is required by PBL has increased over the past six years, as has the proportion who feel it is too demanding. This may reflect increasing demands in the whole optometry course.

In open-ended comments, the students indicated advantages and disadvantages of small-group work and the problem-based approach, compared to traditional lectures.

Advantages

Students are strongly supportive of the interaction allowed by small-group work and the ability to learn from one another. The improved communication between students generates more and different ideas, enables more information to be gathered but spreads the workload. Of interest is the effect of group pressure 'forcing' students to answer the set questions each week because they feel a responsibility to their peers. This has been a striking feature of the classes; students rarely fail to hand in their weekly answers.

The students indicate strongly that the PBL process is much more like real clinical situations (Table 20.1). Understanding is improved because information is retained when students have to find it themselves. The process leads to broad reading around topics and also forces the students to contact outside groups. They report that the process is more interesting, enjoyable and helpful than traditional lectures.

Disadvantages

The comments reflect some concerns about working in groups. These refer to various aspects of group dynamics such as reliance on other members and disagreements within groups. Because of time constraints, information is not always shared or discussed. There is occasional resentment because some group members do more work than others.

Some students indicate discomfort with the process in their comments that there is insufficient direction; they request more feedback on success or failure or are unsure whether all relevant areas have been covered.

My evaluation of the problem-based approach

The advantages and disadvantages of the problem-based approach which I have experienced are similar to those reported by the students.

Advantages

The interactive process with students is most enjoyable and stimulating. The students' approaches vary from year to year, so teaching the same subject each year is no longer boring. Topics have arisen for discussion which I had never previously covered in lectures and students occasionally find new references or make contacts with community groups of which I was unaware.

Disadvantages

There is extra work involved in PBL compared to lectures – as the only person to use this approach in my school, this involved compiling comprehensive resource information and providing overnight feedback on, and copies of, the summaries. It has also been difficult to find a large classroom, as opposed to a lecture theatre, conducive to group discussions.

Most advocates of PBL recommend one tutor per group of eight students. I have one other tutor to assist me with six groups of up to six students. It is difficult to be aware of the interactions between students within each of the groups and ensure involvement of all members. However, there are some advantages in having the groups work without the tutor at times. Students have to take greater responsibility for their work, they may feel less inhibited about suggesting ideas and for the university the cost is lower.

Gibbs (1982) indicated that lecturers are held back from change because of their role perceptions of teachers. These form a number of constraints, but they include the time required to undertake the design of a new approach, and the fear of loss of authority and status. I felt quite insecure when I used PBL for the first time because students have to be trusted to work alone. However, it has been demonstrated that the quality of student learning can be maintained (many say improved) by relying on students' autonomy and personal responsibility and less on formal teaching (Gibbs, 1982) and I have found this to be so.

Future changes

I am currently considering changes to the assessment in this subject. Allocating marks for the weekly summaries handed in by each pair of students may help to overcome the uneven contribution to the work-load which some students have complained about. Similarly, to date I have not given marks for the log or journal which I expect students to keep. Not surprisingly, the journal has not been taken seriously. I have been convinced by the arguments of November (1996) and others, that to enhance reflection on the learning process the importance of the journal should be upgraded by allocating marks.

Summary

All students' comments on the problem-based approach have been positive. They have been supportive of a teaching method which allows:

- development of a number of solutions to a problem;
- appreciation of clinical and real situations;
- discovery of new resources to assist patients;
- investigation of ways to organize patient management;
- thinking about a problem rather than being 'spoon-fed'.

I have had the advantage of working with relatively small numbers of students. Teachers and departments with larger class sizes would have to consider the resource implications in particular before adopting the approach. Overall I have enjoyed the problem-based approach and find that students work very well when given responsibility.

References

Gibbs, G (1982) Better teaching or better learning? In T Habershaw (ed) *Three Ways to Learn*. Occasional Paper 12, Standing Conference on Educational Development Services in Polytechnics: Preston, UK.

November, P (1996) Journals for the journey into deep learning: a framework, *Higher Education Research and Development*, 15, 115–127.

Scheiman M, Whittaker, S and Dell, W (1989) Problem based learning as a potential teaching approach: a literature review, *Journal of Optometric Education*, 15, 9–15.

Staples, D H (1985) *Problem Based Learning*. Report compiled following secondment to Educational Research and Development Unit, Queensland Institute of Technology, Educational Research and Development Unit.

Chapter 21

Problem-based Learning for Architecture and Construction Management

Barry Maitland

Architectural courses around the world have almost universally retained one PBL feature derived from the origins of architectural education in tutelage and apprenticeship to a practitioner. This is the design studio, in which the student is provided with a brief for a building, is periodically tutored over the drawing board in the studio, and finally presents a solution in front of the class to a 'jury' of tutors and practitioners, in a design 'crit'. This studio learning (usually seen by students as the creative part of the educational process) is then traditionally accompanied by formal lectures, tutorials and laboratory classes covering the varied subjects of the curriculum: history and theory; structures, building construction and building science; professional practice, management and law.

The classic problem of architectural courses is how these two parts of the process can be reconciled and integrated. It is a perennial complaint of tutors that students who have successfully passed exams after a course of lectures on, say, structural frame design, then go into the studio and design a frame building as if they had no idea of the principles involved. Equally, students complain that the lecture courses seem to have been devised in isolation from the studio projects, so that information is presented in an incoherent and unrelated way. From time to time, when the situation threatens to get out of hand, the school acts to oblige lecture staff to talk to studio staff, and coordinate at least the major features of their programmes. But the underlying difficulty remains, with its false dichotomy between 'creative' studio and 'academic' lecture room, and, worse still from the point of view of professional competence, between 'exciting' design problems in the former and 'boring' technology problems in the latter.

A comprehensive PBL programme offers a way to cut across this dilemma, and it was this that particularly attracted us to the approach when we came to review the Newcastle course in 1984. In progressively converting all five academic years of the course to a PBL basis over the following three years, we were hoping to achieve a more integrated programme in three respects:

1. integration of discipline areas, and in particular of technical and design areas;
2. integration of the successive stages of the students' design processes, from initial data collection and analysis, through conceptual design to detailed technical resolution;
3. integration of staff inputs.

The problem-based course was developed by building up a sequence of design problems of increasing scale and complexity through the first four years of the course, from the design of a single simple space in Year 1 through to the design of multiple-use developments in complex urban contexts in Year 4. At the same time a theme was adopted to link the problems of each year to a range of building types, so that the student would be exposed to as full a range of types, each with its particular social, economic and cultural context, as possible. For each problem a 'real' client, familiar with that context, presents the problem to the students.

Thus the theme of Year 1 is 'Problems of the workplace', with examples of the design of workstations and small buildings for industrial, office or agricultural work (Donaldson, 1989). Year 2 has 'Problems of the home and community' as its theme, with the design of a private house, of some medium-density group housing, and of a community building such as a primary school. 'Problems of public buildings' is the theme of Year 3, with the design of larger public buildings, such as art galleries, concert halls and theatres as its subjects. And for Year 4 'Problems of the city' is the theme, including major commercial buildings, both medium- and high-rise, in a context of urban design and town planning considerations.

In selecting the problems to fill out this framework, a further consideration was adopted in pursuit of the second integrative objective identified above. It was felt important that students should not only develop expertise in problem solving within each of the several stages of the building design process, but that they should also build up a sense of the overall sequence of these stages, and of the levels of thinking appropriate as one progresses through the typical job-cycle. To do this it was decided that the programme for each year after Year 1 should include one problem which would be taken all the way through from the initial identification of a need to the detailed constructional drawings of the proposed solution. A difficulty with this, however, is that such a process tends to be lengthy, lasting for several months if each stage within it is to be adequately covered.

The pattern of problems which grew from these considerations then runs as follows:

- in Year 1, with a class size of 45 students, a series of problems of about four weeks duration each is developed, culminating in one of about eight weeks in which a conceptual design phase is linked to a technical development stage;
- in Years 2, 3 and 4, with class sizes ranging from 30 to 40 students, one major problem is arranged to last a whole semester, and run through the full cycle of stages, coupled with shorter problems of varying length;
- in Year 5, with a class of about 25 students, a single problem lasts for the whole year.

Year 5 is the culmination of the process, and is different from the earlier years in a number of respects. The students, approaching professional autonomy, select their own problem and must find their own client, with whom they must work through the early problem definition and project feasibility stages. They must also choose an appropriate site for their project.

Running through the five academic year programmes, in the classic matrix pattern of PBL courses, is the requirement for the progressive acquisition by the student of the various areas of knowledge and skill which comprise the syllabus. These discipline areas are fairly precisely identified by the architects' registration boards and professional institute which give professional accreditation to courses, and in the case of the Newcastle course were grouped into 12 'study areas'. Thus the design of the individual problems within the general pattern described above had to ensure that opportunities were given for each of these study areas to be developed to an appropriate standard during the course.

In designing and then running these problems, staff adopt three types of role:

- □ *Consultants* are given responsibility for individual study areas, servicing the problems with their specific expertise as it is required, and ensuring that their part of the syllabus is adequately covered.
- □ *Group tutors* act as generalist design tutors to groups of eight to ten students in Years 1–4 (Year 5 students have individual tutors), with whom they meet for two mornings each week. Their role is to help the students to integrate the input of consultants, to help them to manage their own time, and to provide design criticism. In some ways this role is similar to that of the studio tutor in the traditional course, except that progress in design is now seen in the context of the full range of supporting disciplines. To facilitate this, group tutors are provided each week with a summary of the consultant inputs which students have received during the previous week.
- □ *Year managers* (one or two per year) coordinate the activities of consultants and group tutors within their year, and manage the day to day progress of that year. They set up its timetables, write its phase documents, and ensure that the demands of consultants for contact-time to cover study area material are reconciled with a balanced workload for the student.

With those roles established, the design of individual problems within a year becomes a team process under the chairmanship of the year managers. The general characteristics of the problem are sketched out in terms of the major features which consultants seek. For example, in the case of the major third-year project, the design studies consultant would be looking for the opportunity to develop students' skills in the planning of complex circulation arrangements on a number of levels, the structures consultant would want students to explore the characteristics of a concrete-frame structure, and the building science consultant to introduce the principles of design for acoustics.

From the full range of these requirements the year manager develops the outline of a design problem which should provide the opportunities to meet the study area objectives. One year, for example, the consultants' objectives for the third-year project described above were met by a theatre building, another year by law courts, and another by a motor museum. In each case a client is discovered who can provide a realistic current context for the project, and an outline brief is then developed by reconciling the realities of a development of that type with the needs of the study area consultants for particular features in the programme. From this outline, including time constraints, consultants bid for access time at various stages in the problem as they see the need to offer workshops, lectures or tutorial sessions to support the problem-solving process and develop their study area. Some of these sessions will be pre-planned, involving a pre-arranged speaker, for example, or an exercise designed to develop a skill needed for the project, and some will be a looser offer to be available on call at certain times to respond to students' needs for access to their specialist advice.

Consultants offer these services within a budget provided by the head of department, both of their own time which should be spent on a particular year, and of the part-time resources which they can call upon. Something like 30 per cent of the equivalent full-time staff positions in the Newcastle Department of Architecture are in fact provided in the form of part-time appointments filled by a wide range of practitioners from architectural practices and related disciplines. Practitioners act as both group tutors and consultants, although a full-time staff member always acts as the central coordinator for each study area, even where the majority of its consultants are part-time.

A characteristic timetable emerges from these negotiations between consultants and year managers, in which time in the early stages of the problem (or problem phase) is heavily booked, as students need information and advice during the period of research and analysis. A student's timetable in these first weeks of the project will typically entail 25–30 contact hours per week. Later, as students move towards postulating and drawing up design solutions, their timetable becomes progressively more free, with fixed contact periods reducing to only their group tutorial sessions, and a commitment of about six to ten contact hours per week. This variable contact time is a popular feature with students, who complain in traditional courses of the disruptive effect of study area lectures and submissions during the final intensive all-night draughting sessions of a major design project.

Case Study: 400 George Street, Sydney

One set of objectives of the fourth-year architecture programme relates to familiarizing students with some of the more important town planning, environmental, economic and technical issues raised by high-rise commercial buildings in city centres, and a problem was specifically developed for this purpose. The site, 400 George Street in the centre of Sydney, had already been the subject of a number of development proposals, and was up for sale. The selling agents' brochure formed part of the briefing documents, as did the phase brief, written especially by a senior partner of Peddle Thorp and Walker, one of the most experienced firms of architects for high-rise building in Australia, who agreed to act as client for the project. The situation envisaged was one which the firm had met many times – a client who was considering buying the site required an architectural design for it in order to see how much high-rental development could be got onto its 4698 square metre area, given quite narrow constraints concerning, for example, the avoidance of overshadowing of adjacent Pitt Street Mall, the planning of office floors for fire escape and rental maximization, and many other detailed aspects which were set out in four pages of the briefing document. From a design which answered those questions, a feasibility study would reveal how much (bearing in mind interest rates, rental levels, etc) he could afford to bid for the site. In addition he would need drawings sufficiently convincing to persuade institutional investors to commit funds to the project, and he would need all of these things within six weeks.

These requirements matched our consultants' study area objectives for the project, and these were provided for the students in a phase document (a standard procedure in the presentation of all our problems to students), along with the assessment criteria which would be used. From the overall six-week deadline set by the client a list of intermediate submissions was worked out for the highly compressed design and presentation process, with detailed specifications for each. Around these deadlines a programme of site visits, interviews with the client and lectures, workshops and tutorials with consultants, was constructed to feed the design process. For example, to help students prepare for the visual presentation which the client needed to market the project to financial institutions, a special seminar was arranged with graphic artists who specialize in this sort of work.

At the end of the six-week process each student presented final drawings and a model to the client, and to a panel of tutors, for assessment. A technical report submission was also made, including detailed responses to specific issues, such as the solar control strategy, and calculations for the lift system. An assessment of each student's performance was made in accordance with the process outlined above, with the client as an active member of the design integration jury.

Finally the best and most interesting schemes were put on exhibition in the Sydney offices of Peddle Thorp and Walker, and a number of their partners rounded off the whole project by coming to the school to lead a public discussion on the outcome of the 400 George Street student project, and to give a lecture on the design philosophy of their own practice.

Outcomes

Eleven years after its introduction, the problem-based architecture course at Newcastle continues to operate successfully on these principles. Although there have been many detailed developments of the component parts, the structure and operation remain essentially as established, and especially with regard to the integrated approach to the variety of sub-disciplines contained within an architecture programme (Cowdroy and Maitland, 1994). While that programme represented the conversion of an existing traditional course to PBL, the faculty has subsequently developed a new construction management degree course on the same principles, and offered in both internal and distance-learning modes (Ostwald *et al*, 1993). The commitment of the faculty to PBL has been reinforced by the results of the course experience questionnaire run by the Graduate Careers Council of Australia, which recorded both 1992 and 1993 cohorts of Newcastle students as having the highest levels of overall satisfaction with their course of all architecture students in Australia.

References

Cowdroy, R M and Maitland, B S (1994) Integration, assessment and problem based learning. In S E Chen, R M Cowdroy, A J Kingsland and M J Ostwald (eds) *Reflections on Problem Based Learning*. Sydney: Australian Problem-Based Learning Network, 45–56.

Donaldson, R J (1989) A good start in architecture: problem based learning applied to the first year course in architecture. In B Wallis (ed) *Problem Based Learning: The Newcastle Workshop*. Proceedings of the Ten-Year Anniversary conference, Faculty of Medicine, University of Newcastle, 41–53.

Ostwald, M J, Chen, S E, Varnam, B and McGeorge, W D (1993) The application of problem-based learning to distance education. In B Scriven, R Lundin and Y Ryan, Y (eds) *Distance Education for the Twenty-First Century*. Brisbane: ICDE and QUT Press, 63–67.

Chapter 22

Problem-based Learning in an Integrated Nursing Curriculum

Debra Creedy and Christine Alavi

The health care environment in both developed and developing countries is changing at an unprecedented rate. To be prepared adequately to respond to these demands in healthcare, nurses must exhibit flexibility, independence, critical thinking, leadership and collaboration. Within an integrated service model, nurses need to make optimal use of new technologies while bearing in mind ethical considerations and financial constraints. Meanwhile, there is a growing emphasis on health promotion.

Preventive health care strategies target a diverse patient population and require well-developed communication skills that empower individuals and groups to optimize their health (Meservey, 1995; Oneha *et al*, in press). Furthermore, nurses are required to work efficiently and effectively in teams within the health sector and between the health sector and other socio-economic sectors that influence health. It is nurses who will lead and supervise the health care team, with medical professionals increasingly committed to more specialized and complicated demands (Fagin, 1992).

In meeting these health care demands nurses are now required to possess quite different orientations and competencies. Changes in nurse education are inseparable from the changes in nursing practice. The Australian *National Review of Nurse Education in the Higher Education Sector* (1994) recommends that in the design and delivery of courses, university schools of nursing need to take into account the health care needs of the community, the goals and targets of health

218

services, the requirements of the employers of nurses, and the need for responsive and flexible graduates.

In response to healthcare demands there have been widespread curricular changes favouring PBL in nurse education. At an international conference in 1996 hosted by the School of Nursing at McMaster University in Canada, a panel of eight speakers from countries as diverse as Italy, Thailand and Chile outlined their approaches to PBL within the nursing curriculum, detailing the effectiveness of learning in this way.

In Australia, where nursing has embraced PBL to prepare students for practice, issues such as support, the range of student abilities and reductions in funding have to be confronted. Some schools of nursing which have implemented PBL have done so without necessarily having full institutional support. There is a lack of understanding about PBL and a perception that PBL teaching approaches are more costly. PBL is not necessarily more expensive than traditional courses, but rather nursing has particular requirements, such as clinical practice and nursing laboratory work, which are very expensive. Unlike medical schools, schools of nursing must pay for the clinical facilitation of students within health care agencies.

Recently there has been a general increase in the academic standard of students entering nursing. Although some schools of nursing recruit students in the top 30–35 per cent of the school-leaver population, a wide variety of people who are attracted to nursing. Consequently, teaching-learning strategies within nurse education need to address a wider range of learner abilities, ages, background and motivation for entry than other disciplines such as medicine, law and engineering. PBL can facilitate this diversity because it allows students to progress at their own pace and to read and research as widely as desired.

Reduction in funding to Australian universities means, however, that group sizes in PBL tutorials have increased considerably. It has been important to develop strategies for students to work cooperatively in these large groups to maximize their learning. Such strategies include sub-groups addressing various learning issues and feeding these back to the larger group; peer review and teaching; and increased flexibility of learning materials. What is important in this climate is to ensure that beginning students thoroughly understand PBL and are facilitated in their early learning very skilfully – an issue described more fully in Chapter 13. If this happens, then by the time they reach the third year of the programme students can be almost entirely self-directed in their learning, and facilitator-student contact, primarily initiated by students, is considerably reduced.

PBL and professional practice

PBL prepares students very well for professional work because the processes of learning mirror those required in practice. For example, PBL is a well-established and effective method in the teaching of clinical reasoning. A specific clinical situation becomes the stimulus for identifying what is necessary in order to understand and manage the situation, at a level appropriate for the student at the time. This differs from 'problem solving' which focuses on bringing previously learned information to bear on finding the correct answer to the problem (Kaufman, 1985). Students cope well with learning packages based on clinical situations from the earliest weeks of their course where they face the reality of patients and the complexities of nursing care. Furthermore, students undertake their on-campus learning in groups which also mirrors the situation in the real world where nurses work as members of the health care team.

Not only do the teaching-learning processes mirror the real world of nursing but the unique setting and assessment processes of the nursing laboratory also enhance the students' preparation. The laboratory is a place where nursing, behavioural and scientific concepts and skills can be introduced, practised and reinforced within an environment which is safe and supportive. Elements from problem-based tutorials (PBT) are used to enhance and broaden students' learning: such elements include peer learning and review, self and peer assessment as well as facilitator support.

A typical two to three hour nursing laboratory session is directly linked to concepts addressed in the PBT. Learning materials are from actual case notes which are anonymized and then validated by the clinician who has worked with the client whose situation is being studied. The range of learning packages reflects the clinical situations that students are likely to encounter when they move off-campus. The laboratory uses aspects of the learning package to allow students to develop their nursing practice in context rather than as a set of unrelated skills.

In the first year of the programme one package introduces students to a man who has HIV and whose partner is in the process of dying. The two laboratory sessions associated with this session address such issues as universal precautions, responses to grief and death, confidentiality and documentation. Specifically, students are given a laboratory sheet which they work through in small groups before coming to the laboratory. In order to prepare for the session, one sheet might ask them to think and talk with their colleagues about their responses to death and grief as it has affected them. They may be required to think about what it will be like to work with those who are dying and their relatives. In the laboratory, small groups of eight students are taken through relaxation strategies and a guided imagery where they are exposed to a death. There is time for debriefing and discussion about stress management strategies and the importance of using colleagues to acknowledge and share feelings, and to gather support.

A second laboratory sheet asks students to review their knowledge of universal precautions, and to familiarize themselves with gloves, goggles and the safe disposal of contaminated materials within the context of a client situation. On arrival at the laboratory students are given a number of brief scenarios that relate to the client. Examples of scenarios might include: the client is eating a piece of fruit and cuts himself with a knife; a person who states they are a friend telephones and asks for information about the client; the client dies. Such scenarios might be played out by means of role play and are facilitated by an expert clinician. These laboratory sessions are supported by a clinical workbook which students are able to work through in a self-directed way, and which provides prompts for their work.

Such laboratory work needs careful preparation and expert facilitation, but it deals with the core issues of nursing. The extent to which students are able to develop confidence in a safe setting will determine their ability to continue to deepen and extend their learning in the clinical setting off-campus (Cattoni, 1995). This on-and-off campus dialectic ensures that students see the relevance of their on-campus learning to their off-campus work and that, in turn, their off-campus work can be used to enrich their learning when they return to the university.

Assessment

There are key nursing skills that require assessment prior to off-campus work. Such assessment is important in order for students to feel confident when they move into clinical agencies, but it is also essential to reassure clinicians and accrediting bodies that students have an appropriate understanding underpinning their nursing skills. The assessment of vital signs, medication administration, aseptic technique, fluid management and implementing universal precautions are core nursing activities from which many other skills are derived (Cattoni, 1995). Competency in any one of these areas incorporates important elements of theoretical knowledge, communication and reflection. In the case of universal precautions, for example, it is important to assess not only correct technique in the disposal of bodily fluids, but also the students' understanding of the reasons for taking universal precautions, their awareness of the possible effects of their actions on the patient, and knowledge to generalize these principles across various practice settings and situations.

Assessment in the laboratory may take many forms and may be undertaken by individual students or by small groups. An assessment item in the third year of the programme requires students to role play an actual situation with a client where they have functioned as an advocate. Another assessment in the second year requires students to videotape themselves administering a medication to a client, and then assess their performance.

Changes in the nursing profession are calling for increased self-regulation, accountability, and evidence-based reporting. Peer review processes within the laboratory allow students to engage in practice and assess and judge performance of peers against pre-determined criteria (McAllister and Osborne, 1997). Peer review assessment processes increase personal accountability and have demonstrated improved quality of care and clinical performance.

Such assessment must always support PBL principles. It is self-defeating to tell students that we value critical reasoning and self-direction and then offer a multiple-choice closed-book examination. Assessment must be contextualized and relevant. Since assessment is a powerful driving force for students it is not only important *what* assessment items are chosen, but how the teacher responds to the students' work. Feedback where the teacher enters into a dialogue with students is important so that, in a sense, all assessment is formative, and contributes positively to the students' learning experiences.

Evaluation

Evaluation is central to PBL. As Margetson (1995: 161) outlines: 'evaluation is not a once in a while add-on activity extraneous to a course', but is an important and unifying activity which allows us to see that we are doing what we say we are doing. It is also important that students feel able to contribute to their learning by identifying strategies and activities which they found helpful. Evaluation has a part in all aspects of a PBL course – from the usefulness of a particular learning package or facilitation strategy through to the measurement of student learning outcomes and to inform curriculum changes. Although it is useful, and in nursing mandatory, to have external course evaluation, evaluation as part of the day-to-day running of a PBL course contributes to staff development and orientation, and allows for sharing of experiences and the continual evolution of a vital programme.

As we wrote at the beginning of this chapter, nursing and health care services are changing rapidly. PBL seems to us to be the best way of facilitating student responses to those changes. This makes the use of up-to-date client situations an essential part of student nurses' learning. This learning needs to be supported by relevant and responsive assessment, and evaluated as part of the learning process for both students and teachers.

References

Cattoni, J (1995) Integrating knowledge in the laboratory. In C Alavi (ed) *Problem-Based Learning in a Health Science Curriculum*. London: Routledge, 86–103.

Fagin, C (1992) Collaboration between nurses and physicians: no longer a choice, *Academic Medicine*, 67, 5, 295–303.

Kaufman, A (1985) *Implementing a Problem-Based Medical Education: Lessons from Successful Innovations*. New York: Springer.

McAllister, M and Osborne, Y (1997) Peer review: a strategy to enhance cooperative student learning, *Nurse Educator*, 22, 1, 40–44.

Margetson, D (1995) The role of evaluation. In C Alavi (ed) *Problem-Based Learning in a Health Science Curriculum*. London: Routledge, 141–161.

Meservey, P (1995) Fostering collaboration in a boundaryless organization, *Nursing & Health Care: Perspectives on community*, 16, 4, 234–236.

National Review of Nurse Education in the Higher Education Sector (1994) Canberra: Department of Education, Employment and Training.

Oneha, M, Magnussen, L and Feletti, G (in press) Ensuring quality nursing education in community based settings, *Nurse Educator*.

Chapter 23

Applying Problem-based Learning to Practical Legal Training

Keith Winsor

The College of Law is the main body from which students of graduate status gain a practical institutional qualification as a preliminary to their entering the legal profession in the state of New South Wales. Such qualification requires satisfactory completion of two stages, the first being a practical course offered by the College. The second stage consists of law-related office employment and a series of continuing education activities totalling 60 hours.

The first-stage course at the College is full-time and consists of three phases spread equally over a period of 15 weeks. Phases one and two are designed to develop in students a mastery of tasks and procedures which will develop skills in the methods, systems and strategies of legal practices. It is done using exemplar files. These are sets of documents equivalent to the files of materials which practitioners would typically encounter in law firms. The third phase gives them opportunities to apply those methods, systems and skills in a PBL environment.

In the early phases, the course relies heavily on experiential, transaction-based activities which include problem-solving routines. These are more in the nature of exercises than true PBL. However, PBL techniques are employed in the final or third phase. The other phases may be seen as 'pre-instruction' in vital areas of practice which will lead to the final phase focusing on skills.

The first phase consists of two streams: a short introduction to legal practice including accounting and professional responsibility followed by basic instruction in areas of property or litigation in the alternative. Students change from one stream to the other during the passage of the first phase. The method of instruction is lecture and discussion followed by graded exercises for groups of students, ideally no more than 15 in number.

The second phase follows immediately but now to groups of 30 on a more practice-oriented series of procedures. These include the preparation and completion of files based on given facts and lawyers' bookkeeping and accounting. Assessment of the basic knowledge acquired in this phase is by traditional examinations which take place near the end of the phase. Professional responsibility has already received basic instruction and assessment in the first phase and subsequent contact in the second phase is by way of reinforcement only.

Problem-based learning components

The first two phases may be seen as making students self-sufficient enough to undertake the third phase, which consists not only of PBL but a refinement of skills-based activities already encountered. These include interviewing and advising, advocacy and drafting. PBL is in the major areas of litigation, property and business law. Modules consisting of preliminary lecture and 'base files' are given in areas derived from these subjects. Students are required to work on three files in the subject business law and two in either litigation or property.

The PBL components are introduced by three mornings of lectures on the three major areas of practice. Lectures are given by experts to the whole student body and before each lecture, 'base files' are distributed to students, who become aware of the material relevant to the lectures. They also receive a manual of instructions ('Student set') detailing what the module is about, what materials they will need to be familiar with, and what they will need to do to complete this module. The files are typically realistic of what might be found in practice. Students are then rostered in groups of five to eight in number. They work collectively in teams engaged in self-instruction and research but they are also required to individually comprehend the problems and their ramifications.

The third-phase groups work under the guidance of an instructor of the College whose role is now that of mentor or facilitator. During the course of student investigation, the mentors are available for consultation and advice on methods of investigation as distinct from having a 'teaching' role. The mentor's role is like that of a senior partner in a legal firm who, although not actually handling the details of the workings of the file, needs to be kept up to date on the matter and advised by his 'team' about clients' options and proposed further actions.

In their handling of the PBL files the students are asked to investigate, demonstrate an understanding of how to deal with the problem, to report and finally recommend future action. These activities are influenced by or are dependent upon the following factors:

- nature of the client
- nature of the problem
- possible solutions
- cost impact on the client
- external competencies
- quality of the advice and recommendations given
- restraints imposed by considerations of professional responsibility.

The problem

A typical 'base file' might contain, for example, a memorandum from a supervising partner (to the student) asking for a review of the file and for an opinion or judgement in order to carry the matter forward. The file will typically contain a statement or statements of potential witnesses. Court documents already 'filed' in court and written statements from specialists or experts if such information is relevant are supplied. The following is an example of a 'base file'.

The Oronsay File

Dr Oronsay is being sued for professional negligence and the (student's) firm is acting for her in her defence. At this stage, the client has been interviewed and a full statement obtained which reveals that she has received a Supreme Court Statement of Claim (the initiating document claiming damages), and a Notice of Motion asking the court to order that the name of the plaintiff (the 'opposition') be suppressed from publication. This document is supported by an affidavit sworn by the plaintiff setting out her reasons for seeking the suppression order (namely that her occupation would be prejudiced if her name were made public in the proceedings).

The claim is for negligence in that the doctor treated the plaintiff for superficial injuries arising from a bus accident but failed to diagnose and treat a carcinoma of the right breast of the patient.

The patient, in addition to the legal proceedings mentioned, has complained to the Medical Board in respect of the failure to diagnose the carcinoma to which the doctor has replied in writing to the Board denying the allegations of professional negligence. She has given her solicitors' firm a lengthy statement arising from an interview and all of the relevant documents are present in the file.

Explanation

Nature of the client:	(the student must be aware of material and relevant facts personal to the client and to the particular problem; different clients have different needs and expectations)
Problem:	(apart from the client being sued and the possibility of damages, there are other issues relating to ultimate cost, reputation of client including by peer group and the very real threat to continuation in practice)
Outcomes:	(although seen as part of the problem, possible outcomes will reveal different strategies for both client and lawyer)
External competence:	(any outside experts needed? For example: on medical issues)
Cost:	(ultimate cost to client will involve more than lawyers' costs! For example: investigation and enquiry fees, expert witnesses' fees and so on. How much does the client reasonably wish to spend?)
Quality:	(best strategies all round, for example, to serve the client, the firm, social requirements, personal needs?)
Professional responsibility:	(by what ethical rules is the lawyer bound in constructing possible courses of action?)

(Note: the areas in brackets sometimes overlap, depending on the particular nature of the problem.)

Students as a group must consider the case and be ready to report individually on any aspect to the review panel, which consists of two experienced practitioners and an instructor from the College.

Assessment

Assessment is by *viva voce* examination by the review panel which randomly chooses two of the five 'base files', each from a different major subject worked on by the particular group of students. It is founded on student understanding of issues arising from the files and satisfactory proposals for action based on the same seven areas above used by students in handling the files ('Nature of the client; Nature of the problem; Possible solutions; Cost impact; External competencies; Quality of advice and Professional responsibility restraints'). Each one of these areas is given equal weighting in the assessment procedure and all are explored by the review panel with the student at the *viva voce* examination.

It is intended that the very nature of the assessment procedure will influence the student in his or her approach to the problem-solving routine to be undertaken. Overtly, throughout the course, the student will be guided along certain paths which are familiar to lawyers concerned in the substantive study of law, but beyond that, the PBL episodes in the course foster an heuristic approach useful for all sorts of legal problem solving. One strength of this approach, for example, is recognition of the need to consult with experts in a particular field where students' experience and knowledge in practice would be lacking. The College is providing a model to students in how to be self-reliant in solving problems in practice by using individual case management studies (the 'base files') as the teaching/learning medium.

Rationale for the course

When the new course was framed, it was perceived that there may be difficulties in assessments and course evaluations. These might arise, for example, from the 'Hawthorne effect', that is that students and even instructors as mentors would be conscious of scrutiny in a new and innovative course and either over- or under-react to such scrutiny. From the students' point of view, it is now clear that one of their main concerns is apprehension about the nature of the *viva voce* examination. Strangely, many students expect to be assessed on their knowledge of the law, whereas the course is concerned with the law *in practice*.

This anxiety is partly alleviated by reassurance from their mentors and by an explanatory video. The video shows them exactly what is expected during the final phase and how the assessment with visiting experts will work. The 'Student sets' also give as much information in this area as possible without encroaching on the premise of PBL. Clearly there is a need for proper debriefings with the students as part of their learning experience. In this case, once students realize that the *viva* is in fact a debriefing of their learning and understanding, many inhibitions disappear. This has been confirmed by discussions between researchers and ex-students (Liverani, 1996).

In the College environment where planning and evaluation are the norm, PBL has presented itself as a positive vehicle for the particular type of training established in the curriculum. Recent College trials of this teaching/learning tool confirm it as an ideal medium for the experiential instruction long accepted by the College as being most valuable in its particular teaching environment. It has been perceived that the particular strengths of PBL are associated not only with better outcomes but with increased student motivation compared to traditional methods.

Components of PBL have existed at the College for some time. The College commenced operation in 1974 using an experiential but otherwise traditional form of teaching. Based on different needs in the profession and the major funding body, the Law Society of New South Wales, a new curriculum was established in 1995. In framing the new problem-based curriculum it was important to consider how closely it might follow already accepted course frameworks. For example, the traditional methods, both previously used and those now employed in the three College phases, are based on explicit educational objectives. It is recognized that some educationists have moved away altogether from the use of objectives, but for College purposes, both in traditional methods and for PBL, the way shown by use of objectives seems more useful. It is clear and presents a logical and viable approach connecting present methods to students' previous learning approaches in their undergraduate training. The College has retained in revised and upgraded form the teaching methods and materials which it considers to have been effective in the past and uses them in conjunction with or as an introduction to the PBL components.

Planning the course also requires consideration of whether the PBL components should be restricted to one subject only or whether it should be of a more diverse nature. The latter course has been adopted on the premise of relevance to the particular nature of the desired outcomes. It was decided that in order to approach reality more closely, the problems for the PBL phase should consist of a number of elements which then rightfully could be adjudicated upon as part of the students' assessments. However, some difficulties arose because the particular discipline of legal practice required that students be given an introduction to the PBL components of the course.

These difficulties can be overcome by reference to printed materials such as practice manuals, to video and audio tapes and even by computer-assisted instruction. Such 'pre-instruction' however, tends to render evaluation of the PBL components (where the maxim is often 'Problem first!') more vulnerable. While it is recognized that in problem-based courses instructional material is often associated with the problem-solving exercise, the question remains how much can appropriately be given, and at which stages, without impairing student initiatives and undermining the benefits of PBL? Obviously, some measures of compromise and balance must be obtained and to some extent this can only come about through trial and error for the particular course. Hopefully, the instruction given in the first two phases of the College course gives this balance.

In order to achieve (a) satisfactory assessment of student outcomes and (b) efficient evaluation of courses, the problem-based segment has had to sit comfortably within the curriculum. Problems to be considered in using both traditional methods of teaching and PBL are that students will have to move from completing supervised and guided tasks to self-regulated and self-disciplinary problem solving while instructors must shift from lecturer or teacher to mentor or facilitator.

However, the underlying structure is based on students' skills and competency. With respect to legal education, Schön (1987) argues for a step further than having students 'think like a lawyer', by which he means making legal arguments, clarifying legal issues by adversarial process and making the choice of the most plausible legal precedents. He claims that for several years now, some of the most eminent law schools have argued the need to develop competencies that go beyond thinking like a lawyer, for example, '*skills* (emphasis added) in trial work, client relations, negotiation, advocacy, and legal ethics' (p.14). He argues that the development of such skills amounts to a degree of competency which may be seen as 'professional artistry' and that 'the artistry of painters, sculptors, musicians, dancers and designers bears a strong resemblance to the artistry of extraordinary lawyers'. He concludes: 'It is no accident that professionals often refer to an "art" of teaching or management and use the term *artist* to refer to practitioners unusually adept at handling situations of uncertainty, uniqueness and conflict' (p.16). The College is seeking Schön's ideal of competencies through its PBL approach by having students regard problems in an holistic manner. They must be prepared to approach the problem from a variety of angles rather than trying to 'fit' the problem into a narrow box or pigeon-hole.

Evaluation

Students have indicated the worth of the problem-based approach and members of review panels have signified their approval (Liverani, 1996). Furthermore, from the initial pilot course in 1995 and its successor later in the same year has come an initial study of a qualitative nature (Roper, 1996), with an in-house follow up to that study.

Preliminary results indicate the need to highlight the role(s) of instructors and provide clear guidelines for these roles available both to instructors and students. Student and instructor workloads, it seems, must be more evenly spread in the early phases at least. The need for materials, both printed and electronic, to be shorter, non-repetitious and of the highest quality is of paramount importance for maintaining enthusiasm and motivation. Once the materials are available and after some preliminary instruction, students must be able to understand the nature of the problem and proceed to solutions without further prompting. Over-ambitious pursuit of the objectives can lead to student and instructor frustration resulting in superficial learning. Constant and adequate feedback on ongoing performance by students, particularly when sought or initiated by them, seems to be required to enable success of the programme. On a constructive note, the study indicates that the 'base-file' system employed in the problem-based phase received the highest positive response from students answering a questionnaire about all the learning methods used.

Conclusions

The College is confident from its research and the evaluative responses to date that it has embarked on a valid plan of action with

PBL. So far, apart from needs highlighted by early evaluation, the College has learnt that once they are initiated into PBL, students enjoy the experience and tend to develop not only their legal but also interpersonal skills. This can be considered a bonus which can become vital in the development of skills generally.

The present course will provide further study material for researchers and on present indications the College anticipates that results will confirm what we suspected from earlier short forays into PBL: that it is a good teaching/learning vehicle in this particular field of education.

References

Liverani, M R (1996) 'Very positive results' ... says College of Law on its Panel of Review process, *Law Society Journal*, 34, 7, August, 50–52.

Roper, C (1996) *An Evaluative Review of the Professional Program at the College of Law – Course 95/3*. Sydney: Centre for Legal Education.

Schön, D A (1987) *Educating the Reflective Practitioner*. San Francisco, CA: Jossey Bass.

Chapter 24

Industrial Enhancement Through Problem-based Learning

**John R Usher, David G Simmonds, Iain Mackenzie,
Ken Brown** and **Shirley E Earl**

A specific component of the BSc (Hons) Mathematics and Computing Degree at The Robert Gordon University (RGU) utilizes PBL to educate and train mathematical scientists for careers as 'problem solvers' in industry and commerce. Particular attention is given to group problem solving. The course focuses on the development of interpersonal, modelling, oral and written presentation skills. Since the whole course is designed to relate realistically to post-qualification professional practice, the course team has involved personnel from industry in the production of appropriate material, in student monitoring and student assessment.

Background

In October 1974 The Robert Gordon Institute of Technology (as RGU was then known) started to operate a BSc degree in mathematical sciences. In 1984 a problem-based course, entitled 'Mathematical models and methods', was introduced into the degree programme. The initial development of this course is described in Usher and Earl (1987). Subsequently in October 1988 we introduced an industrial group project as a focal point in the final honours year. In 1996 the title of the degree became 'Mathematics and computing'. All these developments and a comparison with a similar course at the University of Hertfordshire are described in Crouch *et al* (1996).

Right from the conception of the mathematical models and methods course, personnel from industry and commerce have been involved in aspects of the problem-based exercises (which on the course are referred to as 'group modelling exercises'). Latterly, there has been full involvement by industry and commerce in *all* aspects of the operation of the industrial group project, right through from the preparation of material, briefing of students, monitoring student progress, to the final assessment. Aspects of this are discussed by Earl and Hendry (1995).

Development of skills

An effective consultant mathematical scientist must possess technical knowledge in the mathematical sciences and an ability to apply this knowledge to problem solving in an industrial or commercial environment. Nowadays, a consultant mathematical scientist must be able to operate in a group situation where group dynamics and communication skills are of paramount importance.

A good way of providing an undergraduate training for such a person is via a mathematical modelling course whereby students have to work in groups to find practical solutions to problems arising in industry or commerce. Because of the nature of the work that students are likely to undertake on graduation, it is essential that students are placed in the consultant–client situation and are required to give appropriate oral presentations and written reports.

RGU staff and personnel from industry and commerce have combined their skills to devise a curriculum (see Figure 24.1) that facilitates the students' transition from instructor-sponsored modelling and discussion at the beginning of the course to self/peer-sponsored perception of problems and the tender of solutions in language appropriate to the industrial or commercial clients in the latter part of the course.

Early in the second year students are given lectures in the philosophy and methodology of modelling. Subsequently, in the first half of both the second and third years, a lecture course is given where the principles of modelling are presented and demonstrated through the use of appropriate case study material, in many cases the data from industry and commerce being modified in order to achieve particular learning outcomes.

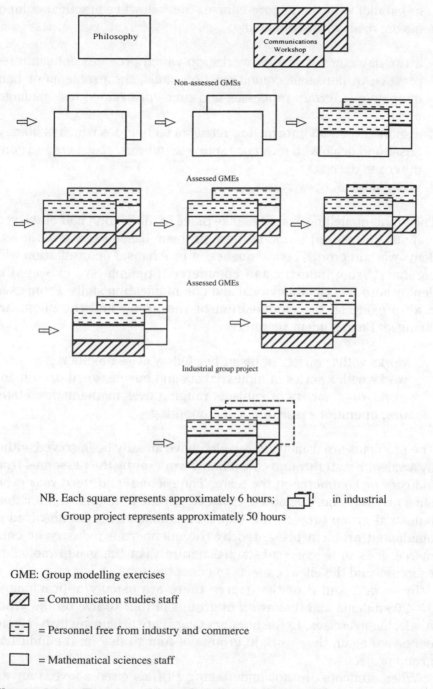

Figure 24.1 *Team-teaching of mathematical models and methods and industrial group project*

In parallel with the lecture course, the following practical components are dealt with sequentially:

1. a two-day communication workshop which provides concentrated practice in pertinent communication skills, the problems of handling people, group processes and time-constrained task management;
2. a short course on information retrieval techniques which is library-based and deals with reference sources, indexes, abstracts and computerized access;
3. group modelling exercises.

The group modelling exercises take place in the second half of the second and in the third years. In these problem-based exercises, the students work in groups on a sequence of problems, in consultation with personnel from industry and commerce. Students are expected to deploy both their mathematical and communication skills. From exercise to exercise the composition of the group and the client are changed. Each student therefore:

- works with a variety of his or her fellow class members,
- works with a series of industrialists and businessmen or women,
- works on a variety of subjects ranging over mathematics, statistics, operations research and computing.

The problems are usually ones which have already been solved, either by academic staff through consultancy work, or by the personnel from industry or commerce in the team. The second- and third-year problems may have been adapted. However, in the honours year, for their industrial group project, the sequence culminates in an unsolved or unadapted problem presented by the client from industry or commerce. It is of a more substantial nature than the group modelling exercises and the client expects to enact the solution.

In years 2 and 3 of the degree there are usually approximately 15–20 students and they work in groups of four to five on the group modelling exercises. In the honours year there are normally 8–12 students and again they work in groups of four to five on the industrial group project.

When students are not undertaking PBL as cited above, they are involved in lectures, tutorials and computing laboratory sessions learning about various areas in the mathematical sciences, eg, calculus, algebra, statistics, computational methods and aspects of operational research, computing, business and management systems.

A typical problem sequence

The sequence of typical problems that follows is taken from four consecutive stages in the mathematics and computing course (see Figure 24.1). It shows the development of assessments from purely formative in the first case to both formative and summative in the others. It also illustrates how industrial involvement develops through the course.

1. Road Survey Problems

Delivery

The non-assessed group modelling exercises are for the most part very short, some of them being designed to last for only an hour or two. In the early days of the course, they were artificial exercises designed by staff to provide practice with simple 'closed' problems. The first two problems are still of this nature, but the introductory session now finishes with a two-week exercise carried out in collaboration with the Roads Department of Grampian Regional Council. Groups are provided with problems associated with the collection of road-survey data, information on the traffic flows in a city centre or through a rural town requiring a by-pass. Students have to recommend methods for obtaining the data, each problem concerning a survey that either has been done or is about to be done by the Council. The students are given a talk by an engineer from the Roads Department before they start the exercises and the same engineer listens to their presentations and is involved in the debriefing.

Assessment

Purely informative. Constructive criticism is given on how groups organize group activity and make oral presentations. Video equipment is used to reinforce debriefing sessions.

Development

We have used the above approach for a number of years and it has proved very successful. The involvement of a 'real' engineer providing 'real' commentary and seeing learning as fun has achieved much higher levels of motivation and presentation in the groups.

2. Quality Control Problems

Delivery

One of the later sets of assessed group problems in the second year of the course is devoted to statistical problems. These were, in the past, exercises devised by staff usually based on problems encountered in consultancy work for industry or commerce. In recent years more direct industrial involvement has been sought and successfully achieved. For example, Wiggins Teape, a local paper-making company, provides problems associated with the quality control of paper manufacture and problems of maintaining acceptable consistency in paper weight, thickness and colour. Engineers act as clients. They supply production data for analysis. They are also involved in assessing student presentations and reports. Before the start of the exercise the whole class is taken on a visit to the company to observe the manufacturing process and absorb necessary technical background to the problems.

Assessment

Each group produces a written report on its findings and also makes an oral presentation. Both are assessed by academic staff and by representatives of the company involved. This collaboration has confirmed the standards set by the course and has helped to motivate the students to achieve these standards. Group activity is assessed by academic staff, with company representatives drawing analogies with their own work experience in the sphere. Debriefing sessions, which include both academic staff and the industrial client, are used to encourage students to improve their performance in later exercises. Video equipment is used to reinforce these sessions.

Development

Again, the direct involvement of industry works well and both students and staff are stimulated by the contact. Similar activities are planned for future years, but academic staff have to balance consultancy aspects of their own jobs with the demands made.

3. A Management game

Delivery

Initially an industrial consultant from Sigma (Scotland) Ltd gives a talk on the purposes of the game, which are, first, to make managers aware of the need for communication, and second, to impart the need for good stock control policies.

Groups of students are provided with the instructions for a management game, the 'Beer Game', as described below, and take part in playing the game with a lecturer or industrial adviser acting as the 'Game Controller'. It should be apparent that 'catastrophic' fluctuations in the supply and demand for beer occur during the game, and that these fluctuations are mainly caused by lack of communication between the participants.

The industrial adviser then explains that he is not satisfied that the game meets his requirements, and requests suggestions from the students for improvements of the existing game, or a completely new game, that will meet his requirements better.

The student groups are encouraged to re-play the 'Beer Game' several times, with changes to the rules, such as varying the lags between orders placed and received. Mathematical models for the movement of 'Beer', using difference equations, may be created and subsequently investigated using spreadsheets.

Additional features may be added to make the game 'more realistic', such as failure of one of the participants to fulfil their role. The students are given free rein to use their own creativity in revising the game.

Instructions and rules for the 'Beer Game'
Beer is produced by a brewery, which is then sold to a wholesale company, which stores the beer in a warehouse until the retailers request it, from where it is sold to the customer. The game is run on a weekly basis.

Rules:
1. The stock levels and forecasting of brewer, wholesaler and retailer are kept confidential.
2. The 'Game controller' acts as the customer and as the 'Beer transporter'.
3. When a retailer places an order, it arrives four weeks later.
4. When the wholesaler places an order, it arrives four weeks later.
5. When the brewer decides to change production of beer, there is a two-week delay.

The initial volume of beer production is ten barrels/week, and the initial stock level at the warehouse is ten barrels, and at each of two retailers five barrels.

Assessment

At the end of the exercise the student groups make an oral presentation of their results to the industrial adviser. Their proposed revisions to the 'Beer Game' should be justified by their own experience of playing the game, backed up by statistics, or mathematical models. The industrial adviser responds with his comments on the proposed revisions. Subsequently the student groups provide a written report on their final versions of the 'Beer Game'.

Development

Similar activities are planned for future years, one game being involved during each session. The overall thrust of serious problem solving remains core.

4. Database Problems

Delivery

In the honours year of the mathematics and computing degree, students spend approximately 50 scheduled hours on their industrial group project, spread over 11 weeks. In groups of four or five they tackle a problem sponsored by local industry. They must organize weekly meetings, properly chaired and minuted, and make interim and final reports and oral presentations. A member of the academic staff acts as a supervisor available to each group, and the client is from industry and plays a dominant part in the exercise. The client provides an initial briefing sheet and a guided tour around their company premises as necessary. The client attends some of the meetings and takes part in the assessment of written and oral reports.

The following group database problem projects have been run in recent years:

Session	Industrial group project	Industrial sponsor
1988/89	Contractors Database using Ingres	BP
1989/90	PC-based Contracts Database	Marathon
1990/91	A Register of Database Systems	Marathon
1991/92	Information Flow from Offshore	BP
1992/93	Oil Extraction Reports using Excel	BP
1993/94	Unifying Payroll Systems	Rockwater
1994/95	Safety Reports Database	Rockwater
1995/96	Critical Factors in Towing Pipelines	Brown and Root

Assessment

Each group produces two written reports with associated oral presentations. The first is a progress report, made four or five weeks after the initial meeting with the client. In this session the groups present their initial functional design for the required software. The second is the final report via which groups present their final design and implementation of the software. Each individual in a group presents a written report at this stage. All reports are assessed by both academic staff and industrial sponsors. Group activity is assessed by academic staff. Debriefing sessions function as in case 2 above. Pro formas are used to help standardize industrial and academic marking, the final mark being achieved by negotiation. Both industrialists and academics have found the system satisfactory and both have been pleasantly surprised to see how little their standards diverge.

Development

It has been found convenient to use each industrial sponsor for two years. This reduces the academic time spent in researching appropriate industrial-based group projects and does not exhaust the goodwill of those partner companies willing to give the students their time and resources.

During the first four years, the timescale for the industrial project was set at 16 weeks and its operation was reviewed in Usher *et al* (1992). However, other academic subjects were being squeezed timewise, so a condensed schedule of 11 weeks was agreed. This has resulted in increased emphasis on analysis and design rather than on full implementation. No educational objective has been lost.

Conclusion

Internationally, PBL has become a natural feature of many degree courses in mathematical sciences, computing, applied science and engineering (see Crouch *et al*, 1996). Students are being exposed to many more 'raw' problems associated with the main-stream subjects of their degree programmes. This reflects industrial and commercial demands for 'problem solvers', and increasingly close employer-education partnership.

At RGU, the major benefit of industrial and commercial enhancement of the problem-based mathematical models and methods course has been increased student motivation. The students are able to relate their undergraduate studies directly to post-qualification professional practice. They see how important group presentation and technical skills are. One of the 'problems' resulting from the industrial and commercial involvement is that some students have been so highly motivated in trying to produce a polished product for their industrial client that excessive time spent on their industrial group project has adversely affected other studies. By careful student counselling the course team has tried to minimize this effect. In the view of the course team, there is no doubt whatsoever that the benefits of industrial enhancement on the problem-based mathematical models and methods course far outweigh any disadvantages. Professional bodies respond positively to the approach.

Acknowledgement

The authors wish to thank all members of the teaching team who have helped to develop and to successfully operate the mathematical models and methods course and the industrial group project at RGU, together with the industrialists who have willingly provided their time and effort. Without all this help, this chapter would not have been written.

References

Earl, S E and Hendry, I (1995) Peer assessment of group problem-solving and group writing. In G Gibbs (ed) *Assessing Student Centred Courses*. Oxford Centre for Staff Development, Oxford.

Crouch, R, Davies, A, Usher, J R, Mackenzie, I and Forrest, E (1996) Working in groups: personal and professional skills. In C Haines and S Dunthrone (eds) *Mathematics Learning and Assessment Pack, Sharing Innovative Practices*, Section 1C in Book One. London: Edward Arnold.

Usher, J R and Earl, S E (1987) Group modelling and communication. In J S Berry *et al* (eds) *Mathematics Modelling Courses*. Chichester: Ellis Horwood.

Usher, J R, Brown, K and Masterton, S (1992) Industrial enhancement of problem-based learning, *First Scottish Enterprise Conference in Higher Education*.

Chapter 25

Experiences With Problem-based Learning in Business and Management

Alan Gilbert and **Stephen F Foster**

This chapter discusses issues that arise when planning and implementing PBL in business, management and economics studies in higher education. Experiences in a ten-year-old Dutch university economics and business administration faculty, originally founded on the basis of PBL, are described and comment is made on recent planning and testing of new problem-based modules within existing traditional programmes in England. In both settings dissatisfaction with traditional instructional forms and contextual pressures suggested trying new alternatives.

The University of Maastricht approach to PBL has been discussed elsewhere in some detail (eg, Foster, 1990; Gijselaers, 1995; Schmidt, 1983). Thus we give only a brief sketch here. In Maastricht groups of ten to 12 students meet regularly over a series of intensive eight-week blocks. They apply a structured seven-step approach to study problems (see Figure 25.1) embedded in written situations presented in a 'block book' which also contain lists of library references and other study aids.

Students work in groups that change membership between blocks. They must identify one or more problems within the text, decide what they need to learn and form a plan for acquiring the necessary information to solve the problem(s). Progress therefore is determined by decisions taken within each group. Problems identified and addressed by students may be either practical or theoretical in nature but ideally revolve around comprehension issues, ie, explanations of phenomena,

A. Context: Groups of 8–12 participants receive a (usually written) statement describing a situation or condition. The group selects a discussion leader, sometimes a recorder, and applies the 'seven steps' to find, analyse and solve the problem(s). The steps are:

1. discuss and agree on working definitions of unclear words and concepts.
2. identify one or more problems in the statement, agree on which phenomena require explanation or discovery of underlying causes.
3. analyse problems into components, implications, possible explanations or solutions, and develop working hypotheses. This is like a 'brainstorming' phase with evaluation suspended while explanations or solutions are written on a flipchart or chalkboard.
4. discuss, evaluate and organize hypotheses and tentative explanations.
5. formulate learning goals including: how to resolve conflicting ideas, incomplete, incongruent or unclear explanations; what further information is needed; how can this information best be obtained?
6. develop study plans to discover needed information; identify individual or sub-group study tasks; adjourn meeting to carry out these study activities.
7. meet to consider and synthesize newly acquired information; try to apply it to the problem(s); test the results against alternative explanations or applications; agree on the best solution(s).

B. Types of problem-based learning tasks

1. *Problem explanation task*: invites students to plan and execute out-of-group study activities to discover underlying processes, structures or reasons for problem(s).
2. *Study task*: invites students to undertake independent study.
3. *Discussion task*: invites students to compare and combine their individual knowledge, beliefs and attitudes to focus on one or more specific problems often involving values or societal norms.
4. *Action tasks*: (a) field; (b) strategy; (c) simulation/role play
   (a) Field task – stimulates students to undertake *in vivo* investigations.
   (b) Strategy task – invites students to design a problem investigation, ie describe how to handle the problem in a real situation, or to perform a 'mental experiment'.
   (c) Simulation/role play – encourages a symbolic exercise to see how problem issues feel or can be explained in microcosm (simpler, safer setting).

C. Characteristics of problem-tasks amenable to problem-based learning

Problems:
1. ideally involve comprehension goals, eg explanations for why or how phenomena or relationships occur (and what might be done).
2. require combinations of information often from different sources or disciplines for satisfactory solutions.
3. are not always obvious, may require transformation, reformulation and partitioning to solve.
4. often have ethical or value aspects requiring identification and consideration.

Figure 25.1 *Seven-step problem finding/solving (after Schmidt and Bouhuijs, 1980)*

relationships or events. Often problems require knowledge from more than one discipline to produce an adequate solution. In this approach, students are assigned the problem statements in a given sequence; they must then identify problems within the statements which they choose to work on.

Instructors avoid the role of information-giver or conductor. Instead they monitor, provoke and evaluate group progress, periodically stimulating students with questions rather than giving out answers. In the first one to two years of study, faculty tutors need not be subject matter specialists in the field of the block. Tutoring skills are more important than content area skills at this level. Advanced students are increasingly used in tutor roles as student numbers have risen faster than full-time teaching staff.

Groups have a large measure of autonomy and must exercise considerable group and personal discipline to identify and work through problems successfully. Groups working on the same exercise often identify different problems or approaches and thus produce markedly divergent results.

An extensive system of tests charts student knowledge after each block, and progress evaluations assess integrative knowledge growth over time. Both types of tests employ a multiple-choice (extended true-false item) format and computer scoring and feedback to students and staff. Source evaluation is regularly undertaken as well. Considerable administrative support is required to service these activities.

Some subjects are not taught by PBL (eg, statistical analysis) since the 'Maastricht approach' is regarded as not being equally effective for all types of objectives, and particularly less for those which deviate from 'comprehension', as defined above. An illustration of a sample problem statement from beginning economics is shown in Figure 25.2. (Note: this type of statement is used in training new faculty and students in PBL. Typically problem statements are embedded in longer narratives.)

Constraints

The main contextual constraints centre upon three foci: the participants – staff and students; the content – business and management and subjects; and the social-financial-political environment. All three of these sources contain elements that augur well or poorly for success with PBL. Available space does not permit a thorough development of

Problem:

Jan has always proved to be a dependable employee. Whenever given a pay rise he responded by working even more. The last time he received a rise however he resolved to work less. His friends find his behaviour irrational. How do you explain this situation?

Commentary:

Students are free to identify the problem in terms of Jan's change, or in terms of his friends' reactions or (ideally) both. When they do the latter it is possible to apply both economic and behavioural science explanations to this statement. The discussions among students as to how to proceed involve considering assumptions (Are Jan's friends also co-workers? What kind of work does he do? etc) and can be as valuable, from a learning perspective as the solution to the problem(s) chosen.

Figure 25.2 *Sample (demonstration) problem*

all of the 'good and bad news' associated with these constraints but a number of the more pronounced elements are identified here. Gijselaers (1995) provides extensive critical evaluation of the Maastricht experience in economics and business administration.

Participants come from varying backgrounds but largely with educational experiences of a more traditional nature (eg, lecture-discussion formats). Some may be dissatisfied with the old approaches but few have had experience with PBL before arriving at university. A number of students select Maastricht because of its reputation for a student-centred teaching and learning system. Unlike other Dutch universities, Maastricht continues to attract increased numbers. This motive could be less operative in the case of new faculty members, some of whom are probably just trying to find a good academic position. PBL is featured in the annual open house days and other information directed to secondary school graduates, and it is typically mentioned in notices for new faculty positions.

On arriving in Maastricht, students receive a week's induction into the PBL educational process and new faculty are required to attend workshops on the system before participating with their first student group.

The future prospects of the two groups also differ. For students, it is said that their skills in group communication, problem solving and disciplinary integration are prized in the business settings where they may find future employment. For faculty, career prospects with respect to their involvement in PBL are less rosy. Their academic future is seen as being determined by research and publication lists, not by how well they learn to tutor PBL groups. Other universities or institutes where they may work in future are likely to use traditional teaching methods. Programme evaluation in the faculty also includes focus on student ratings of tutor performance. This could have a positive effect on staff motivation and performance. Faculty time, real and perceived, remains a key limiting factor to incorporating the PBL process into educational institutions where efficiency of resource utilization over-rides pedagogical discussion. Similarly, the Research Assessment Exercise of Higher Education in the UK has refocused faculty priorities to research activities.

Some colleagues and students probably long for a return to lectures. Business and economics faculty are oriented toward efficiency perhaps more than are medical faculty (who regard effectiveness as a *sine qua non*). Lecturing to large classes looks efficient compared with meeting large numbers of small groups. A good lecture may inform students, elucidate difficult areas in their study and even inspire deeper thought and study. Lectures in general provide the same kinds of facts that can be found in textbooks whereas the attainment of deeper approaches to learning (Marton, 1984) is served by a focus on applying those facts to solve 'comprehension' problems. It is the promotion of these deeper approaches, coupled with social problem-solving skills and attitudes, that characterizes what is meant by effectiveness as in PBL, where the learning process is continually in focus and participants are encouraged to integrate and apply their growing skills to identify, analyse and (re)solve increasingly complex situational problems.

The financial climate surrounding higher education, the growth in distance learning programmes and development of Internet degrees present real challenges for PBL.

Case studies have a long history in business and management education. Case study can be considered to be an early 'proto-' form of PBL. Although PBL is often described as 'imported' from medical education, the 'Harvard case study method' in management is probably best considered to be PBL's 'grandparents'. Case study traditions are weaker for general economics where some faculty members frankly state that PBL is not compatible with the ways they organize their field. Other colleagues express doubts that students are motivated to study anything that may not appear directly on their examinations. Furthermore, the reported gain in student abilities in group communications and problem solving are said by some to be at the expense of developing their skills of written expression also prized by potential employers. These questions need to be addressed further in educational research and evaluations of PBL.

Current stage of development

The status of PBL after ten years of implementation in Maastricht finds the faculty in a continual curriculum restructuring process that includes an explicit commitment to preserve and improve the practice of PBL. This contrasts sharply with the situation in England where PBL been subject to some consideration for business management studies departments. Given the financial climate in English tertiary education, the need for some sort of cost-benefit analysis is clearly evident, particularly in the context of 'privatization and the efficiency squeeze'.

In England, as in The Netherlands, motives for considering PBL in tertiary education are often dissatisfaction or doubts about the educational value or effectiveness of more traditional methods. As in Maastricht, hesitancy about PBL in England often centres on efficiency questions and perceptions of students' extrinsic motives and rapidly increasing student numbers.

The vocational nature of most postgraduate management education, where the majority of learners are part-time, provides opportunities for the application of PBL. The direct links between the PBL process and career/organizational benefits for employed management students could be developed through integration with the action learning process developed by Revans (1980). Action learning involves organizing exchanges so that a manager experienced in one organization is placed in another to solve a particular set of problems. There are several essential ingredients if the convergence between PBL and action learning is to occur in the management education process.

First, the action must be in the real world rather than simulated; second, the activity must involve the participation of others who are working on the same or quite different projects; third,emphasis on the learning, not merely the taking of action. This combination ensures the academic learning required for a postgraduate qualification is based on 'grounded' theory. The diverse nature of course members attending management education programmes provides rich experience and perspectives to tackle real problems and provide sponsoring organizations with recognizable added value and corporate partnership in applied education.

The evolution of the PBL approach in the MBA programme at Ohio University is briefly explained in Gijselaers (1995) and emphasizes the development of strategic, communicative, analytical and financial skills when dealing with actual cases in organizations.

Requirements for long-term success

Considering faculty viewpoints coloured by experience in business and economics, and the funding climate for education both in The Netherlands and in England, there may be a need for cost-benefit analyses of PBL to convince (potential) users of its viability, despite the fact that educational decisions are rarely made on the basis of such information. Arguments and even evidence for educational effectiveness, *per se*, do not provide justification for doubters who regard efficiency as an important goal. If PBL were shown to facilitate 'deep structure' conceptual learning in business and economics, as it may do in medicine (Coles, 1985) and in ways that lecture-discussion methods do not, a stronger case could be made for the 'efficiency ' of this approach and hence its adoption as an educational investment. Industries spend large sums on both technical and management development training and savings would result if graduates arrived better prepared for their roles as a result of practical problem-solving skills.

Similarly, studies exploring the dimensions of student (and staff) commitment are needed to address cynical or oversimplified interpretations. In the absence of real intellectual challenges or convincing prospects of long-term gain, students (and staff!) may default to using pragmatic strategies, such as studying for tests rather than learning skills for longer term use, especially if tests emphasize memorization of facts.

The task of writing problem texts and compiling block books that challenge students to active study within and outside the group is not easy, nor is the generation of test items tapping the comprehension skills the system requires. Moreover, academic staff members feel conflicting claims for time no less than their counterparts at more traditionally organized faculties. We need to know more about the dimensions and dynamics of student and staff motivations and attitudes to address resistance to innovations such as PBL. Clear exemplars of successful implementations are also needed (eg, Boud, 1985; Gijselaers, 1995).

Information about PBL in business and economics is small but growing and evidence from studies is needed for the heuristic value in providing examples of the method, and for the informative nature of the findings. This is not to say holistic PBL practised in medicine has been adopted without any modifications in management or business, or that the 'Maastricht approach' is directly exportable without taking account of situational factors. Indeed, it was not directly imported either from McMaster or from the Maastricht Medical School, but rather adapted to local needs. We would argue that the approach be designed to fit the particular context and a planned evaluation scheme be carried out to check on local applicability.

A stakeholder's linkage analysis model would provide a systematic approach to examine the forces, and their relationships, affecting the adoption or continuation of PBL. This model forms the basis for a critical evaluation of stakeholder influences on the process and effectiveness as perceived by participants. In the current climate, competencies which offer employability are the longer-term outcomes desired by course members.

None of the above is to suggest that PBL has not been successful in business, management and economics studies in Maastricht, or that it lacks interest and potential support in England or elsewhere. On the contrary, the Maastricht faculty undertook curriculum restructuring in the early 1990s and continues to 'fine tune' the system. Similarly in England it is not difficult to find those willing to discuss or even to begin planning pilot studies with problem-based modules. Numerous issues remain to be addressed, however, and many of them are discussed elsewhere in this book (and Gijselaers, 1995). Analyses of the types of content and goals best addressed by PBL, and those better handled by other methods, are needed. Long-term success for PBL of the kind reported in medical education requires concerted collaborative effort, innovative strategies to tackle financial constraints and strong commitment from senior institutional staff over a period of years. Planning and pilot projects are only the beginning.

References.

Boud, D (ed) (1985) *Problem-Based Learning in Education for the Professions*. Sydney: HERDSA.

Coles, C R (1985) Differences between conventional and problem-based curricula in their students' approaches to studying, *Medical Education*, 19, 308–309.

Foster, S F (1990) Problem-based learning as practised in faculties other than medicine. In C van der Vleuten and W Wijnen (eds) *Problem-Based Learning: Perspectives from the Maastricht Experience*. Amsterdam: Thesis Press, 83–94.

Gijselaers, W H (1995) Perspectives on problem-based learning. In W H Gijselaers, D T Templaar, P K Keizer *et al* (eds) *Educational Innovations in Economics and Business Administration: The Case of Problem-Based Learning*. Norwell, Mass.: Kluwer.

Marton, F (1984) Approaches to learning. In F Marton, D Hounsell and N Entwistle (eds) *The Experience of Learning*. Edinburgh: Scottish Universities Press.

Revans, R W (1980) *Action Learning – New techniques for management*. London: Blond and Briggs.

Schmidt, H G (1983) Problem-based learning: rationale and description, *Medical Education*, 17, 11–16.

Schmidt, H G and Bouhuijs, P A J (1987) Validation of a new measure of clinical problem-solving. *Medical Education*, 213–218.

Part V
Student Assessment and Programme Evaluation

Judging the success of a new kind of curriculum is more complex than we usually care to admit. We still expect students to demonstrate their knowledge and skills as part of the annual ritual. We hope they feel satisfied with their achievements, but although these are vital measures of success, the results of assessment of students' performance are certainly not the only outcomes of such programmes. Likewise, the overall evaluation of a new curriculum involves more than just the measurement of outcomes. It can depend as much on what goes into it, and by whom, as on what it achieves.

The two main issues for consideration which emerge from Part V are the assessment of students' performance and the evaluation of the educational programme. Evaluation is undertaken for many reasons. Most commonly it is used to contribute towards improving the programme which is being evaluated. All the different approaches included in this book have been subjected to such formative evaluation; some in a very substantial way. A second, common, pragmatic reason for the evaluation of programmes is justification. Can present practices be justified in terms that will satisfy critics of the programme, be they internal or external? Such justification needs to address the immediate needs of the audiences who are concerned and often appears very selective to external readers. The third reason for evaluation is the most important for external groups: how does the programme compare with others which are pursuing similar objectives? This is an area which is often neglected, at least in the early stage of development characterized by sensitivity (to any feedback), and pragmatism (in making it work). Innovators need to produce a good working model – true to course goals and objectives – *and* rectify real or perceived defects to gain its acceptance by both students and faculty. Refining the innovation using more robust feedback, and publicly matching it against other more established models occurs at a later stage.

Typical evaluation studies of problem-based curricula have focused on student outcomes, including their perceptions of specific courses or the institution as a learning environment. Even in this part, most chapters illustrate the importance of defining our measurement, or refining our understanding of problem solving. Kaufman (1985) at New Mexico, and more recently Kruseman (1996) at Maastricht, have each gone beyond that – looking at faculty attitudes and institutional costs and benefits of tutorials. Quantitative and qualitative evaluation studies have slowly accumulated under this broader frame of reference, leading to a different concern for potential adopters of PBL – how to make sense of all this information? Some evaluative data relate to well-established problem-based curricula; other studies derive from individual problem-based subjects embedded in conventional curricula; and a third set evolve from psychological or other fields of research not specifically geared to PBL. Although there have been several major reviews (and meta-analyses) of quantitative studies in medical education since our first edition, each review presented quite different interpretations – paradoxically adding to both our understanding and confusion! Here are some of the main challenges.

The challenge of evaluation design and justification

First, good quality evaluation studies of PBL programmes incorporating both longitudinal and cross-sectional data are still hard to find; those on institutional cost and benefit comparisons are even scarcer, but recent analyses indicate that problem-based curricula are still competitively priced and valued (Des Marchais, forthcoming; Kruseman, 1996).

Second, it is not simply a matter of devising suitable designs for such studies. There are other considerations. One is the lack of time and opportunity to devise ethical studies (ie, which don't play games with students' education) utilizing experimental or even quasi-experimental research designs. Another is the question of whether it is possible to undertake research on programmes which pursue quite different goals from each other. While it might be possible to agree on the general desirability of producing competent practitioners, when it comes to defining what is meant by competence, the possibility of agreement across philosophies recedes and the quest for operationalization has to be abandoned.

Third, even for pilot projects the pressures to conform, or to offer the same resources or support to the 'traditional' students, are very real and taxing (Kaufman, 1985; Ramos and Moore, 1987). Comparative studies involving other 'traditional' programmes or students are equally difficult to justify or interpret. Research into students' approaches to learning acknowledge these difficulties for inter-school comparisons within one profession (Coles, 1985; Newble and Clarke, 1986) but there is other evidence of a general effect on students' approaches to learning through problem-based curricula (Feletti *et al*, 1988) and of the need to refine courses in the light of students' conceptions (Duke *et al*, submitted for publication).

The challenge of measurement, and interpreting assessment of problem solving

Another major challenge for evaluation of PBL programmes is that good, universally accepted outcome measures are hard to find; indeed, they may not exist. Whether or not there is a generic problem-solving skill (inferred from correlations between such performances across different subject areas) has been carefully researched over the last decade by teams led by Geoff Norman at McMaster University, Henk Schmidt at Maastricht University, and Paul Feltovitch at Southern Illinois University. Norman's chapter reflects a shift in his thinking on aspects of assessment and evaluation, based on his review of more recent evidence. He offers sensible criteria for selecting and using different instruments for student assessment, according to the specific purpose and institutional context.

Dathe, O'Brien and colleagues at Alverno College once again provide important new perspectives on assessment of problem solving, through their reflection on student performance. In brief their evaluation of student assessment has led to further revision of their philosophy and implementation of a curriculum which is *not* problem based, but which is committed to developing students' problem solving *in different disciplines*, and to a degree of systematic improvement which would be hard to match in any other institution. Like Norman's research findings, their faculty realized that problem solving must be taught (learnt) in discipline-specific contexts, although students must also recognize their existing range of problem-solving strategies; a well-balanced education will see them develop an effective repertoire from both sources.

In fact, all chapters in this part stem from a common interest in assessment of problem solving, rather than active involvement in problem-based curricula. Their unique and collective strength originates from the not-so-radical viewpoint that the 'assessment tail wags the curriculum dog'. Individually, the authors of the three chapters describe different kinds of phenomena. As already stated, Dathe and his colleagues' chapter shows how a steady-state process of student assessment can inform curriculum planners. The respective chapters by Barry Maitland, and Dave Swanson and colleagues, each show how different curriculum models can benefit from developing new, matching kinds of student assessment. Swanson's chapter describes some of those assessment instruments, plus some recent initiatives in graduate certification examinations aimed at reducing the tension between psychometric requirements (for sufficient testing time or number of examination items to ensure sound competency decisions) and feasible, humane limits to comprehensive performance testing. Maitland's chapter illustrates and emphasizes the value of continuous grading of project work in architecture, using peer groups and design juries to evaluate design integration at the end of a problem phase, and how this tradition of presenting and defending one's work is just as nerve-wracking but rewarding for architecture faculty seeking accreditation of new courses, as it is for their PBL students.

The challenge of evaluating innovative educational programmes like PBL

Challenges relating to evaluation of educational programmes in general, and problem-based medical curricula in particular, are addressed in a new chapter contributed by Christel Woodward from McMaster University. She focuses on some of the challenges raised earlier in trying to find an acceptable common definition of PBL in terms of its main curriculum objectives, how these might be evaluated both during the course and after graduation, and the main areas and pitfalls for comparative curriculum evaluation. A number of other challenges arise. One is that course evaluation is typically the prerogative of the course director – which means that the nature, scope and ramifications of evaluation may be sorely restricted. It also may explain why most published research focuses on student assessment. A second, related challenge is that any such evaluation may be prejudged or genuinely biased because of the (traditional and conflicting) nature of assessment adopted. Even the results of *national* tests of professional competence (eg, medical licensing in the USA and Canada) may give misleading impressions of the relative merits of PBL or traditional programmes, due to a wide range of other influences (eg, students' independent studies, or strong preparatory courses aimed specifically at such examinations – see Kaufman, 1985, Chapter 10).

A final challenge for evaluating PBL is the overall interpretation of 'influence' attributable to the new curriculum. Longitudinal and cross-sectional studies together should at least differentiate the Hawthorne effect (or short-term gain when participating in something new) from longer-term outcomes. Clarke *et al* (1984) have showed students' consistent, high satisfaction with their five-year problem-based medical curriculum. Nolte *et al* (1988) demonstrate students' performance and attitudinal changes in a modified form of problem-based neurobiology course in an otherwise traditional curriculum.

Although the scientists' prayer, that 'more PBL research needs to be done' has been taken seriously by many more disciplines and institutions world-wide in the last decade, there is still much room for improvement. Robust qualitative methods and evaluation studies are needed to address the preponderance of quantitative reports (and subsequent meta-analyses) which constitute the current research literature. Broader, institutional studies are also needed – ones reporting on the 'big picture' developments at all levels and beyond graduation, not just refinements in teaching technology, curriculum development or student assessment issues. And faculty must be willing to accommodate unexpected outcomes from programme evaluation studies into revised curriculum models, like those resulting from routine assessment of problem solving at Alverno, so that the PBL literature benefits from truly dynamic and trans-disciplinary research efforts rather than seeming like 'more (or less) of the same'.

References

Clarke, R M, Feletti, G I and Engel, C E (1984) Student perceptions of the learning environment in a new medical school, *Medical Education*, 18, 321–325.

Coles, C R (1985) Differences between conventional and problem-based curricula in their students' approaches to studying, *Medical Education*, 19, 308–310.

Des Marchais, J (forthcoming) Curriculum change for sustaining social adaptation of medical programs and institutional responsibilities. In M Magzoub, H Schmidt, G Feletti and Z Nooman (eds) *Handbook of Community Based Education: Theory and Practices*.

Duke, M, Forbes, H, Hunter, S and Prosser, M (submitted for publication) The conceptions of problem-based learning held by undergraduate students of nursing.

Feletti, G I, Drinan, J, Trent, F and Maitland, B (1988) Students' approaches to learning and satisfaction with problem-based curricula for four different professions, *Assessment and Evaluation in Higher Education*, 13, 2, 163–176.

Kaufman, A (ed) (1985) *Implementing Problem-Based Medical Education*. New York: Springer.

Kruseman, N (1996) 'A cost benefit analysis of problem based learning', invited address, Third International Conference on Problem-Based Learning, Durban, South Africa, 22 September.

Newble, D and Clarke, R M (1986) The approaches to learning of students in a traditional and in an innovative problem-based medical school, *Medical Education*, 20, 267–273.

Nolte, J, Eller, P and Ringel, S P (1988) Shifting towards problem-based learning in a medical school neurobiology course. *Proceedings of the 27th annual conference on Research in Medical Education*. Washington DC: Association of American Medical Colleges, 66–71.

Ramos, M B and Moore, G T (1987) Harvard Medical School, USA: the New Pathway to Medical Education. In *Innovative Tracks at Established Institutions for the Education of Health Personnel*. WHO Offset Publication No.101. Geneva: World Health Organization.

Chapter 26

Accreditation and Assessment in Architecture

Barry Maitland

The account in Part IV of the original intentions in adopting a problem-based approach in the Newcastle architecture course emphasized the importance given to the possibility of integrating aspects of architectural education which elsewhere have tended to grow apart. In particular, integration of discipline areas was sought, and especially that of technical and design areas, so that students would come to see the whole evolution of a building project as an unfolding design process, rather than as a creative initial conceptual design stage followed by a tedious technical resolution stage.

This priority given to the integration of discipline areas within the design process, as well as the length of time required to work through this process in an architectural project, led to the view that examinations independent of the problems encountered during the year would be an inappropriate way of assessing student progress and performance. Instead, assessment takes the form of a continuous grading of work through the year, with mid- and end-of-year reviews and a final compilation of assessments into a single graded year result.

The mechanics of this process reflect the twin priorities of design integration and development of new areas of knowledge and skill within the study areas, the former being the province of group tutors and year managers (whose roles were described in the earlier account in Part IV), and the latter of the study area consultants.

Design integration is assessed by design juries who review students' work at the end of a problem phase, and sometimes at an intermediate stage as well. The juries comprise the group tutors for that year, together with invited guest critics. They have a checklist of the design objectives for the project, and are advised on the way in which each student undertook the process by the relevant group tutor. Each student makes a presentation of their submission to the jury, and responds to questions, discussion and criticism. The process is open to the whole year (and sometimes other years as well) and students join in the debate. The jury then goes into closed session to review all the projects once more, and to give them grades, which are published.

Progress in the study areas is assessed by the relevant consultants in two ways: through the main design submissions, and through separate assignments. The latter are designed to equip students with the knowledge or skill they will need for the solution of the problem. Thus a consultant who has it as an objective for a particular problem phase that the students should be able to present a proposal in the form of a two-point perspective drawing, say, will have held a workshop on how this is done, will have set a practice exercise which may include an assessed assignment, and will then assess the final project submission purely from the point of view of the success of that particular feature. At the start of each problem phase such objectives are provided to students, and at the end consultants complete a feedback sheet with comments for each student against each objective.

At the end of each semester each student's results for both study areas and design integration are reviewed by a panel chaired by the relevant year manager, with the student present. Students are expected to reach at least a pass standard in all study areas, and a student with an area of weakness may be given a remedial programme in it. At the end of the year, study area results, weighted according to the notional time a student is anticipated to spend on each area, are aggregated with design integration results, similarly weighted according to phase length, to give a single overall graded year result.

Both normative and summative assessment are integrated into the overall process (Kingsland, 1995), which is backed up by a flow of supporting documentation, providing the objectives, assessment criteria and feedback appropriate to the stage (Kingsland, 1989). Architectural design involves the resolution of objectives which are often in conflict and whose effects and relative values are difficult to quantify. This makes it important for the student to learn to make value judgements and to form strategies for the creative reconciliation of opposing criteria, and these skills are best tested and developed in an interactive way with tutors. The formal assessment process is then seen as an extension of the learning experience, in which the assumptions and choices made by the student in the process of arriving at a design solution are questioned and defended, and the skill of the student in making the most of the opportunities presented by those choices is debated in front of the student.

The process of presenting and defending one's work is traditional to architectural courses, and has some value in preparing students for similar situations in practice, although it can be a nerve-wracking experience. Internal evaluations of students' responses to the course have not identified this as a particularly problematic part of the assessment process as far as students are concerned. Overall, the Graduate Careers Council of Australia's annual Course Experience Questionnaires have shown Newcastle graduates to be among the most satisfied of architecture graduates in terms of their perceptions of the assessment process.

An important external evaluation of architectural courses in Australia lies in the accreditation procedure undertaken by the Royal Australian Institute of Architects, together with the Architects Registration Board for each state, and the Commonwealth Association of Architects. Accreditation panels include both practitioners and academics, and state and national representatives, together with a student member. They visit an architectural school over a period of three days, during which time they inspect portfolios of best, median and lowest pass work for the previous two years, assess teaching in each discipline area, inspect facilities, and meet with students and staff.

The joint accreditation panel may accredit a school for the purposes of professional recognition of its degree for up to five years, and since the Newcastle school was due for such an inspection in the third year of its conversion to PBL, when all five academic years of the course were operating on that basis, it was seen by both the school and the profession, which had been advised of changes at Newcastle, as an important test. This perception was heightened by the fact that panels visiting other schools during the previous couple of years had taken a tough line in a number of cases, withholding full five-year terms of recognition in favour of shorter periods, and taking issue with schools on questions of relevance of courses to practice, and of integration of discipline areas.

Perhaps these preoccupations of the panel predisposed it to the full endorsement which it eventually gave the new approach. In the final meeting at the end of its visit, a somewhat intimidating experience (especially for the head of school) in which a draft of the panel's criticisms and recommendations is read out before the whole school, staff and students gathered together, the panel chairman referred to the confidence and competence of students, and of standards of work comparable with the best seen in other schools. The panel had also been impressed by a sense of vitality in the school, arising no doubt in large part from the galvanizing effect of trying something new, which had gripped the school for the previous few years.

Ironically, the panel's reservations concerned the possible limitations of too much realism and an overwhelming attention to integrating conceptual and technical design. Perhaps there was insufficient scope for the students' imagination to soar above the humdrum facts which tied practitioners to the ground, and which the problem-based approach tended to bring to the fore?

This doubt echoed a concern in the minds of the staff with the way in which the detailed technical resolution phases of the larger projects, with comparatively long periods of time needed to become familiar with new technologies, tended to dominate the conceptual design phases. Often this would slow down the whole programme, restricting the number of design problems which students would meet during the course and so restricting their opportunities to develop the sort of facility in conceiving and exploring design options which comes from constant practice.

The accreditation panel suggested that the difficulty might be overcome by introducing a number of very short problems, ranging in duration from a few hours to a week, and aimed particularly at developing conceptual design skills. This has subsequently been done and has proved very successful, especially with those short problems set simultaneously across the whole school, and with student groups formed from mixed years.

References

Kingsland, A J (1989) The assessment process in architecture at Newcastle. In B Wallis (ed) *Problem Based Learning: The Newcastle Workshop*. Proceedings of the Ten-Year Anniversary conference, Faculty of Medicine, University of Newcastle, 121–130.

Kingsland, A J (1995) Integrated assessment: the rhetoric and the students' view. In P J Little, M J Ostwald and G Ryan (eds) *Research and Development in Problem Based Learning*, 3. Sydney: Australian Problem-Based Learning Network, 309–324.

Chapter 27

Assessment in Problem-based Learning

Geoffrey R Norman

A starting point in the development of an assessment method is a careful consideration of exactly what one wishes to assess. I am not an advocate of detailed behavioural objectives as a precursor to any exercise in assessment; such an approach is the antithesis of problem-based, self-directed learning. But at a philosophical level, it is worth pausing to ask whether we expect the graduate of a problem-based school to be different from or better than a graduate from a 'traditional' school.[1] Unless one takes the outrageous position that teachers at the 'other' schools are deliberately intent on producing ill-equipped, outmoded, passive-aggressive physicians, a plausible starting point must be that the graduates of problem-based and other schools are more similar than different. Indeed, the literature suggests just this (Vernon and Blake, 1993); graduates of problem-based schools appear to have a comparable or slightly inferior knowledge base, similar level of skills in other areas, and are primarily identifiable by a less jaundiced view of their undergraduate experience. It may be argued that the lack of difference simply reflects the inadequacy of our measures, and we certainly do not have an overabundance of good measures of, for example, community orientation or self-directed learning. Still, we should reflect that our first responsibility to society is to demonstrate with conviction that our graduates are no worse than others in those areas central to clinical competence, and hopefully better than others in areas, such as self-directed learning or group skills, which are embraced by PBL schools.

If this is so, then the task of identifying the issues of assessment in PBL schools becomes somewhat simpler. We can begin by presuming that issues of assessment are basically no different here than else-where, and then begin to refine our questions from a relatively common starting point. I expect that this position is somewhat foreign to those who are more radical disciples of PBL. As many of the writings in this book demonstrate, there is no unanimous position about the nature of PBL, and it would seem nihilistic to ignore the many purported benefits of the approach by beginning at the lowest common denominator. As a result, permit me to elaborate further in defence of this position.

One position is that the central role of PBL is the acquisition and nurturing of problem-solving skills, which are applicable to a wide variety of clinical problems. If so, then we should devise some methods to measure problem-solving skills, more or less independent of knowledge. There have been numerous examples of such measures over the years, beginning with paper-based problems like the Patient Management Problem (PMP) (McGuire and Babbott, 1967) and currently seen in the proliferation of computer-based simulations.

With the exception of PMPs, there has been little study of the reliability and validity of these assessment methods. However it is possible to draw some general conclusions from the literature. In particular, I do not believe that there is any real evidence to support the claim for problem-solving skills independent of knowledge. While the originators of the first PBL curricula may have believed in such a dichotomy, I think the evidence from the last two decades of research overwhelmingly argues against this premise (Ericsson and Charness, 1994; Norman *et al*, 1987; Perkins and Salomon, 1989). At this level, PBL is not about general skills; it is really about knowledge, learned in the context in which it will later be used so that hopefully transfer can be facilitated. It then follows that it is impossible to gain any useful information about a student's abilities from a few cases (Swanson *et al*, 1995) since the successful solution of one problem requires a complex interaction between knowledge about the problem and some highly specific procedural skills. As a result, scores on one problem are typically poorly correlated with scores on a second problem, even when the two problems are closely matched for content (Norman *et al*, 1983).

Since knowledge and problem solving are closely related, then we may unapologetically ask that our students know something, and we may and should test for knowledge. In doing so, there are two major concerns: first what is, from a psychometric perspective, the best way to assess knowledge gleaned from a PBL experience, and second, what is the impact of such knowledge tests on learning. In response to the first question, we are unequivocally on the side of multiple-choice questions (MCQs). Short-answer questions have not been shown to measure anything distinct from MCQs (Frederiksen, 1984; Norman *et al*, 1987), and inevitably sacrifice efficiency. Recent work has attempted to use MCQs which are embedded in a rich clinical stem, presuming that such formats may involve higher order skills, and hence be more discriminating. However, at least one study (Case *et al*, 1996) has not shown any advantage to this format.

However, the issue of assessment does not begin and end at the choice of a format for the final examination. Indeed, there is reason to be concerned about the use of final examinations, regardless of format, in PBL schools. It is well documented that examinations have a massive steering effect on the curriculum (Newble and Jaeger, 1983), and the effect is present at least as strongly in PBL schools (Blumberg and Daughterty, 1989), despite any philosophical tendencies of faculty to dismiss its importance. As one colleague put it, 'The curriculum tells you what the faculty are doing; the examination system tells you what the students are doing!' Nevertheless, we are constrained by the necessity to demonstrate the competence of our students; either on national licensing examinations or, where there are none, on equally rigorous internal examinations (Verwijnen *et al*, 1982). The real art, then, comes from using assessment methods to appropriately steer students' learning.

One solution to the potential steering effect of examinations is the progress test, pioneered at the University of Maastricht (Verwijnen *et al*, 1982) and the University of Missouri, Kansas City (Arnold and Willoughby, 1990) and recently adopted at McMaster. The test is administered several times per year, unrelated to the beginning or end of any curriculum blocks, and items are drawn from all of medicine. Studies we have conducted (Blake *et al*, 1996) show conclusively that it has no steering effect on student learning, either at the level of individual learning approaches, learning style (memorization vs concept learning) or tutorial function. However it is a reliable measure of student knowledge acquisition in medical school, with test-retest reliability over successive tests of the order of 0.6–0.7, which has enabled us to identify students who are having continuing difficulty with knowledge acquisition. The test also has predictive validity, demonstrated by a correlation of about 0.6 between the progress test and performance on the national licensing examination written several months later.

There is one final point about the particular issues of assessment in PBL curricula. I have suggested that we must take the assessment of knowledge seriously, and demonstrate that our students can do as well as others in this arena. But we demand more of our students, and if we do not assess these other qualities, they will have as much substance, in the eyes of the students, as the fabled emperor's clothes. In part, this is an easy task. Many schools are engaged in the assessment of clinical skills, using simulated patients, objective structured clinical examinations or other performance tests. Indeed, in North America, both licensing bodies, the National Board of Medical Examiners and the Medical Council of Canada (Reznick *et al*, 1993), have been engaged in massive efforts to introduce performance assessment into the licensing process. We need only follow this lead and introduce such methods into our schools as well.

But there are other domains that are not so straightforward. There are a number of areas where we differ in our objectives from mainstream schools and, for that matter, from each other. Nevertheless, if we wish our students to learn the skills and knowledge associated with a community orientation, health promotion, population and public health, critical appraisal, lifelong learning, interdisciplinary learning or self-appraisal, then we are obliged to assess these objectives in a meaningful, reliable and valid fashion. I recently looked at the literature on interprofessional education, and have attended numerous conferences on community-based education. While these areas have no shortage of demonstration projects and armchair advocates, it is virtually impossible to identify any evidence that these curriculum strategies result in intended changes, mainly because reasonable methods to assess these components do not presently exist. Therein lies a research agenda particular to our institutions, and we should devise strategies to collaborate in this enterprise.

In summary, many of the challenges facing educators in PBL schools are the same as those faced by educators everywhere. Some issues are unique. But we must be aware that assessment is not done in isolation, and that there are 'side effects' of the drug. The intelligent use of assessment to help students to learn appropriately those things we consider appropriate remains a substantial challenge.

Note

1. An apology is necessary, since the use of the adjective 'traditional' carries with it a pejorative meaning. As I hope will become clear, this is not my intent.

References

Arnold, L and Willoughby, T L (1990) The quarterly profile test, *Academic Medicine*, 65, 515–516.

Blake, J M, Norman, G R, Keane, D R, Mueller, C B, Cunnington, J P W and Didyk, N (1996) Introducing progress testing in McMaster University's problem based medical curriculum: Psychometric properties and effect on learning, *Academic Medicine*, 71, 1002–1007.

Blumberg, P and Daughterty, S (1989) 'Good student or good physician: what are we trying to encourage?' Presented at the American Educational Research Association Annual Meeting, San Francisco.

Case, S M, Swanson, D B and Becker, D F (1996) Verbosity, window dressing and red herrings: Do they make a better test item? *Academic Medicine*, 71, 528–530.

Ericsson, KA and Charness, N (1994) Expert performance: Its structure and acquisition, *American Psychologist*, 49, 725–747.

Frederiksen, N (1984) The real test item bias, *American Psychologist*, 39, 193-202.

McGuire, C H and Babbott, D (1967) Simulation technique in the measurement of problem solving skills, *Journal of Educational Measurement*, 4, 1-10.

Newble, D I and Jaeger, K (1983) The effect of assessment and examinations on the learning of medical students, *Medical Education*, 13, 263–268.

Norman, G R, Tugwell, P, Feightner, J W, Muzzin, L J and Jacoby, L L (1983) Knowledge and clinical problem solving, *Medical Education*, 19, 344–356.

Norman, G R, Smith, E K M, Powles, A C P, Rooney, P J, Henry, N L and Dodd, P E (1987) Factors underlying performance on written tests of knowledge, *Medical Education*, 21, 297–304.

Perkins, D N and Salomon, G (1989) Are cognitive skills context bound? *Educational Researcher*, 18, 16–25.

Reznick, R, Blackmore, D, Cohen, R *et al* (1993) An objective structured clinical examination for the licentiate: Report of the pilot project of the Medical Council of Canada, *Academic Medicine*, 67, 487–494.

Swanson, D B, Norman, G R and Linn, R L (1995) Performance based assessment: Lessons from the professions, *Educational Researcher*, 24, 5–11.

Vernon, D T A and Blake, R L (1993) Does problem based learning work? A meta-analysis of evaluative research, *Academic Medicine*, 68, 550–563.
Verwijnen, G M, Imbos, T, Snellen, A *et al* (1982) The evaluation system at the medical school at Maastricht, *Assessment and Evaluation in Higher Education*, 3, 225–244.

Chapter 28

Strategies for Student Assessment

David B Swanson, Susan M Case and **Cees P M van der Vleuten**

While many educators have emphasized the impact of student assessment on learning (Bouhuijs *et al*, 1987; Case, in press; Entwistle, 1981; Frederiksen, 1984; Newble and Jaeger, 1983; Swanson and Case, 1992; van der Vleuten *et al*, 1989), there is little agreement on methodologies for assessment among PBL advocates. Specific instruments have been proposed for use in problem-based contexts, but few complete, integrated systems have been presented. Exceptions are described in Feletti *et al* (1983), West *et al* (1985), and van der Vleuten and Verwijnen (1990).

In this chapter we review a variety of approaches to assessment for PBL, drawing on examples from health professions education and experiences of the last named author at the University of Maastricht (formerly University of Limburg). The first section identifies two types of problem-based curricula that differ somewhat in assessment needs. The second section reviews assessment methods that focus on the learning process. The third section discusses use of traditional paper-and-pencil measures to assess learning outcomes. The last section provides recommendations for improving assessment practices in PBL programmes.

Types of problem-based curricula: open versus guided discovery

Although all problem-based curricula emphasize the learning process, learning how to learn, student responsibility for their own learning, and preparation for lifelong learning, there are important variations among programmes that have implications for assessment. Using terminology associated with 'discovery learning' in science education (Shulman and Keislar, 1966), in programmes following the 'open discovery' approach, students have responsibility for determining what to learn, as well as when and how to learn it. Learning to apply broad principles in problem-solving situations is most important, with minimal guidance from instructors and maximal opportunity for exploration by students.

In contrast, for programmes following a 'guided discovery' approach, specific learning objectives are identified by curriculum developers for each problem; these objectives are provided to instructors who use them to organize group discussion and student learning. These curricula may be highly structured, with careful sequencing of instructional experiences. Students may or may not be aware of the structure and the specific objectives: their experience may be quite similar to students in programmes using the open discovery approach. In practice, the open and guided discovery approaches are probably best viewed as opposite ends of a continuum. Programmes vary along the continuum, and, within a programme, problems (and groups) also vary.

Assessment in programmes using the open discovery approach often focuses on process variables such as self-directedness, motivation, effort, problem-solving, and attitudes. Assessment of learning outcomes is generally viewed as problematic because, in effect, each student is encouraged to pursue a somewhat different curriculum. Traditional multiple-choice tests, in particular, are viewed as inappropriate, since they may cause students to 'study to the test' and thus discourage students from self-determination of the material to be learned and the process for learning it.

Assessment of learning outcomes poses fewer problems for curricula using the guided discovery approach, because the same learning objectives that guide problem development may also guide test development. Nevertheless, multiple-choice tests may still be viewed with some suspicion, typically because they are viewed as inadequate for assessment of highly valued problem-solving skills. As a consequence, assessment in 'guided discovery' programmes may also be focused on the learning process.

Assessment methods

Process-oriented assessment methods. What processes should be assessed?

Problem-based curricula generally emphasize communication skills in tutorial groups, acceptance of responsibility for learning, learning to learn, appropriate selection and use of a wide range of learning resources, and development of problem-solving skills. Consequently, process-oriented assessment methods generally focus on one or more of these. Three categories of methods are reviewed below.

Tutor, peer, and self-ratings

Tutor, peer, and self-ratings are commonly used to assess a broad range of skills, including effort, self-directed learning, group cooperation, and communication skills. Use of ratings from tutors and peers is based upon the belief that co-workers are in a good position to evaluate each other. Use of self-ratings is nicely congruent with PBL's emphasis on judging the state of your own knowledge as an essential element of the learning process. However, there are well-known psychometric and practical problems with the use of ratings.

As an example of the problems that may occur, when peer ratings were used formatively by the School of Health Sciences at the University of Maastricht, students either did not take them seriously or refused to complete them. When they were used summatively, ratings were uniformly high and not useful. Steps to force some variation into ratings (eg, by forced ranking) elicited so much resistance from students that they had to be discontinued. The School of Medicine at the same university has never used tutor or peer ratings because of a belief that the teacher and assessor roles are incompatible; interpersonal relationships take on a different meaning when teachers are involved in assessment, and it is difficult for co-workers to be objective.

These results are consistent with research that has found that peer and tutor ratings (especially when focused on process) carry little measurement information and have poor validity (Boud, 1989; Rezler, 1989). Generally, inter-item correlations are very high, suggesting that raters can only provide an overall impression, without much differentiation of distinct skills. In addition, raters commonly vary in stringency, so that variation in ratings across students may simply reflect differences in rater standards. Similar problems exist for self-ratings.

Unobtrusive measures

Student assessment may also be based upon unobtrusive measures of the process of learning (Webb *et al*, 1966) such as library records of books and articles that were checked out and computer records of literature searches that were done. Alternatively, students may be asked to keep logs or diaries summarizing their learning activities. Because of difficulties in capturing and standardizing such information, however, these techniques are more commonly used for curriculum evaluation, rather than student assessment, since the former only requires that measurements be precise for groups, not individuals.

Learning exercises

In the final category of process-oriented assessment techniques, a learning exercise is posed for students to complete; both process-oriented and outcome-oriented elements may be considered in marking. The classic example is the 'triple jump exercise' (Painvin *et al*, 1979). Individual students are presented with a problem situation; they discuss the problem and their learning needs with an oral examiner. They then locate and review resource material. Last, students meet with the original oral examiner, discussing conclusions reached about the problem, resources consulted, and the quality of their performance. Problem-solving skills, self-directed learning skills, and knowledge of the problem area are then rated.

Thus, the exercise resembles the learning process that takes place in PBL, but under more controlled and standardized circumstances. While only limited psychometric research has been conducted (Painvin *et al*, 1979; Powles *et al*, 1981), it seems likely that a student's performance will vary extensively from problem to problem because of the content-specificity of medical problem-solving skills – a consistent result across a wide range of measurement techniques (Swanson, 1987; Swanson *et al*, 1987; van der Vleuten and Swanson, 1990). Tests including only one or a few problems will not provide reproducible, accurate assessments of students' skills.

These results may well generalize beyond medical education to other areas. The student-to-student variation in learning experiences promoted by problem-based programmes (particularly open discovery approaches) might be expected to produce similar psychometric problems, since students would have varying knowledge of the problem area(s) selected for the learning exercise.

Outcome-oriented assessment methods. What outcomes should be assessed?

Over the long term, it is reasonable to expect that differences in students' self-directed learning skills and motivation to learn, coupled with differences in general ability, will result in marked variation in learning outcomes. Given similar educational goals and opportunities to learn, better students (brighter, more highly motivated, more self-directed) will learn more than poorer students and, as time goes on, this effect will increase in size. Use of outcome-oriented assessment procedures capitalizes on this trend: the quality of the learning process is measured indirectly by testing the results of that process after it has been in operation for some period of time. But what kinds of outcomes will provide the most appropriate indicators of the quality of the learning process, given the goals of PBL?

Development of problem-solving skills is a major focus of PBL, so assessment of these skills seems like a natural choice. However, research has shown that medical problem-solving should not be thought of as a unitary, consistent, content-independent skill that increases over time (Elstein *et al*, 1978; Norman, 1988). The effectiveness of the process depends upon details of the structure and organization of knowledge and skills that support the problem-solving process, not in gross characteristics of the process itself. Possession of factual knowledge of an area does not guarantee successful application of that knowledge in solution of problems. This is, in fact, a major element in the rationale for PBL: knowledge is better remembered in the context in which it is originally learned (Norman, 1988).

Recent research in medical education has suggested that learning progresses through a series of levels as expertise develops (Norman *et al*, 1989). At the lowest level, the novice learner has 'dispersed knowledge': list-like knowledge of isolated facts with little conceptual integration. More advanced learners possess 'elaborated knowledge': facts and principles of basic biomedical science, pathophysiological concepts, and medical information are richly organized to support use in the solution of clinical problems. At the highest level of expertise, knowledge is 'compiled' (in a computer sense) and condensed: clinical cues and contextual information are instantly and automatically recognized and processed. Individuals function at various levels of expertise depending upon the content area; a learner may possess only dispersed knowledge in some areas, but elaborated knowledge in others.

The notion of 'levels of expertise' is useful for thinking about assessment in a problem-based context. Deliberate assessment of dispersed knowledge is acceptable only if it is necessary to determine if students have memorized basic information; focusing on assessment of dispersed knowledge is not generally compatible with the curricular goals of PBL or even of most traditional curricula. However, strictly from a psychometric perspective, the resulting rank-order of students might well be appropriate, since good learners will probably have greater mastery of basic facts, as well as better problem-solving skills.

Elaborated knowledge is a more appropriate focus for assessment. Test items should require examinees to apply their knowledge to the solution of real problems. In medical education, where PBL is generally used for pre-clerkship instruction, test items might ask students to predict or interpret the results of a laboratory experiment, to explain pathophysiological relationships between a disease process and the findings that result, or to identify the most likely diagnosis and appropriate treatment when presented with a case description. To respond to such 'test tasks' successfully, students must analyse the presented situation and reason out a solution, recalling relevant facts as necessary in the process. Thus, items should require examinees to apply their knowledge to commonly occurring and important problem-solving situations.

Assessment of compiled knowledge is generally not of interest for problem-based curricula, since such knowledge develops over a long period of time in response to experience in the real problem-solving environment. At least in medical education, this typically occurs later in (or following) training, after initial PBL has taken place.

What assessment methods should be used?

Several assessment methods may be used to measure learners' use of elaborated knowledge in solving problems. Within medical education, there have been advocates for written and computer-based clinical simulations, essay exams, multiple-choice exams, and short-answer tests. Each of these is reviewed briefly below.

Written and computer-based clinical simulations

Written and computer-based simulations usually begin with an 'opening scenario' that briefly describes a patient situation. Examinees then proceed through a series of 'scenes' in which additional information is gathered (often history-taking, physical examination, and laboratory scenes) and patient management activities are initiated (McGuire and Solomon, 1976). For written simulations, a 'latent image' pen is used to select options and reveal the consequences of the selections; for computer simulations, the keyboard and screen play a similar role.

Depending upon the complexity of the simulation, all examinees may proceed through the same series of scenes in a linear fashion or pathways may vary (branch) as a function of examinee decisions. The simulated patient may improve, complications may develop, or the patient may die, depending upon the quality of the decisions made.

Until the mid-1980s, clinical simulations were frequently used for assessment of problem-solving skills, both by medical schools and certifying agencies. However, psychometric research demonstrated a number of shortcomings: scores were unduly influenced by the response style of examinees; very long tests (ten to 40 cases and four to ten hours of testing time) were needed to obtain stable, reproducible scores; and correlations with scores on multiple-choice tests were quite high (Swanson *et al*, 1987). As a consequence, most medical schools and certifying agencies have discontinued the use of clinical simulations for assessment purposes, though there is continued interest and research on computer-based simulations (Swanson *et al*, 1987; 1995). It is likely that the same shortcomings would be present for assessment of problem-solving skills in other content areas; careful psychometric research is clearly desirable prior to adoption.

Essay exams

Essay exams are a popular choice for assessment in problem-based curricula because the format can provide an in-depth assessment of problem-solving skills. Essay questions encourage students to integrate their insights into a systematic framework, rather than simply recall isolated facts. There are major problems, however, if scores are to be used for summative assessment (Norcini *et al*, 1990). Questions are often too vague, forcing students to 'guess what the teacher wants'. Because each essay question requires substantial time for examinees to answer and faculty to mark, essay exams typically include only a small number of questions. Because sampling breadth is limited, the generalizability of scores may be poor because of content specificity. Thus, essay exams may provide very accurate information about students' understanding of the topics actually included, but very inaccurate impressions of the broader domain from which questions are sampled. To reduce this problem, it is better to include a larger number of short essays, rather than a small number of longer ones (eg, twelve ten-minute essays, instead of two 60-minute ones).

Multiple-choice exams

Traditional multiple-choice questions (MCQs) are often rejected for use in PBL programmes, because of the belief that they can assess only factual knowledge (Newble *et al*, 1979; Pickering, 1979; West *et al*, 1985) and, as a consequence, may have an adverse educational impact. We feel that this is just plain wrong. While some MCQs do focus purely on recall of isolated facts, it is quite possible to prepare MCQs that require examinees to apply their knowledge in problem-solving situations (Case and Swanson, 1996; Page and Bordage, 1995). Concurrently, such tests retain the usual benefits associated with MCQs: broad, efficient sampling of content, high reliability, and ease of scoring.

The task posed for examinees by a test item is paramount. The first three sample items in Figure 28.1 illustrate this point. The first item assesses recall of an isolated fact (dispersed knowledge); the second and third items assess application of knowledge. (It is not clear if the second and third items assess elaborated or compiled knowledge. This depends on the cognitive processes used by the examinee, not just the content of the item.) The second item parallels traditional 'top-down' instruction: given a lesion, what patient findings are expected? The third item requires the 'bottom-up' reasoning of clinical practice: given patient findings, what is the underlying cause? In other items assessing application of knowledge with a 'bottom-up' focus, a patient description may be followed by lead-in questions such as: what is the most likely cause of the problem? What laboratory tests should be ordered next? What is the most appropriate initial management?

Critics of MCQs often focus on the 'cueing' inherent in the MCQ format: they argue that examinees need only recognize the correct answer, rather than work through the problem and construct it. This is a legitimate concern, but it is generally straightforward to reduce cueing by increasing the number of response options. Items 4 and 5 in

1. Which of the following nerves innervates the triceps muscle?

   (list of nerves)

2. Transection of the radial nerve would reduce ability to (extend the forearm; flex the arm, etc)

3. A 20-year-old man is stabbed in the arm with a knife. There is anaesthesia of the dorsum of the forearm and the dorsum of the hand between the thumb and forefinger. The extensors of his wrist are paralyzed. He cannot extend his thumb at the metacarpophalangeal or interphalangeal joints. Which of the following has been damaged?

   (list of nerves)

4. A 26-year-old man has insidious onset of low back pain associated with early morning stiffness. The pain alternates from side to side and occasionally radiates into the buttocks and back of the thighs, but not below the knees. The patient has acute anterior uveitis, diffuse tenderness of the low back and sacroiliac, and restricted range of motion at the hips. Erythrocyte sedimentation rate is 40 mm/hr, latex fixation test is negative, and mild hypoproliferative anaemia is present. What is the most likely diagnosis?

(A) Ankylosing spondylitis	(E) Osteoporosis
(B) Intervertebral disk infection	(F) Spinal stenosis
(C) Multiple myeloma	(G) Spondylolysis
(D) Myofascial pain	(H) Tuberculosis of the spine

5. A 40-year-old black man has the sudden onset of severe headache, dizziness and vomiting. His blood pressure is 260/130 mm Hg; he has encephalopathy and grade IV retinopathy. Treatment with which of the following is most appropriate?

(A) Alpha agonists	(G) Central sympatholytics
(B) Alpha blockers	(H) Direct vasodilators
(C) ACE inhibitors	(I) Negative inotropic agents
(D) Beta agonists	(J) Thiazide diuretics
(E) Beta blockers	(K) Vasoconstrictors
(F) Cardiac glycosides	

Figure 28.1 *Sample items*

Figure 28.1 provide illustrations. Given modern technology, there is no reason not to include all or most of the options present in the real environment (Case and Swanson, 1993; Case *et al*, 1994). In some assessment situations, an exhaustive list of options (eg, all relevant diagnoses, laboratory tests, and drugs) may be prepared for use with all questions (Veloski *et al*, 1988).

Critics of MCQs also argue that, in some real-world problem-solving situations, physicians must consider more than a 'single best answer' (eg, preparing a list of diagnostic possibilities to be 'worked up'). This task may also be modelled with MCQ items; for example, an item might describe a clinical situation and ask examinees which three diagnostic studies should be ordered (Ripkey *et al*, 1996).

Short-answer tests

Short-answer questions (SAQs) may also be used for assessment in PBL programmes (de Graaff *et al*, 1987; Feletti, 1980); psychometric characteristics should be similar to those for MCQs (Norman *et al*, 1996), though more time and effort will be involved in grading. As with MCQs, the skills assessed by SAQs depend crucially upon the task posed for examinees. In Figure 28.1, it matters little whether item 1 is posed in MCQ or SAQ format; the item is poor because it focuses on recall of an isolated fact. Items 3 to 5 are much better, regardless of the response format used. Whether a particular item is followed by the traditional five MCQ options, by a longer list including all relevant possibilities, or by a blank that examinees must complete, is largely a logistical issue. The primary effect of altering the number/presence of options is on item difficulty (poor examinees derive some benefit from a limited number of options) and discrimination; the rank-ordering of students is not greatly affected, nor is the ability of the test to identify students' strengths and weaknesses. There is no direct relationship between response format and skills assessed (McGuire, 1987); it is not format, but examinee task that matters.

When should outcome assessment take place?

Because problem-based curricula using a guided discovery approach have specific objectives associated with each problem, timing of outcome assessment poses no particular problems. Tests may be given after each problem, at the end of each course or academic year, or as a part of graduation requirements.

Timing of tests is more problematic for open discovery curricula. For example, during the mid-1970s, the University of Maastricht School of Medicine used end-of-course tests for summative assessment. It was difficult to construct the tests, because the content covered by individual students varied and, in contrast to the intended open discovery approach, students studied the content that they expected to see on tests, rather than pursuing their own learning goals. In response, the school continued the tests, but only as formative assessments: students' scores were no longer considered in grading or promotion decisions.

In addition, the 'Progress test' was introduced (van der Vleuten and Verwijnen, 1990) as a comprehensive examination used for promotion decisions. Four times each year, a new form of the test is administered to all students, across the six years of the medical school curriculum. Each test contains 250 to 300 items, based upon a fixed content outline covering basic biomedical, clinical and behavioural sciences. Because the exam is comprehensive, the direct relationship between the educational programme and test content is severed. Students are unable to prepare specifically for the test, individual study routes are not penalized, and students gain insight into their weaknesses and strengths through detailed profile scores. Unlike conventional course-related tests, where performance generally declines after a course ends, scores on progress tests rise as students advance through the curriculum.

Use of such comprehensive exams allows different study sequences, reinforcing the PBL emphasis on self-assessment of learning needs; the profile of scores can facilitate self-diagnosis of areas of strength and weakness, as long as the exams are sufficiently long and include an appropriate and representative sample of the domain to be learned. Moreover, the tests can provide a wealth of longitudinal information, both for individual students and for programme evaluation. If tests are too short or if too little of the content is appropriate for beginning students, sub-scores will not be reliable and will not provide an accurate index of performance in individual content areas. This led at least one problem-based programme to abandon the progress-testing approach (West *et al*, 1985).

Conclusions and recommendations

Instruments used for process-assessment are very closely linked to the problem-based approach and are structured to have a beneficial effect on student learning. However, most of the techniques are psychometrically suspect, and basing major promotion decisions on scores from process measures should be avoided. At the very least, other assessment information should be used as well.

In contrast, techniques for outcome-oriented assessment are well developed and have many psychometric advantages. As long as tests focus on application of knowledge in problem-solving situations, and undesirable influences on student learning are avoided, these techniques can play an important role in problem-based programmes. MCQ-based tests, in particular, if constructed and used appropriately, can provide an effective and efficient method for making promotion decisions and for identifying patterns of student strength and weakness.

References

Boud, D (1989) The role of self-assessment in student grading, *Assessment and Evaluation in Higher Education*, 14, 20–30.

Bouhuijs, P, van der Vleuten, C and van Luyk, S (1987) The OSCE as a part of a systematic skills training approach, *Medical Teacher*, 9, 183–191.

Case, S (in press) Assessment truths that we hold as self-evident and their implications, in A J J A Scherpbier, C P M Van der Vleuten, J J Rethans and A S W Van der Steeg. *Advances in Medical Education*. Dordrecht, The Netherlands: Kluwer Academic Publishers.

Case, S and Swanson, D (1993) Extended matching items: a practical alternative to free-response questions, *Teaching and Learning in Medicine*, 5, 2, 107–115.

Case, S and Swanson, D (1996) *Constructing Written Test Questions for the Basic and Clinical Sciences*. Philadelphia: National Board of Medical Examiners.

Case, S, Swanson, D and Ripkey, D (1994) Comparison of items in five-option and extended matching format for assessment of diagnostic skills, *Academic Medicine*, 69, 10, S1–S6.

de Graaf, E, Post, G and Drop, M (1987) Validation of a measure of clinical problem-solving. *Medical Education*, 21, 213–218.

Elstein, A, Shulman, L and Sprafka, S (1978) *Medical Problem Solving*. Cambridge, MA: Harvard University Press.

Entwistle, N (1981) *Styles of Learning and Teaching*. Chichester: Wiley.

Feletti, G (1980) Reliability and validity studies on modified essay questions, *Journal of Medical Education*, 49, 666–672.

Feletti, G, Saunders, N and Smith, A (1983) Comprehensive assessment of final-year medical student performance based on undergraduate programme objectives, *The Lancet*, 34–37.

Frederiksen, N (1984) The real test bias: influences of testing on teaching and learning, *American Psychologist*, 39, 193–202.

McGuire, C (1987) Written methods for assessing clinical competence. In I Hart and R Harden (eds) *Further Developments in Assessing Clinical Competence*. Montreal: Heal Publications.

McGuire, C and Solomon, C (1976) *Construction and Use of Written Simulations*. Chicago, IL: The Psychological Corporation.

Newble, D and Jaeger, K (1983) The effect of assessments and examinations on the learning of medical students, *Medical Education*, 17, 165–171.

Newble, D, Baxter, A and Elmslie, R (1979) A comparison of multiple choice and free response tests in examinations of clinical competence, *Medical Education*, 13, 263–268.

Norcini, J, Diserens, D, Day, S, Cebul, R, Schwartz, S, Beck, L, Webster, G, Schnabel, T and Elstein, A (1990) Free-response formats for evaluating clinical judgement, *Academic Medicine*, 65:9 (supplement), S41–S42.

Norman, G (1988) Problem-solving skills, solving problems and problem-based learning. *Medical Education*, 22, 279–286.

Norman, G, Swanson, D and Case, S (1996) Conceptual and methodological issues in studies comparing assessment formats, *Teaching and Learning in Medicine*, 8, 4, 208–216.

Norman, G, Allery, L, Berkson, L *et al* (1989) Research in the psychology of clinical reasoning: implications for assessment. *Proceedings of Cambridge Conference IV*. Cambridge: Cambridge University Press.

Page, G and Bordage, G (1995) The Medical Council of Canada's key features project: A more valid written examination of clinical decision-making skills, *Academic Medicine*, 70, 2, 104–105.

Painvin, C, Neufeld, V, Norman, G, Walker, I and Whelan, G (1979). The triple jump exercise: a structured measure of problem-solving and self-directed learning. *Proceedings of the 18th Annual Conference on Research in Medical Education*, 73–77.

Pickering, G (1979) Against multiple choice questions. *Medical Teacher*, 1, 84–86.

Powles, A, Wintrip, N, Neufeld, V, Wakefield, J, Coates, G and Burrows, J (1981) The triple-jump exercise: further studies of an evaluative technique. *Proceedings of the 20th Annual Conference on Research in Medical Education*, 73–79.

Rezler, A (1989) Self-assessment in problem-based groups, *Medical Teacher*, 11, 151–156.

Ripkey, R, Case, S and Swanson, D (1996) A new item format for assessing aspects of clinical competence, *Academic Medicine*, 71, 10, S14–S16.

Shulman, L and Keislar, E (1966) *Learning by Discovery: A Critical Appraisal*. Chicago, IL: Rand-McNally.

Swanson, D (1987) A measurement framework for performance-based tests. In I Hart and R Harden (eds) *Further Developments in Assessing Clinical Competence*. Montreal: Heal Publications.

Swanson, D B and Case, S M (1992) Trends in written assessment: A strangely biased perspective. In R Harden, I Hart and H Mulholland (eds) *Approaches to Assessment of Clinical Competence*. Norwich: Page Brothers, 38–53.

Swanson, D, Norcini, J and Grosso, L (1987) Assessment of clinical competence: written and computer-based simulations, *Assessment and Evaluation in Higher Education*, 12, 220–246.

Swanson, D, Norman, G and Linn, R (1995) Performance-based assessment: Lessons from the health professions, *Educational Researcher*, 24, 5, 5–11, 35.

van der Vleuten, C, and Swanson, D (1990) Assessment of clinical skills with standardized patients: state of the art, *Teaching and Learning in Medicine*, 2, 2, 58–76.

van der Vleuten, C and Verwijnen, G (1990) A system for student assessment. In C van der Vleuten and W Wijnen (eds) *Problem-Based Learning: Perspectives from the Maastricht Approach*. Amsterdam: Thesis-publ.

van der Vleuten, C, van Luyk, S and Beckers, A (1989) A written test as an alternative to performance testing, *Medical Education*, 23, 97–107.

Veloski, J, Rabinowitz, H and Robeson, M (1988) Cueing in multiple choice questions: a reliable, valid and economical solution. *Proceedings of the 27th Annual Conference on Research in Medical Education*, 195-200. Washington DC: Association of American Medical Colleges.

Webb, E, Campbell, D, Schwartz, R and Sechrest, L (1966) *Unobtrusive Measures: Nonreactive Research in the Social Sciences*. Chicago, IL: Rand McNally.

West, D, Umland, B and Lucero, S (1985) Evaluating student performance. In A Kaufman (ed) *Implementing Problem-Based Medical Education*. New York: Springer.

Chapter 29

Learning from the Assessment of Problem Solving

David Dathe, Kathleen O'Brien, Georgine Loacker
and **Mary Georgia Matlock**

When we began the educational programme, which we have had in place at Alverno College since 1973, PBL was not our aim. We sought to provide students with an environment that would assist them to use knowledge as they develop it. Since that time, our students are required, as a basis for advancing and graduating, to develop and demonstrate abilities in a context of whatever discipline or profesional field they are studying. The abilities include problem solving, among others like communication and aesthetic response (Alverno College Faculty, 1989).

Unlike PBL, where problems organize the course and/or curriculum, in our programme the abilities central to a given area of study do the organizing. Like PBL, at the design stage our faculty build into the learning situation the need for whatever concepts and abilities they consider essential to practice in the field. However, students do not always begin their learning with a problem. Some faculty still consider it important and pedagogically sound for students to begin their learning with some concepts before working with actual situations, primarily because of the necessity of beginning where students are and because of varied learning styles that need expanding and gradual diversifying. In their teaching our faculty carefully consider this question in regard to the nature of each ability, which they approach in an explicit pedagogical sequence in terms of specific levels for the students. Through their academic programme students are assessed on the development of the identified abilities and time is provided for practice of these abilities at all levels.

In working out the implementation of the programme, we have gradually made explicit its underlying principles and their implications for our practice (Alverno College Faculty, 1985). We began articulating a theory out of our practice, which in turn keeps informing further practice. For example, the more we saw how self-assessment develops over time and how it makes an important contribution to a student's development of autonomy as a learner, the more we found strategies for building it into the curriculum as a developing ability (Loacker *et al*, 1986). In the process of inferring principles and putting them into practice, one thing we see happening is the ongoing identification of areas in the curriculum and specific contexts where a form of PBL is functioning or would enhance the learning situation if it were. This is hardly surprising, since some of the major conceptual elements of our programme are also those of PBL: contextualization, integration, inquiry skills, and self-directed learning, although we organize them in a different framework. The main point of this chapter, therefore, is to show how, through ongoing evaluation of actual student performance, faculty can develop principles by which they can improve their practice while they improve the theory that informs it. We will also show how, in our case at least, these principles lead, in appropriate contexts, to approaches like that of PBL.

Improving our approaches to learning through research: faculty involvement

Through a study of student performance and how faculty-designed learning experiences and assessments elicit those performances, we continually learn what makes best pedagogical sense. This kind of study is one focus of the group of faculty who are members of what we call the Problem Solving Department. This is one of eight departments – one for each corresponding ability – that are composed of those faculty from varied discipline departments who are interested in the development and evaluation of learning and assessment strategies for the ability they represent.

It has been the particular aim of the Problem Solving Department to study student performances to determine how learning experiences and assessments can be improved. For the past two years we focused attention on the courses in the disciplines that most frequently offered learning experiences and assessments for problem-solving ability.

These included courses in psychology, social science, the natural sciences, business and nursing. We made some important discoveries (Loacker and Jensen, 1988). Most of the students had previously shown that they were able to identify the stages in the scientific method when asked to name them in the abstract. They could also list some of the important assumptions and limitations. When they listened to an actual research report, however, they often could not accurately match the appropriate stage of the process with the actual activity of the researcher.

We found that students had this same difficulty on a general assessment designed for all students who had completed at least one semester at Alverno. In this assessment, students were asked to identify the stages that their group went through in solving a problem involving the selection of images of the United States to show to a group of visiting Russian engineering students. Again, though they could describe the process they used to generate their selection of images, they were frequently unable to relate their actions to problem-solving methods.

From our study of these assessments and of sample assessments from a number of other disciplines, we concluded that when the problem-solving process was embedded in the concrete context of a specific discipline, beginning students could not separate out a process from the specific procedure and details of the problem solver or researcher. Furthermore, we realized that students at this level were only beginning to be able to attend to the significant activities of the problem-solving process and needed more practice in carefully observing how expert problem solvers in different contexts or discipline areas move through the process. We also discovered that they learned the most when they involved themselves in a problem. Therefore we reconceptualized the learning framework at the early levels (*Faculty Handbook on Learning and Assessment*, 1986). We decided to focus first on the learners' ability to develop their own typical problem-solving approaches, not by learning theoretical approaches and then trying to observe them in action, but rather by delving into problems themselves with awareness and reflection.

Reconceptualized framework for developing problem-solving ability

Specifically, as a result of our ongoing study of how students learn problem solving, we rewrote the levels as follows:

Level 1

Previous definition: The student articulates and evaluates her own problem-solving process.

New definition: The student articulates her problem-solving process when given a problem by making explicit the steps she takes to approach the problem.

Level 2

Previous definition: The student defines problems or designs strategies to solve problems using discipline-related frameworks.

New definition: The student practises with discipline problem-solving frameworks to approach problems.

Level 3

Previous definition: Student selects or designs appropriate frameworks and strategies to solve problems.

New definition: Given a problem in a discipline, the student uses a discipline problem-solving framework to develop a solution.

Level 4

Previous definition: The student implements a solution and evaluates the problem solving process she used.

New definition: The student independently examines, selects, uses and evaluates various approaches to develop solutions.

The result of this review of our problem-solving, teaching and assessment strategies by the Problem Solving Department led us to emphasize not only self-assessment but put the problem, embedded in its discipline context, at the focal point of our teaching-learning strategies as opposed to stressing the knowledge of a specific problem-solving process such as the scientific method.

Learning activities are now directed to developing the students' awareness of the attitudes, activities and thinking processes they each use as they solve less sophisticated problems in beginning level courses. Faculty have increased the use of logs, thinking-out-loud exercises, and other self-reflective activities. For instance, in the freshman-level integrated science course, students are now asked to design a simple experiment to test some aspect of the biological concepts they are learning, keep logs of the process they go through, and after implementing their test, and with the help of their instructor, evaluate the process they used for its effect on the test they designed.

One advantage of Alverno's inclusion of departments like the Problem Solving one and the overall administrative structure of the college is the ease with which curricula changes can be made. Because Problem Solving Department faculty took the leadership in researching our practice and worked with samples of assessments from faculty who teach and assess this ability, implementation of the sequence changes into the curriculum was almost immediate.

Placing our emphasis on self-assessment in the student's beginning problem-solving work in a discipline has meant that we needed to put the solution of a problem embedded in its context at the starting point of the learning process. Thus two conceptual elements of PBL, contextualization and self-directed learning, receive increased initial emphasis in our revised curriculum. Our practice of teaching learners how to self-assess their problem-solving abilities has also led to an emphasis on teaching our students how to determine what inquiry skills are their strengths and how to identify those that they need to develop. This practice has re-emphasized our efforts to teach students inquiry skills that are relevant to specific problem contexts, another important element of PBL.

The process of redefining the levels of problem solving was based on an exploration of the question of how problem solving was being taught across the disciplines. At the time, there were two issues we were aware of that faculty were having trouble with: first, distinguishing between levels 3 and 4, the intermediate levels of problem solving, and, second, understanding the application of the levels.

The basic difficulty was that the levels of problem solving, as then defined, seemed to 'carve up' a problem-solving process into various components and equate these components with levels. Yet we clearly saw that students were encountering a variety of problems at all levels. We realized that students were attempting a complete problem-solving process at all levels.

In redefining the problem solving levels, we worked within the institutional framework: Alverno's academic framework of levels and the developmental nature of the ability.

Primary sources for the revision process

We used three major sources in redefining the levels of problem solving. They are, in order of importance:

1. Our teaching practice. We are always analysing, reflecting and assessing what we are doing in the classroom. In fact, it was this reflection process (self-assessment) that prompted us to change the levels in the first place. We saw that we were not teaching the levels as they had been defined. (A strong case can be made that the majority of curriculum change arises out of our collaborative self-assessment of our teaching practice.)
2. Our understanding of the characteristics of a beginning (levels 1–2), developing (levels 3–4) and experienced (levels 5–6) problem solver. We devoted several meetings to brainstorming and discussing, in frank terms, the characteristics we saw in our students as beginning, developing and experienced problem solvers. Listing the specific characteristics allowed us to see clearly the developmental nature of problem-solving ability.
3. Literature research. After considering how we were teaching problem solving, we looked at the 'theory' of problem solving for additional insights. We developed a bibliography of all books relating to problem solving in Alverno's library. After reviewing several of these texts, each department member selected a variety of articles for other members to read. As a result, we each developed a personal library of problem-solving articles. Meetings were used to discuss and reflect on ideas developed from the readings. One of the most significant findings of the literature is that solving problems in discipline-specific ways helps students develop domain-specific knowledge – knowledge that may not transfer to other situations unless attention is given to more general heuristics (Perkins and Salomon, 1989). This and other such findings reinforced our practice of having students carefully self-assess their own approach and disciplinary approaches to solving different kinds of problems, comparing and contrasting across different situations. This literature review also led us to build in for the students more problem-solving experiences, in particular disciplines at all four levels of the ability, not just at the last two.

Three fundamental questions guided our work on redefining the levels:

□ Is there a general or generic problem-solving process applicable to every problem or is problem solving discipline-specific? Our teaching practice showed that different disciplines define and approach problems differently. Consequently, we looked at problem solving within a discipline framework.

□ What, if any, is *the* generic problem-solving process? The literature describes several problem-solving models. Our main concern in answering this question is whether a generic process can be split into components. We firmly believe that it cannot. Students attempt a rather complete problem-solving process immediately; the developmental nature of problem solving must lie somewhere else, not in simply progressing sequentially through a process.

□ What types of problems are there? The literature discusses two fundamental types of problem: well-structured and ill-structured. We saw that students encounter all types of problems at all levels of problem solving. In fact, some disciplines, such as social science, seem to have only 'messy' problems! Clearly it is impossible to relate the levels of problem solving to the types of problems encountered.

Two conclusions developed from our exploration of the above questions. First, students apply a complete problem-solving process (either generic or discipline-specific) to a problem whether they are beginning, developing or experienced problem solvers. Second, students encounter a variety of problems at all levels of problem solving. These two conclusions form the underlying basis of our redefinition of the levels.

Terminology

Three terms are used throughout the revision of the levels: approach, framework and strategy:

□ *Approach* is any or all parts of a generic problem-solving process. This may include: defining the problem, developing and selecting a strategy for solution, implementing the solution, and evaluating the process.

□ A *framework* is any disciplinary problem-solving process.

□ A *strategy* is a problem-solving plan. We view a problem-solving strategy as a subset of a framework. For example, in solving a problem in a discipline, a student may use a general framework (eg, the scientific method), but have a choice of several strategies (plans) within that framework to solve the problem.

Levels

The revised levels of problem solving represent our view of how students learn to solve problems and, consequently, how we teach students to do that.

Level 1   The student articulates her problem-solving process when given a problem by making explicit the steps she takes to approach the problem. At level 1 the student needs to be introduced to, and use appropriately, a problem-solving vocabulary. She is also introduced to a problem-solving process (either generic or discipline- or profession-specific).
Example from Instructional Syllabuses. Psychology 101/ General Psychology (Paul Smith): 'The purpose of this assignment is for you to demonstrate your ability to discuss and evaluate your own preferred processes for solving problems.'

Level 2   The student practises discipline or professional problem-solving frameworks to approach the problem(s). At level 2, the student develops a basic understanding of problem solving within a discipline by being presented with typical problems from within a discipline. This includes practising problem-solving frameworks within the course context, practising various strategies within a specific discipline framework, understanding problem definition in the context of the discipline, and using discipline problem-solving vocabulary.
Example from Instructional Syllabuses. A 136/Studio Art 2: Two-Dimensional Design (Nancy Lamers): 'You are able to discern in both structured and unstructured assignments what the problem is, and you are able to clearly state what your goal is. You are able to identify alternative strategies for problem solving and can defend your decision-making reasons. This means in this context that you demonstrate an ability to: 1) Identify the types of problems that are charac-

teristic of art making; 2) reformulate problems into smaller component parts; 3) create and visualize potential solutions; 4) interpret and redefine the problem.'

Example from Instructional Syllabuses. Psychology 101/General Psychology (Paul Smith): 'The purpose of this assignment is for you to demonstrate your understanding of how psychologists approach problem solving. You will apply your understanding in finding and summarizing research published in a professional psychological journal.'

At levels 1 and 2, ideally the problems should be solvable. If the students can arrive at an answer they are better able to articulate their problem-solving process and understand how a discipline framework is used to solve a problem. If this is not possible, the instructor should define under what conditions the problem will be considered solved.

Level 3 Given a problem in a discipline or profession, the student uses a discipline problem-solving framework to develop the solution(s).

The major difference between levels 2 and 3 is meta-cognition. At level 2, the instructor is demonstrating and explaining – and the student is practising – discipline problem-solving frameworks and strategies. At level 3, the student becomes more aware that she is a problem solver. Rather than practising a discipline problem-solving framework (level 2), she selects and uses discipline problem-solving frameworks and strategies. The student develops self-awareness as a problem solver, makes decisions among various frameworks, makes decisions among various strategies, questions the solution(s), and brings together analytic thinking and problem solving.

Example from Instructional Syllabuses. Education 225/Integrated Reading Curriculum 1 (Jackie Hass): 'Student selects or designs appropriate frameworks and strategies to solve problems.'

Level 4 The student independently examines, selects, uses and evaluates various approaches to develop solutions. The emphasis of level 4 is that the student independently chooses the framework and strategy she perceives to be most appropriate to develop solutions. She then evaluates her selections and problem solutions.

Example from Instructional Syllabuses. Biology 251/Microbiology (Leona Truchan): 'Problem solving, level 4 will be partially achieved using a problem-solving process to select and implement procedures that will lead to the identification of your unknown organism. You must be able to explain your problem-solving approach'.

Example from Instructional Syllabuses. Dance 340/Dance Composition and Performance 1 (Cate Deicher): 'You will invent, employ and evaluate problem-solving techniques as you work through the choreographic process. This will introduce you to choreography as a revisioning process and will involve such skills as deep listening, (consulting your intuition), risk taking, peer consultation and cooperation.'

Longitudinal research findings

Research by our Office of Research and Evaluation has told us that our students develop problem-solving ability to increasingly complex levels (Mentkowski and Doherty, 1987). Students attribute their development of that ability to their learning experiences at Alverno, which include primarily simulations, immersion in problems, performance assessments, internships, and other forms of learning by doing. We have also learned that such experiences have assisted them to become self-sustaining learners, to transfer abilities across settings, and to expand their repertory of ways of thinking. As in the investigations of the Problem Solving Department, the major source of these data has been the study of student performances, with the addition of their later performance after graduation. Performance has been one focus of our triangulated model for programme evaluation, including the longitudinal study that produced the above findings. Within these findings, we keep looking for other specifics that can tell us about learning patterns that can enable us to improve our teaching.

Future work

As we continue to study student performances, our concern now is how the changes in our framework will contribute to the students' beginning work in problem solving as an improved basis for more advanced work. For example, we will be carefully studying performances in programmes like business and management to examine the results of early immersion in problems accompanied by self-reflection and self-assessment.

Our long-term goals are to investigate other, more general, aspects of problem solving. In particular, we will pursue five questions:

☐ What role does prior knowledge and experience play in problem solving? Does this develop 'intuition'?
☐ How does creativity affect problem solving? Can creativity be taught? Assessed?
☐ How is problem solving in a group situation different from independent work?
☐ How does problem solving differ when the consequences are more 'real'?
☐ How can students become more aware of the moral dimensions of their problem solutions?

Our ongoing commitment to examine student performance across the curriculum constitutes our main means of finding better ways to assist students to develop problem-solving ability.

References

Alverno College Faculty (1985) *Assessment at Alverno College*, 2nd edn. Milwaukee, WI: Alverno Productions.

Alverno College Faculty (1989) *Liberal Learning at Alverno College*, 4th edn. Milwaukee, WI: Alverno Productions.

Faculty Handbook on Learning and Assessment (1986) Alverno College, Milwaukee, WI: Internal publication.

Loacker, G and Jensen, P (1988) The power of performance in developing problem solving and self assessment abilities. *Assessment and Evaluation in Higher Education*, 13, 128–150.

Loacker, G, Cromwell, L and O'Brien, K (1986) Assessment in higher education: to serve the learner. In C Adelman (ed) *Assessment in Higher Education: Issues and Contexts*. Washington DC: US Department of Education.

Mentkowski, M and Doherty, A (1987) *Careering after College: Establishing the Validity of Abilities Learned in College for Later Careering and Professional Performance*, 2nd edn. Milwaukee, WI: Alverno Productions.

Perkins, D N and Salomon, G (1989) Are cognitive skills context-bound? *Educational Researcher*, 18, 1, Jan–Feb.

Chapter 30

What Can We Learn From Programme Evaluation Studies in Medical Education?

Christel A Woodward

Evaluation of the outcomes of PBL is not a simple endeavour. Three papers that recently appeared in the medical education literature (Albanese and Mitchell, 1993; Berkson, 1993; Vernon and Blake, 1993), each reviewing a highly similar set of studies about PBL, came to quite different conclusions. The outcomes of their analyses ranged from a ringing endorsement of PBL (Vernon and Blake, 1993), through the suggestion that PBL (even given whole curriculum innovation) produces graduates who are indistinguishable from their traditional counterparts (Berkson, 1993), to concern that PBL may have adverse effects on the learner (Albanese and Mitchell, 1993). This chapter provides an overview of programme evaluation related to PBL and attempts to put these three reviews in perspective. It explores why this diversity of opinion regarding PBL exists and identifies substantive issues regarding programme evaluation of PBL curricula. It suggests that better theory and increased methodological rigour are needed to advance our efforts to evaluate PBL-based educational programmes and improve the educational process.

Defining problem-based learning

In order to evaluate PBL, first the necessary and sufficient conditions to classify a curriculum as PBL need to be identified. The invariants in any definition of PBL are that a set of problems is used to engage the

294

learner in the learning task and that discussion among learners occurs to identify the features of the problem, the areas in which they lack information needed to understand the nature of the problem and how it can best be approached and managed. The learners then engage in a variety of independent learning activities which help them explore the constructs, issues, theories and mechanisms involved in obtaining a deeper understanding of the problem and how it can be managed. The results of these learning activities are again brought to the group for further discussion to elaborate the problem and its implications.

Faculty have major responsibilities in the learning process, but their tasks differ significantly from their more traditional role. They must develop the problems used to ensure that issues, ideas, etc discussed are relevant to the overall learning objectives. They must facilitate group process. Finally, faculty other than tutors may act as expert resources and/or help ensure such resources are available for students to use.

How should PBL be evaluated?

The field of programme evaluation suggests that we review the objectives of the programme to decide how to assess outcomes. To establish the objectives of PBL, we must examine the reasons given by the 'founding fathers' at McMaster for designing such a curriculum which was a radical departure from their own medical education. Discussion with them indicates that they wished to make education more enjoyable for the learner. They sought to put the emphasis on learning rather than teaching by:

1. making the student an active partner in the learning process,
2. increasing the perceived relevance of what is being learned,
3. focusing more on conceptual or deep understanding than rote memorization, and
4. having less scheduled time in the curriculum.

In their deliberations about how to achieve these objectives, they noted that medicine had become a great deal more fun for them once they had moved beyond the initial education period, which had been largely lecture-based, and entered a phase of their education when learning centred upon the problems presented by patients. Relatively unschooled in education theory, these innovators decided to create a curriculum that mirrored the types of learning they had found most rewarding, which for them had mainly occurred in their postgraduate education and beyond. Not surprisingly, they decided to use patient problems as the cornerstone of curriculum planning.

They postulated that PBL might increase the problem-solving skills of the learner, make the curriculum more flexible and open to change, and allow integration of basic and clinical sciences education. Further, it might produce physicians who, because they learned around the problems that they encountered, would continue to seek out new information to solve problems that they encountered in practice and become 'lifelong, self-directed learners'. (For a more detailed account, see Spaulding and Cochrane, 1991.)

What is the evidence that PBL has met the goals set by its originators?

Although as programme evaluators we should include the many questions of stakeholders and be open to examining unintended effects of PBL, let us examine first the evidence relevant to assessing an over-riding goal of PBL: to put the emphasis on learning rather than teaching and thus make learning more enjoyable. All of the studies reviewed by Albanese and Mitchell (1993: 63) suggest 'that students generally perceive PBL environments in a positive light; certainly these curricula are not perceived as less humane'. Vernon and Blake (1993: 554), who formally developed effect size and vote counting procedures to categorize the studies that they reviewed, agree: 'No sample was found in which the students' attitudes did not favor PBL to some degree'. Some more recent studies not included in these reviews continue to concur with this assessment (Regan-Smith *et al*, 1994; Vasconez *et al*, 1993). Students in PBL curricula report spending far less of their time engaged in rote learning without conceptual understanding (Moore *et al*, 1990; Regan-Smith *et al*, 1994). An examination of the time formally scheduled with classes and labs for traditional curriculum and PBL students invariably finds that PBL students have more time to engage in self-initiated learning activities (Kaufman, 1985; Moore *et al*, 1990).

A final piece of evidence that PBL is more enjoyable comes from the satisfaction of the learners with their education. Satisfaction, however, can occur even when little learning has been achieved. Thus, greater satisfaction with the learning experience among PBL learners when learners had had an opportunity to assess PBL and traditional curricula in light of their subsequent education and current professional activities provides more compelling evidence than satisfaction during or immediately after the experience. In a recent survey of all practising Ontario-based members of the College of Family Physicians of Canada who were certified between 1989 and 1991 and graduated from an Ontario medical school (N=320), significant differences were noted among physicians' satisfaction with 'the extent to which medical school has prepared you for practice' (Woodward *et al*, 1994). PBL graduates (McMaster) were much more likely to report being satisfied or very satisfied (65.7 per cent compared to 39.7 per cent) and fewer (10.4 per cent) were dissatisfied than graduates of the other four schools (25.5 per cent). This question, buried among other questions, forms one of 16 items of a Professional Satisfaction Scale for physicians developed at the Rand Corporation (McGlynn, 1988).

But, meeting this original goal may not be sufficient; the justifications given for using PBL methods should also hold up to careful scrutiny. Here, the evidence about PBL becomes much more mixed. How these objectives are operationalized and measured is much more varied. In fact, one rationalization, that PBL increases problem-solving skills, is not likely to be true. Both in medicine and other fields, educators no longer believe in the existence of a general problem-solving skill that can be taught and learned (Norman and Schmidt, 1992), a notion that was popular among educators in the 1960s. The importance of content-specificity, the variability in problem-solving performance across problems (which is related to the extent of prior knowledge of the specific problem area) is now clear (Elstein *et al*, 1978). There is no evidence that any curriculum enhances problem-solving skills independently of knowledge acquisition.

Measurement difficulties face evaluators who try to operationally define constructs important to assessing claims about potential benefits of PBL. This will be illustrated using studies that have attempted to measure 'lifelong learning'. Some investigators have reasoned that if PBL is to create lifelong learners, we must first show that students actually exhibit self-directed learning skills during their education (to assume that they are acquiring such skills). They studied the library behaviour of students in PBL and traditional curricula or tracks (Anderson *et al*, 1990; Blumberg and Michael, 1991; Marshall *et al*, 1993; Saunders *et al*, 1985). The range and number of resources consulted by PBL students is larger than that of students in traditional curricula who are more likely to use course notes, syllabuses and assigned texts for study purposes. Such studies have been criticized for assuming that students successful in gaining medical school entry have not already acquired self-directed learning skills (Berkson, 1993). Further, most PBL programmes offer their new students short courses in how to use the library. Could such a course alone be responsible for any difference seen? (See Berkson, 1993, for an elaboration of these arguments.) However, the weight of the available evidence suggests 'a greater degree of independent study in the PBL programs than in traditional programs' (Vernon and Blake, 1993: 554).

Two studies, involving physicians after they had entered practice, have also tried to address 'lifelong learning'. One study observed no difference in the continuing education (CE) activities graduates of a traditional medical school (Ottawa) and a PBL school (McMaster) using survey methods (Tolnai, 1991). The graduates participated equivalently in CE. Here, the question becomes whether the amount of formal CE activities is the best way, or even a good way, to operationally define a lifelong learner. Will a lifelong learner do more or less CE? It can be argued either way. If PBL graduates do less, it may be because they use more informal CE mechanisms or because they do CE more efficiently. If they do more, it may be because they are more motivated to keep current in a number of areas. Even if they spend the same amount of time, the crucial questions remain: what prompts CE? How well do their search strategies work? Does CE lead to behaviour change?

A second study's operational definition of lifelong learners was: physicians who display up-to-date medical knowledge in areas of medicine in which practice has changed since their medical graduation (Shin *et al*, 1991). It compared primary care physicians who had graduated from a PBL school (McMaster) and a traditional school (Toronto) five to ten years earlier. The McMaster graduates were more familiar with new developments in the management of hypertension. While we are unlikely to quibble with this definition of a PB learner, the area of medicine chosen for study (hypertension) raised some questions about generalizability of study findings. Cardiovascular research is one of the fields where McMaster University's medical school faculty has distinguished itself. Would similar results be likely if other medical conditions were examined? Do the results need to be consistent across all fields? Further, the reasons for the effect may also be more complex. We know that McMaster graduates display a higher interest in providing education to learners as part of their professional activities (Ferrier and Woodward, 1987). Even if they are more up-to-date than a comparison group, is being up-to-date a *direct* result of enhanced lifelong learning skills or is it an indirect effect, mediated by being more involved in teaching? Clearly, operationally defining and measuring a relatively simple construct, 'lifelong learner', is a major challenge. Deciding whether to attribute any differences in knowledge, if found, to lifelong learning skills or propensities must also be done with caution.

A mixed review for PBL is also provided by studies that attempt to address whether PBL curricula allow better integration of basic and clinical science learning. One study (Patel *et al*, 1991; 1993) asked PBL (McMaster) and conventional school students (McGill) to solve a clinical problem and then integrate three passages of relevant basic science knowledge in their explanations. PBL students advanced more causal explanations and were better able to integrate clinical with basic science knowledge at all educational levels. Yet, because they made more clinical inferences (when in some cases the other group of students made none), a higher proportion of the hypotheses made by PBL students were incorrect.

In a second study of PBL and conventional curriculum effects on knowledge integration (Boshuisen *et al*, 1990), pre-clinical students from two Dutch medical schools were asked to explain how a specific metabolic deficiency and a specific disease might be related. An expert group of biochemists and internists also completed the task. The PBL students and biochemists usually first explored the problem's biochemical aspects and later linked these to its clinical aspects. A more memory-based approach was noted among conventional curriculum students and internists. They tended to search their memories for a direct answer to the question. This latter strategy worked less well, producing more errors.

The two studies, taken together, suggest PBL students tend to offer more casual explanations about pathophysiological process underlying disease which tie together basic science and clinical knowledge. Why overall errors in problem solution were higher for the PBL group in one instance and lower in the other is unclear. It may relate to the problems chosen or other features of measurement. The difference observed also may be a product of the way PBL and conventional education are operationalized in the curricula examined. Replication of these studies in different settings with a greater number of problems is required to sort out whether the finding is consistent.

Why does PBL work?

An interesting line of research that is gaining popularity involves examining 'how come' PBL works. Efforts are made to understand how PBL relates to theories of learning. Three studies suggest PBL promotes long-term (three months to two years later) recall of information studied (Coulsen, 1983; Eisenstadt *et al*, 1990; Tans *et al*, 1986). The mechanisms by which this may occur are unclear. The immediate knowledge of PBL students was somewhat less in all studies. Eisenstadt *et al* (1990) invited randomly selected students to participate in a PBL course rather than a lecture-based hematology-transfusion medicine segment of a second-year pathophysiology course. Over a three-year period, 59 students participated in the PBL course. PBL students, consenters to PBL and non-consenters, did not differ in socio-demographic characteristics or prior performance. In the end-of-course objective examination, PBL students scored lower; but, their performance remained near their original level two years later, by which time the performance of the control group had declined and matched the PBL group.

Similar results are reported by Tans *et al* (1986), who studied physiotherapy students randomly assigned to PBL or lectures for a muscle physiology course. PBL students' scores were significantly lower on a multiple-choice exam directly after the course. When asked to recall core knowledge gained in the course in a free-recall situation six months later, PBL students remembered up to five times more concepts than the lecture group. Coulsen (1983) reported somewhat poorer initial performance by PBL students, but a more precipitous drop-off in information retained among conventionally taught students. A study by Martensen *et al* (1985), has also been used to suggest better retention for PBL. However, the way PBL was put into operation does not meet the usual definition of PBL. Further, in measuring longer-term recall, length of time since exposure to the material was confounded with type of instruction.

Two possible reasons for poorer immediate recall by PBL students are posited. The phenomenon observed may be a measurement artifact; it is difficult to test exactly what students have learned in PBL because they may venture far from the 'prescribed' curriculum which lectures cover more reliably. On the other hand, PBL students may learn less but retain more. Using measures that allow free recall of information (rather than constraining recall to multiple-choice or other structured questions) both initially and later would provide information to help decide which of these hypotheses, if either, is correct.

Norman and Schmidt (1992) describe the state of current knowledge about how memory is enhanced and suggest aspects of PBL which may be responsible for improved long-term recall. They note that *activation of prior knowledge facilitates the subsequent processing of new information* and suggest that small-group discussion of a problem, a feature of PBL, may be a powerful method of activating relevant prior knowledge. Yet, evidence is lacking that small-group discussion provides a better or more efficient way of activating prior knowledge than methods often used by lecturers. They also note that *elaboration of knowledge at the time of learning enhances subsequent retrieval*. Tutorial discussion and use of knowledge to solve problems may facilitate knowledge elaboration in a PBL curriculum. Yet, such activities as note-taking, answering the occasional question, preparing for examinations, etc, prevalent in conventional curricula, also may facilitate knowledge elaboration. Finally, they note that *similar context facilitates recall*. Here, at least on the surface, PBL should provide an advantage. However, how discrete aspects of PBL may promote better long-term recall than memory prompts used by teaching in conventional curricula has not yet been studied. We are far from being able to illuminate how the 'black box' of PBL works.

Norman and Schmidt also hypothesize that PBL may facilitate the formation of a larger number of mental images (instances) of prototypical problem situations in medicine, essential to the competent diagnostician. PBL students may develop a larger repertoire of patterns which they can use to assist them in the solution of new (similar) problems. Much of problem solving is actually pattern recognition. It is rare that the expert must resort to reasoning from basic principles, although when called for by the situation, experts do so with facility. Their hypothesis has yet to be tested.

Goal-free PBL evaluation

Not all studies of the outcomes of PBL focus on seeing whether or not PBL has met its original goals or try to analyse the way PBL works. In the spirit of Scriven (1974), who advocated goal-free evaluation, studies have been done using either (a) measures that exist and are considered benchmarks by which conventional curricula measure themselves or (b) other measures that might illuminate difference, or lack thereof, between PBL and conventional curricula not previously considered.

Perhaps because these are the easiest types of studies to mount, a number of investigators have examined PBL and conventional curricula or tracks, using examinations required for graduation or licensure. Berkson's (1993) review suggests no difference is seen in academic achievement as measured by such tests. Albanese and Mitchell (1993) separated basic science knowledge from clinical knowledge in their review. They found no consistency across studies (and perhaps implementations of PBL) regarding whether or not PBL students differed from conventional students in basic science knowledge, although when a difference was found, it often favoured the conventional curriculum. Vernon and Blake (1993), whose review also separated consideration of basic science knowledge from clinical knowledge, report that greater heterogeneity in basic science test results exists for PBL curricula than for conventional ones. They suggest that implementation differences, rather than PBL itself, are responsible for any difference (positive or negative) in basic science knowledge. Both reviews concur that there is a slight trend for PBL curricula students to outperform conventional students on clinical examinations.

Others have sought information about the career choices or practice patterns of their medical school's graduates (eg, Ferrier and Woodward, 1987; Kaufman *et al*, 1989; Woodward *et al*, 1990) and examined the output of a particular medical school. Often, the effects of PBL cannot be isolated from effects of major differences in admission criteria, types of clinical placements or predominant philosophy of care that are also present. Caution must be observed not to attribute all differences to PBL.

The results of some studies have been erroneously used in arguments about the effects of PBL when it is more likely that the effects found are due to selection and philosophy of care differences. For example, one study (Woodward *et al*, 1990) showed that McMaster graduates who are primary care physicians, compared to their matched contemporaries from other Ontario medical schools, bill the health care system less, see fewer patients, do fewer minor assessments (very quick visits) and more psychotherapy and are less likely to practise in emergency rooms. They appear to spend more time with their patients. Understanding illness in the context of their patients' lives, the role of psycho-social issues in health and well-being, and the primacy of caring in primary care medicine were emphasized throughout their medical education at McMaster. If spending more time with people to understand the context in which their symptoms present and to provide a listening ear leads to better or worse health outcomes in the long run, or is more efficient or inefficient health care delivery, can be debated. However, this debate is not about PBL's effects because not all PBL programmes emphasize this philosophy of care.

Other questions regarding PBL that may be of interest to stakeholders

Little empirical work has been done to examine whether or not the contents of PBL curricula are easier to alter than in conventional curricula. The notion has face validity. Change in a PBL curriculum may be as easy as changing the relative emphasis given to identifiable issues in a problem, adding a new wrinkle to a problem or substituting one problem for another. Cost savings may result during the maintenance and updating phase of a PBL curriculum. Answers to this question may be of interest to faculty and administrators.

Three other potential longer-term outcomes of PBL may be of interest to faculty and students. First, PBL may make the transition from education to practice easier or less stressful. The evidence to support this idea is scanty yet compelling enough for me to want to take a look at this issue. As a faculty adviser to medical students who grapple with PBL, I have noted that they initially complain that they never know if/when they know enough about a topic. Within the first year of PBL, these students develop their own comfort levels about information needed related to a problem. About two years ago, while conducting a focus group of family physicians, then five to eight years in practice, about their early practice years, several physicians mentioned their initial anxiety about not knowing enough to practise effectively. The two McMaster graduates in the group demurred. For them, this type of anxiety had faded within the first year of medical school. Is this observation generalizable to other PBL students and schools? No information is available.

Second, the interpersonal learning that occurs in small PBL tutorial groups is likely to be an underrated aspect of PBL. The numerous interactions with peers in work groups which occur during their medical education may refine PBL students' communication skills and make them more aware of how they react to others and how people react to them. One PBL graduate, when asked what was the most important learning that she attributed directly to PBL, said that it helped her learn to get along with people she did not like, an important skill. Research that probes such interpersonal learning is needed.

Finally, PBL creates a more egalitarian learner/teacher relationship than is typical in conventional curricula. Does this have an impact on the kinds of relationship PBL-educated physicians form with their patients? No evidence is available, but the question is important.

Conclusions

The educational experience that PBL provides is different from conventional education and is often valued more highly by learners and teachers. An understanding of how a PBL curriculum facilitates learning, what kinds of learning are best facilitated and if and how such a curriculum produces longer-lasting effects remain on the programme evaluation agenda. The search for lasting effects is difficult, given the crudeness of our measuring devices, the passing of time and number of confounding intervening variables (events) that have occurred (Friedman *et al*, 1990). Further, the ability of bright people to learn what they need to know despite any curriculum cannot be discounted. These factors add to the challenge facing programme evaluators. Yet, an important and large research agenda remains if we are to understand what PBL does and does not do, and how come it does what it does. The answers to the questions posed are likely to be complex. They are unlikely to emerge from a single study or site and require greater cooperation among education researchers across different curricula. While looking for consistency of evidence from a variety of studies, evaluators should carefully examine and learn from inconsistencies in the evidence which may help refine our theories and sharpen our questions.

Acknowledgement

This chapter is based on a previous paper by the same author entitled 'Problem-based learning in medical education: developing a research agenda' that appeared in *Advances in Health Sciences Education*, 1996, 1, 83–94.

References

Albanese, M A and Mitchell, S (1993) Problem-based learning: A review of literature on its outcomes and implementation issues, *Academic Medicine*, 68, 1, 52–81.

Anderson, S, Camp, M G and Philp, J R (1990) Library utilization by medical students in a traditional or problem-based curriculum. In W Bender, R J Hiemstra, A Scherpbier and R Zwierstra (eds) *Teaching and Assessing Clinical Competence*. Groningen, The Netherlands: Boekwerk Publications, 77–80.

Berkson, L (1993) Problem-based learning: Have the expectations been met? *Academic Medicine*, 68, 10, S79–S88.

Blumberg, P and Michael, J A (1991) The development of self directed learning behaviours in a partially teacher-centred, problem-based learning curriculum, *Teaching and Learning in Medicine*, 4, 3–8.

Boshuisen, H P, Schmidt, H G and Wassamer, I (1990) 'Curriculum style and the integration of biomedical and clinical knowledge'. Paper presented at the Second International Symposium on Problem Based Learning, Yokyakarta, Indonesia.

Coulsen, R L (1983) Problem-based student-centred learning of the cardiovascular system using the problem-based learning module (PBLM), *Physiologist*, 26, 220–224.

Eisenstadt, R S, Barry, W E and Glanz, K (1990) Problem-based learning: Cognitive retention and cohort traits of randomly selected participants and decliners. In *Research in Medical Education*. 1990 Proceedings of the 29th Annual Conference (M B Anderson, compiler). Washington, DC: AAMC, S11–S12.

Elstein, A S, Shulman, L S and Sprafka, S A (1978) *Medical Problem Solving: An Analysis of Clinical Reasoning*. Cambridge, MA: Harvard University Press.

Ferrier, B M and Woodward, C A (1987) Career choices of McMaster University medical graduates and contemporary Canadian medical graduates, *Canadian Medical Association Journal*. 136, 39–44.

Friedman, C P, deBliek, R, Greer, D S, Mennin, S P, et al (1990) Charting the winds of change: Evaluating innovative medical curricula, *Academic Medicine*, 65, 8–14.

Kaufman, A (ed) (1985) *Implementing Problem-Based Medical Education: Lessons from successful innovations*, New York: Springer.

Kaufman, A, Mennin, S, Waterman, R, Duban, S et al (1989) The New Mexico experiment: educational innovation and institutional change, *Academic Medicine*, 64, 285–294.

McGlynn, E (1988) Physicians' job satisfaction: Its measurement and use as an indicator of system performance. Unpublished doctoral dissertation. Santa Monica, CA: Rand Graduate School.

Marshall, J G, Fitzgerald, D, Busby, L and Heaton, G (1993) Study of library use in problem-based and traditional medical curricula, *Bulletin of the Medical Library Association*, 81, 299–305.

Martensen, D, Eriksson, H and Ingelman-Sundberg, M (1985) Medical chemistry: Evaluation of active and problem-oriented teaching methods, *Medical Education*, 19, 34–42.

Moore, G T, Black, S and Mitchell, R (1990) A randomized trial evaluating the impact of the New Pathway Curriculum at Harvard Medical School. Report to the Fund for the Improvement of Post-Secondary Education. Cambridge, MA: Harvard Medical School.

Norman, G R and Schmidt, H G (1992) The psychological basis of problem-based learning: A review of the evidence, *Academic Medicine*, 67, 557–565.

Patel, V L, Groen, G J and Norman, G R (1991) Effects of conventional and problem-based medical curricula on problem-solving, *Academic Medicine*, 66, 380–389.

Patel, V L, Groen, G J and Norman, G R (1993) Reasoning and instruction in medical curricula, *Cognition and Instruction*, 10, 335–378.

Regan-Smith, M, Obenshain, S, Woodward, C, Richards, B, Zeitz, H and Small, P, Jr (1994) Rote learning in medical school, *Journal of the American Medical Association*, 17, 1380–1381.

Saunders, K, Northup, D and Mennin, S (1985) The library in a problem-based curriculum. In A Kaufman (ed) *Implementing Problem-Based Medical Education: Lessons From Successful Innovations*, New York: Springer, 71–88.

Scriven, M (1974) Pros and cons about goal-free evaluations. In W J Popham (ed) *Evaluation in Education: Current Applications*, Berkeley, CA: McCutchan.

Shin, J H, Haynes, R B and Johnston, M (1991) The effect of a problem-based self-directed undergraduate education on life-long learning, *Clinical Investigative Medicine*, 14, A82.

Spaulding, W B and Cochrane, J (1991) *Revitalizing Medical Education: McMaster Medical School, The Early Years 1965–1974*. Philadelphia: BC Decker, 27–34.

Tans, T W, Schmidt, H G, Schade-Hoogeveen, B E J and Gijselaers, W H (1986) Sturing van her Onderswijsleer-proces Door Model van Problemen: Een Veldexperiment (Directing the learning process by means of problems: A field experiment), *Tijdschrift voor Onderwijs Research*, 11, 35–46.

Tolnai, S (1991) Continuing medical education and career choice among graduates of problem-based and traditional curricula, *Medical Education*, 25, 414–420.

Vasconez, H C, Donnelly, M B, Mayo, P and Schwartz, R W (1993) Student perceptions of the effectiveness of a problem-based surgery curriculum, *Academic Medicine*, 68, S28–S30.

Vernon, D T A and Blake, R L (1993) Does problem-based learning work? A meta-analysis of evaluative research, *Academic Medicine*, 68, 550–563.

Woodward, C A, Cohen, M, Ferrier, B M and Williams, A P (1994) The relative importance of undergraduate and postgraduate education to the practice decisions and attitudes of young family physicians practicing in Ontario. ACMC Medical Resources Conference, Vancouver, April 24 also Hamilton, Ont.: McMaster University Centre for Health Economics and Policy Analysis (CHEPA) Working Series paper.

Woodward, C A, Ferrier, B M, Cohen, M and Goldsmith, A (1990) A comparison of the practice patterns of general practitioners and family physicians graduating from McMaster and other Ontario Medical Schools, *Teaching and Learning in Medicine*, 2, 79–88.

Part VI
Beyond Problem-based Learning

Introduction

The preceding chapters have provided an overview of the wide range of practices in problem-based learning. They bear witness to the creativity and dedication of teachers in the ingenious ways in which they have been introduced, the rejuvenated forms of implementation, and the painstaking methods of assessing students' competence. Many more issues have been raised than resolved, adding a mischievous twist to the term 'problem-based' curriculum.

All these are issues within the overall framework of problem-based learning where much fruitful development is still occurring. Rather than leave the book on this point, though, we wanted to look beyond the present stage of development to where professional education might be headed in the light of the substantial impetus given by the problem-based learning movement. Is there an area beyond problem-based learning which we can meaningfully discuss?

Our final three authors represent a perspective which can be regarded as that of interested observers of the problem-based learning scene. All have been involved in major innovations in professional education, two of whom (Richard Bawden and John Drinan) have wrought a revolution in agricultural education in Australia. They are committed to the improvement of professional education, but do not have a personal stake in problem-based learning.

Colin Coles challenges us to consider whether problem-based learning is the best way to arrange a curriculum to provide the kind of learning required for professional practice. He believes that important work has been done by the proponents of problem-based learning and that many versions of a problem-based approach are effective. However, he is also of the view that problem-based learning is not the only, or even perhaps the most desirable, way to go. From his analysis of research on student learning and his experience of innovation at the University of Southampton, he has developed a model which can be used to underpin not only problem-based learning, but other curricular arrangements. He identifies the educational conditions necessary for effective learning and explores ways in which these can be manifest in course designs.

Richard Bawden has been involved in the conceptualizing of new approaches to the enterprise of agriculture and agricultural education from a perspective of experiential learning in a systemic context (Bawden *et al*, 1984; Bawden, 1985). He is concerned about dividing the world into 'problems' to be solved. The focusing of students' attention on relatively straightforward problems may represent a diversion away from a more complex and potentially more important set of issues. He emphasizes the notion of situation improvement as the organizing concept. This idea, from soft systems theory (Checkland, 1981), prompts one to see the solving of problems as not the central issue and one which in the long term may prove counterproductive. There is even a hint of the view that this may also not be ethically defensible. With his former colleague, John Drinan, he believes that he is a co-learner with his students and does not assume that the curriculum can be either defined unilaterally by teachers or be fully knowable to the extent that it can be exhaustively specified. This is a profoundly disturbing notion from an instructional design perspective which calls into question much of the technology of problem-based learning.

Finally, John Drinan points to the dangers of the mechanical application of problem-based learning strategies through the over-prescription of problems and methods for dealing with them. 'Problem' implies reactivity and a mind-set which encourages active intervention to satisfy the needs of the practitioner as much as that of the problem situation (or patient in medical terms). For example, it might be questioned whether a problem-based view is the most suitable for dealing with preventative medicine which eschews the idea of treatment of individuals or those aspects of health care concerned with caring. He sees problem-based learning as a sub-set of experiential learning and plots an area of interest which moves beyond what he sees to be the limits of the former strategies, towards a more holistic conception of knowledge and learning; this moves us to the realm of a self-critical profession which is intimately in touch with the unity of the world.

References

Bawden, R J (1985) Problem-based learning: an Australian perspective, in Boud, D (ed) *Problem-Based Learning in Education for the Professions*, Sydney: Higher Education Research and Development Society of Australasia, 43–57.

Bawden, R J, Macadam, R D, Packham, R G and Valentine, I (1984) Systems thinking and practices in the education of agriculturalists, *Agricultural Systems*, 13, 205–225.

Checkland, P B (1981) *Systems Thinking, Systems Practice*, Chichester: John Wiley.

Chapter 31

Is Problem-based Learning the Only Way?

Colin Coles

'And what is the use of a book,' thought Alice
'without pictures or conversations.'
(Lewis Carroll, *Alice in Wonderland*)

This chapter will take a somewhat oblique and challenging look at problem-based learning. The conclusion will be that problem-based learning is not the only way to arrange a curriculum to promote the kind of learning needed in professional education, and it might not even be the best way to do it. To start with, we shall briefly review recent research largely in medical education, and link these findings with what we now know from cognitive psychology concerning how people learn. Out of this will emerge an educational model which seems to underpin not just problem-based learning but other curricular arrangements. It will be argued that the proposals made here will apply to professional education generally.

Approaches to studying

During the 1970s several researchers attempted to identify the optimum approaches for studying in higher education. Marton identified what he called deep and surface processing (Marton and Säljö, 1976a). Deep processing was said to occur when students understood the meaning of what they were learning, and was associated with high scores on tests of their knowledge. Surface processing occurred when students merely memorized what they were studying, and was associated with poor test scores.

In the UK, Entwistle measured various learning approaches, and proposed a mathematical model (Entwistle, 1981): students' scores on approaches contributing positively towards their learning success were added, while those shown to be counter-productive were subtracted. He called the resultant score a prediction of success, which he claimed correlated positively with students' examination grades.

In the early 1980s the Entwistle learning inventory was used with medical students, and the first study comparing conventional and problem-based medical schools was reported in 1985 (Coles, 1985a). Further studies demonstrated comparable results (Martenson, 1986; Newble and Clarke, 1986). Students studying under the conventional curriculum arrangement showed a deterioration in their approaches to studying, while those in a problem-based curriculum did not, and indeed might actually improve (De Volder and de Grave, 1989).

These findings supported other studies (Coles, 1985b; Maddison, 1978; Mountford, 1989; Simpson, 1972) which suggested at the very least that the conventional curriculum arrangement was educationally unsound, and some researchers went further to claim support for a wider introduction of problem-based learning (Newble and Clarke, 1986). However, both of these conclusions are overly simplistic, as we shall see later.

What kind of learning is needed?

Arguably, the kind of learning students should engage in, not just in higher education generally, but more particularly when preparing for a profession, should reflect 'deep processing'. People going into a profession should understand the meaning of what they are learning. However, there are several reasons why this may not be so.

While empirical studies have shown that students who adopt a surface approach to processing do rather badly in their courses, they have not clearly shown that those who adopt a deep approach do well (Coles, 1985b; Newble and Clarke, 1986). In one study, a surface approach was relatively easy to induce experimentally in students but not a deep one (Marton and Säljö, 1976a).

The deep and surface processing analysis has not been supported by a clear theoretical explanation, nor has it been shown what are the mechanisms that could be operating educationally in situations which purport to induce one approach or the other. Attempts have been made to describe a theoretical basis for problem-based learning (Schmidt, 1983), but these have had to draw rather widely on diverse theoretical structures which lack cohesion.

Evidence now exists that deep processing students are less successful than those who elaborate their knowledge – that is who see the interconnections and links between different knowledge areas (Coles, 1990a) – who not only gain the highest scores in examinations which test that knowledge but are more able to retrieve and use in some novel situation the information they have learnt. Broadbent (1975) argues that remembering is more likely when the learner has 'multiple routes of access' to the stored information. The greater the network of knowledge and multiplicity of linkages between stored information, the more likely will be its retrieval and use. Mayer (1979) also argues that what he calls 'the far transfer of knowledge' is only possible when there has been 'elaboration to schema'.

This kind of learning also seems necessary for professional practice. Norman (1988) suggests that 'there is an accumulation of evidence that problem solving in medicine is dependent on ... elaborated conceptual knowledge', and the work of Gale and Marsden (1983) and Bordage and Zacks (1984) shows that successful clinical reasoning is dependent upon having access to an appropriately structured memory comprising a deep, rich knowledge

The educational conditions for effective learning

However, elaborated learning is rare under normal educational conditions, though it was found when medical students revised their basic science knowledge for an examination not at the end of the pre-clinical years but one year after beginning their first clinical attachments, and also (Patel and Dauphinee, 1984) when re-taught a basic science course during their final clinical attachments. In both cases the educational mechanisms are the same and embody three elements.

First, students needed a concrete context for their learning which was provided for them by their first-hand experiences. Second, they had available related theoretical information, provided in one case by their revision notes and in the other by a taught course. Third, students had the opportunity of handling this abstract information in such a way as to relate it to their clinical experiences. This analysis suggests a generalizable model which has been called 'contextual learning' (Coles, 1985b; 1990a).

The contextual learning model

Before discussing further the implications of the contextual learning model for professional education it might be useful to describe its three elements further.

1. *The context of learning*

Perhaps the most important feature of contextual learning is the establishment of an appropriate context in which learning can take place. Once such a context has been established, elaboration will almost inevitably (though not necessarily) occur. Why is this, and how can it be created?

For students to be able to acquire the kind of rich knowledge described earlier, they first need to have had something to which that information can be related. Some students bring with them prior knowledge, conceptualizations, and even experiences from the past which help their understanding of what they now need to know. This may well explain why mature students tend to perform well educationally in professional courses (Coles, 1988). However, curriculum planners should not assume that students enter courses already possessing the necessary contexts to enable them to acquire the abstract information they are likely to be taught. That is a task for the curriculum planner.

The context forms a basis or framework within which learners can receive the information they need to know. It begs questions, and enables learners to enquire. It creates an instability in the learner's mind, a wish to learn, a desire to create (Rogers, 1960), and a want (as opposed to a need) to know something more about the subject. In a word, it is motivating.

Contexts for learning exist at different levels of concreteness. Perhaps the highest is actual experience and may be the most universally appropriate, though contexts at lower levels of concreteness may be appropriate in certain circumstances. For example, students could be shown an activity being performed or experienced by someone else, such as a demonstration either in person or through a film or video. (It is perhaps worth noting that a recorded demonstration is at a rather lower level of concreteness than one in person.) Contexts for learning can be provided at even lower levels of concreteness. Students might be given a written case study or set of notes concerning some relevant situation, or be provided with some kind of framework or theoretical structure (such as the periodic table in chemistry) as an attempt to make concrete some otherwise theoretical information. Often teachers use analogies as a way of making concrete otherwise abstract ideas, and this too illustrates an attempt to contextualize learning.

What then are the implications of this for the curriculum planner? When students have little knowledge in the area, or no experience of a relevant situation, or the theoretical information they are expected to learn is novel and highly complex, the context being provided through the curriculum needs to be at a higher level of concreteness than if students have some previous experience or knowledge of the subject. Thus, curriculum plans should incorporate contexts for learning at an appropriate level of concreteness for students' current state of understanding and the nature of the knowledge they need to acquire.

2. *Information*

By its very nature, the kind of information students are being taught, and which they are expected to learn, is likely to be of an abstract nature. On its own, it probably carries little meaning for many students. Yet this is information which students are expected to acquire to help them to practise effectively. Curriculum planners need to consider very carefully the nature of this information and its relationship to the context for learning already established.

When attempting to contextualize learning, the most important feature of the information being provided is that potentially it should be relatable to the already established learning context. In many cases, this will mean that the choice of content will be determined by decisions already made concerning those contexts, and it should be recognized that this is likely to be the reverse of the decision-making process in conventional curricula, where the choice of content usually lies in the hands of individual teachers – especially those teaching theoretical courses. The choice of content and of contexts can and should be closely negotiated by all interested parties.

Once the content has been agreed, there are other considerations such as the way in which the information is to be made available to students, and how to present it. Behind these decisions lies a concern about how much information students should be expected to gather for themselves and how much they should be given. In the early stages of a course, or where the information is novel and complex and perhaps from a variety of distinct sources, the information could be suitably packaged and provided for students. Later in courses, or in areas where students have some background experience and knowledge, and have already identified sources of the necessary information, then students could be expected to gather information for themselves. In that case, consideration needs to be given to the amount of support and guidance students receive.

Reading lists, guided and annotated reading, previously prepared hand-outs and notes, and even lectures are certainly ways of making information available, and the choice of what is most appropriate will depend on local circumstances, as well as factors concerning the nature of the course, the level of student development, the availability of appropriate contexts, and the complexity and novelty of the information itself. The choice of textbooks to support learning is also important, and it is worth noting that these can vary greatly in the way they structure knowledge (Kriel and Hewson, 1986), so care must be taken to ensure that a preferred or recommended text helps rather than hinders the aims of the course planners.

Information relating to professional practice, however, poses a sterner problem. Much of it is intuitive, being hidden from even the professional's view, and embedded in one's practice. It comprises more than formal knowledge. Know-how crucially informs practice, as do assumptions, attitudes, beliefs and values. Professionals need the opportunity to unearth their practical knowledge, not just to make it available to learners, but to develop their own practice further (Eraut, 1994). Insider practitioner research is one approach for achieving this (Fish and Coles, 1997).

3. Opportunities for handling the information

In a conventional curriculum, students often say they are unclear about what they should be doing with the information they are being taught. It is the responsibility of the curriculum planners to build into the curriculum suggestions about how students should be making sense of what is being taught. For elaboration to occur, students should see their task as linking together aspects of knowledge both within and between subjects, and relating what they are learning now to what they already know. Students should be 'structuring' the information they are acquiring. They should be making connections, and in professional courses perhaps the most important consideration is the linking of theory and practice (Coles, 1990a). Where students have an appropriate learning context and the necessary information, they report 'things coming together' (*ibid*). This is the very essence of elaboration but it does not occur automatically. Thought should be given to providing opportunities which allow students to handle the information and relate it to their prior knowledge or experiences so that elaboration will occur.

An important feature of this handling of information is that students should do it for themselves. However much their teachers may have elaborated their own knowledge, it is for the students to make the connections in their own minds. It is for this reason that learning must be an active process on the part of the learner (Rogers, 1960).

While elaboration is something only an individual student can do, it can of course occur when students work in groups (Walton, 1973). The contribution of group work to each student's elaboration processes is that it allows the opportunity to articulate one's thoughts in a safe environment, and to receive constructive feedback from peers (Coles, 1989). The role of the teacher is to facilitate this elaboration, and this often requires considerable patience as students grapple for themselves with their uncertainties.

Perhaps what is equally important is that curriculum planners make absolutely clear to students what their tasks are in elaborating their knowledge, and these could include private study, essay writing, problem solving in groups, preparing and-presenting a paper or case, computer-assisted learning, and even examination revision.

How does contextual learning relate to other innovative educational approaches?

The three features of the contextual learning model clearly relate to what can occur in problem-based learning. At the beginning of a problem-based learning sequence, students are presented with a case or problem. This could well establish an appropriate context for learning. At the very least it allows students to raise questions in their own minds concerning why the problem is occurring, what is going on, and what the resolution might be. Then, in a problem-based curriculum, students acquire information in order to understand that problem more fully, and possibly to solve it. This represents the second phase of the contextual learning model. Following this, students have the opportunity, often in groups, to solve the problem, or at least to work towards its resolution. Clearly this is a curriculum strategy which closely relates to providing opportunities for handling the information in such a way that students can elaborate their knowledge.

Having said this it is also clear that the problem may not always provide an appropriate context for learning, and there is some evidence to suggest that this can occur to the detriment of students' knowledge acquisition (Haas and Shaffir, 1982; Olson, 1987). Perhaps one difficulty is that often the problem comprises a paper and pencil case which earlier was described as being at a lower level of concreteness than some other contexts, such as first-hand experience or even a live or recorded demonstration. Also, in problem-based learning students are often expected to acquire the information for themselves, but under certain circumstances it might be appropriate to make the information available to students. Similarly, the problem-solving activity in problem-based learning can, but does not necessarily, provide an opportunity for handling the information in such a way that elaboration occurs for all the students involved.

Thus, though problem-based learning might ideally seem to reflect the three essential characteristics of the contextual learning model, it might not do so if a specific effort were not made to ensure that these activities do in fact occur.

The contextual learning model also seems to relate closely to what has been called experiential learning. Kolb (1984) describes the ideal learning cycle as proceeding from concrete experience to observations and reflections, and then through the formulation of abstract concepts and generalizations to testing the implications of these concepts in new situations, and thus new experiences. The first stages of this cycle could be related to the establishment of an appropriate context for learning. Formulating abstract concepts and generalizations parallels the information element of the contextual learning model, and the testing of their implications in new situations is clearly an opportunity for elaborating one's knowledge. Thus the experiential learning cycle can be explained in terms of the contextual learning model, but just as with problem-based learning it does not necessarily mean that this is what will occur since, unlike that model, it does not indicate how to apply it.

A third innovative approach to education which closely resembles the contextual learning model has been called reflection on practice, as seen especially in the work of Schon (1983; 1987) and of Boud (Boud *et al*, 1985). Reflection on practice is made possible because of the learner's prior experiences, and this clearly relates to establishing an appropriate context for learning. This provides a basis for the generation by the learner of abstract thought in relation to those experiences, which equates with the information phase of contextual learning. The outcome of reflection is that the learner gains new perspectives on experience and has the possibility of changing behaviour. This phase has been called 'resolution' in which learners experience 'a coming together or creative synthesis of various bits of the information previously taken in' (Boyd and Fales, 1983), which seems closely to relate to what has been called elaboration here.

Contextual learning, then, provides a model which seems to underpin these various innovative approaches to education, and this gives strength to the model in terms of its generality, but it also suggests they will not inevitably lead to elaboration occurring. The contextual learning model takes these innovations further, and can be applied even to more conventional forms of education as we will now see.

Applying the model

A recurring theme in this chapter has been that the curriculum which students experience is the greatest determinant of the kind of learning that occurs (Coles, 1985b), and sadly many curricula in professional education do not have the conditions necessary for generating elaborated learning. An appropriate context for learning is rarely set, information presented to students is often highly abstract and only relevant in the long term, and few opportunities are provided within the curriculum for students to handle the information appropriately. Indeed, it seems that often a hidden curriculum operates where grapevine messages from other students determine the study habits that develop, many of which are likely to be inappropriate or even counter-productive (Snyder, 1971). The contextual learning model can provide a basis for curriculum planning if those responsible provide for students a course structure which embodies the three elements described here.

Individual teachers too can, whatever the nature of the curriculum, reformulate their own teaching to embody the principles of contextual learning. Someone giving a lecture could provide, at the outset, some example or illustration, possibly graphically demonstrated, of a situation which provides a context for students to learn what the lecturer wishes to present, allowing them to raise in their own minds questions they would like the lecture content to resolve. The lecturer can then proceed to present information, and to provide opportunities both during and after the lecture for students to handle this information and to elaborate.

Similarly, teachers can modify their small group work seminars and tutorials to incorporate the principles of the contextual learning model. In practical situations this is relatively straightforward. Students could experience for themselves some practice, and then proceed to establishing its theoretical or abstract basis and to make links with what they already know or need to know in future. The role of the teacher would be to ensure that the context has been established, to facilitate students' accumulation of the necessary information, and to encourage elaboration. Teachers need to guard against attributing blame to those students who find information retrieval difficult, but rather recognize it is not always easy to recall in novel situations information learnt earlier in a different setting. The learning process is often one of recontextualizing previously acquired information.

Students themselves can also adopt the contextual learning model and apply it to their own studying (Coles, 1990b). Lecturers often present abstract information and then give examples or use analogies to illustrate their point. To recontextualize this, students may need to reverse the teaching sequence (abstract before concrete) into a more appropriate learning sequence (concrete to abstract) by recalling the example or illustration given, and then relating to it the information which preceded it in the lecture.

When students undertake practical work, they frequently have difficulty in seeing what their task should be, often seeing it as a time for merely acquiring skills, and not for revising previously taught theoretical information. They should be encouraged to elaborate their knowledge by relating theory and practice. To do this they will need to draw on a variety of sources since theory courses are often organized round academic disciplines rather than the problems encountered in practice. Importantly, students should be encouraged to seek information even from courses which they do not immediately remember as being relevant. Often they will say they did not realize until now just how relevant were those early courses.

Conclusion

This chapter has looked at what and how we teach from the viewpoint of learners and the ways they learn. It has briefly reviewed work on study approaches and the kind of learning needed for effective professional practice. Out of this has emerged the concept of elaboration. Students need to be formulating more and more complex networks of knowledge relevant to their field of study.

It has also been suggested that elaboration is unlikely to occur under the conventional curriculum arrangement, and does not necessarily occur during problem-based learning or other innovative schemes. A generalized model has been proposed called contextual learning. This suggests that elaboration can occur if three conditions are met: students must have an appropriate context for learning; they must be provided with or acquire information potentially relatable to that context; and they should have opportunities to so handle the information that they make connections.

It has been shown how this model can be applied in conventional educational settings through curriculum design, in improving one's teaching, and in helping students learn more effectively.

So where does all of this leave problem-based learning. The implication is that problem-based learning is an unnecessary complication to the educational scene. It has been an interesting and worthy experiment but now that we know about the contextual learning model we no longer need to reinvent it. Certainly conventional courses should not be abandoned in favour of problem-based ones. Rather they should be helped to evolve in line with the principles of contextual learning outlined here.

References

Bordage, G and Zacks, R (1984) The structure of medical knowledge in the memories of medical students and general practitioners, categories and prototypes, *Medical Education*, 18, 406–416.

Boud, D, Keogh, R and Walker, D (1985) Promoting reflection in learning: a model, in Boud, D, Keogh, R and Walker, D (eds) *Reflection: Turning Experience into Learning*, London: Kogan Page.

Boyd, E M and Fales, A W (1983) Reflective learning: the key to learning from experience, *Journal of Humanistic Psychology*, 23, 99–117.

Broadbent, D E (1976) Cognitive psychology and education, *British Journal of Educational Psychology*, 45 (2), 162–176.

Coles, C R (1985a) Differences between conventional and problem-based curricula in their students' approaches to studying, *Medical Education*, 19, 308–309.

Coles, C R (1985b) A Study of the Relationship Between Curriculum and Learning in Undergraduate Medical Education, PhD thesis, University of Southampton.

Coles, C R (1988) Medicine: not a job for the boys! *Medical Education*, 22, 78 (abs).

Coles, C R (1989) Self-assessment and medical audit: an educational approach, *British Medical Journal*, 299, 807–808.

Coles, C R (1990a) Elaborated learning in undergraduate medical education, *Medical Education*, 24, 14–22.

Coles, C R (1990b) Helping students with learning difficulties in medical and health-care education, *ASME Medical Education Booklet, No 24*, Dundee: Association for the Study of Medical Education.

De Volder, M L and de Grave, W S (1989) Approaches to studying in a problem-based medical programme: a developmental study, *Medical Education*, 23, 262–264.

Entwistle, N J (1983) *Styles of Learning and Teaching*, Chichester: John Wiley.

Eraut, M (1994) *Developing Professional Knowledge and Competence*, London: Falmer Press.

Fish, D and Coles, C (1997) *Developing Professional Judgement in Health Care: Learning Through the Critical Appreciation of Practice*, Oxford: Butterworth Heinemann.

Gale, J and Marsden, P (1983) *Medical Diagnosis: From Student to Clinician*, Oxford: Oxford University Press.

Haas, J and Shaffir, W (1982) Ritual evaluation of competence: the hidden curriculum of professionalization in an innovative medical school program, *Work and Occupations*, 9, 131–154.

Kolb, D A (1984) *Experiential Learning: Experience as the Source of Learning and Development*, Englewood Cliffs, New Jersey: Prentice Hall.

Kriel, J and Hewson, M (1986) Conceptual frameworks in preclinical and clinical textbooks, *Medical Education*, 20, 94–101.

Maddison, D C (1978) What's wrong with medical education? *Medical Education*, 12, 111–123.

Martenson, D F (1986) Students' approaches to studying in four medical schools, *Medical Education*, 20, 532–534.

Marton, F and Säljö, R (1976a) On qualitative differences in learning I – outcome and process, *British Journal of Educational Psychology*, 46, 4–11.

Marton, F and Säljö, R (1976b) On qualitative differences in learning II – outcome as a function of the learner's conception of the task, *British Journal of Educational Psychology*, 46, 115–127.

Mayer, R E (1979) Twenty years of research into advanced organisers: assimilation theory is still the best predictor of results, *Instructional Science*, 8, 133–167.

Mountford, B (1989) Teaching and Learning Medicine: A Study of Teachers and Learners in a Young Medical School, PhD thesis, University of Southampton.

Newble, D and Clarke, R M (1986) The approaches to learning of students in a traditional and in an innovative problem-based medical school, *Medical Education*, 20, 267–273.

Norman, G R (1988) Problem-solving skills, solving problems and problem based learning, *Medical Education*, 22, 279–86.

Olson, J O (1987) The McMaster philosophy: a student's perspective on implementation, *Medical Education*, 21, 293–296.

Patel, V L and Dauphinee, W D (1984) Return to basic sciences after clinical experience in undergraduate medical training, *Medical Education*, 18, 244–248.

Rogers, C R (1960) *On Becoming a Person*, London: Constable.

Schmidt, H G (1983) Problem-based learning: rationale and description, *Medical Education*, 17, 11–16.

Schön, D A (1983) *The Reflective Practitioner*, New York: Basic Books.

Schön, D A (1987) *Educating the Reflective Practitioner: Towards a New Design for Teaching and Learning in the Professions*, San Francisco: Jossey-Bass.

Simpson, M A (1972) *Medical Education: A Critical Approach*, London: Butterworth.

Snyder, B R (1971) *The Hidden Curriculum*, New York: Knopf.

Walton, H J (1973) *Small Group Methods in Medical Teaching*, Medical Education Booklet. Dundee: Association for the Study of Medical Education.

Chapter 32

Towards a Praxis of Situation Improving

Richard Bawden

Introduction

The professional agriculturalist faces two interdependent worlds of immense complexity. There is the 'natural' world of soils, plants and animals which the primary producer manipulates in order to produce quality foods and fibres. And there is the 'social' world of families, labour, markets and cultural mores which greatly influence the modes of production and the distribution of the outputs.

The major career areas of graduate agriculturalists lie in those industries which provide services to the producers; both abstract, in the form of research findings and market intelligence, and concrete in the form of technologies. Whatever their niche, agriculturalists deal with issues that are complex and dynamic, and therefore their education should prepare them for that. In the vast majority of instances, it does not.

Conventional agricultural curricula are noted for their constellations of subject disciplines from the physical, biological and social sciences. To the expositions of theories is then typically added a whole collection of laboratory and field exercises. And all of these endeavours are invariably presented in a lock-step matrix of pre- and co-requisites. It can be posited that the linear thinking, the deductive and inductive logic, and the sheer fragmentation of effort which characterizes such educational environments is really counter to the development of those competencies demanded by professional practice.

Yet rather than having constructive debates about change, education for agriculturalists, like that for many professionals, is invariably reduced to fruitless arguments between those who believe that theories are prime and those who support the primacy of the practical.

On praxis

A decade or so back, our faculty decided to escape this dichotomy between theory and practice by exploring a third dimension. Being a professional agriculturalist, we decided, is much more than knowing the theories of agriculture, and doing it in practice. Experience combines with theory and with practice to form a dynamic praxis – an evolving set of interrelationships with the 'whole' (praxis) being different from the sum of its interdependent parts (theory, practice and experience). One way of focusing on education for effective praxis, is to base curricula on the problem-solving strategies that graduates use in their professional practice. Inspired by our colleagues at the medical school at the University of Newcastle, we decided to explore a problem-based approach in the quest for education for effective praxis (Bawden *et al*, 1984). Unfortunately, we soon ran into problems with problems!

Problems with problems

Dividing the world into convenient problems reduces complex situations in ways which are themselves problematical. The idea of a problem always seems to connote trouble – worrying concerns that what is actually happening is somehow a wrong that can be righted. Moreover, the nature of any recognizable problem so often appears to be determined by the pre-existing solution.

Now it is true that many aspects of agriculture can be considered as troubling, and it is also true that a host of relatively simple problems with potential solutions can be identified. Deficiencies in the nutrient status of crops and livestock are not that difficult to recognize, or fix. The same can be said of a host of pests and diseases for which control treatments are available, and of mechanical breakdowns which can be repaired. But none of these 'problem/solution sets' reflects the ever-evolving, dynamic complexity that characterizes the relationships that exist in agriculture between people and their environments. Attention to the more straightforward problems may indeed represent a diversion away from a much more complex set of problematic issues.

Following an idea of Checkland (1981), we decided that learning to improve situations was a more constructive competency for professional agriculturalists to master than learning how to solve problems. Not only did this provide a much more comprehensive focus for the design of feasible educational strategies, it also encouraged a much more positive and creative atmosphere within the faculty itself. In our own work as designers of new educational systems, we saw ourselves as being in our own unknown, unpredictable, complex, even chaotic world where it was much more relevant to seek to create improvements than to select out problems and solve them. Accordingly we recognized that each of us needed to develop our own situation-improving competencies in order to improve the quality of our learning environment and the relationship each of us bore to it.

The richness of the notion of praxis soon became evident to us as we found ourselves in a veritable whirlpool of new experiences, new practices and new theories. We discovered that we needed not just new knowledge, but new ways of knowing – and most importantly, we also discovered that we needed to develop new ways of knowing about new ways of knowing. If these notions of differences in ways and 'levels' of knowing were essential to the development of our own praxis, then logic dictated that the same would pertain to our students. Indeed as we would be learning as a result of helping others to learn, then it would be more accurate to express the teacher/student relationship as a learner/learner one. In our evolution we had progressed from exploring problem-based learning to improving complex learning systems where such systems comprised people collaborating together to explore issues and events of common concern.

Ways and levels of knowing

Reason and Heron (1986) have provided a model of ways of knowing which is consistent with the notion of distinctions among theory, practice and praxis. Experiential knowledge (for being) is gained through direct encounters with people and places, and where our sensory experiences of the world act as the foundation and focus for the knowledge we create – the meanings that we make. Practical knowledge (for doing) is that which can be demonstrated in such a way that it can be emulated and where we learn how to do things by doing this. And finally, propositional knowledge (for knowing) is public knowledge which can be shared through conversation, either directly or through the literature, of meanings, concepts and theories proposed by others.

Clearly each individual is capable of gaining knowledge in each of these three manners and indeed each way of knowing can clearly motivate the need for the others. Reflections on the knowledge gained in each way and the processes by which it was gained are crucial in this regard. This constant interplay between different ways of knowing, where each informs the other, can be described as a recursive relationship. There is no primacy among theories, practice and experience in education for professional praxis, for each is interdependent with the others. This means that it is legitimate to 'enter' any situation-to-be-improved from any locus of learning: the only imperative for effective praxis is to explore the differences that exist between these three ways of learning and exploit the synergy that emerges from their interrelationships.

In order to exploit multiple ways of knowing, it is obviously important that one is both conscious of the choices available and competent at both being able to choose when each is most appropriate and then how each leads to the need for the others. Thus in addition to knowing about agriculture, the professional agriculturalist must also know how to know about agriculture; and this suggests that just as one can recognize different ways of knowing, so too is it useful to recognize different 'levels' of knowing.

From the above, we can distinguish between using a particular method for situation improving to improve a situation, and using a method to select or even design another method. We can also use methods to investigate the assumptions we accepted in choosing between two methods, or designing new ones. Together these represent a 'hierarchy' of three interdependent levels of knowing – knowing how to use a method, knowing how to choose a method, and knowing how to muse about the way we choose and use methods! This interplay between the ways of doing and the philosophies and logic which underpin them, is referred to as methodology.

A final dimension to be introduced here is that which suggests that not only are there different types of knowledge reflecting different ways and levels of knowing, but that there are also different reasons for wanting to know – a hierarchy of different interest constitutions as Habermas (1972) has put it. Crudely expressed, we learn in order to be more efficient, in order to be more effective, or in order to be emancipated.

This talk of knowledge and knowing is not whimsy, but philosophy-for-action. Our use of particular methods for improving agricultural situations is informed by thinking about those methods, which in turn is informed by thinking about the methodological assumptions upon which thinking about methods is based. In equivalent terms this is like saying that technology is informed by science is informed by philosophy, and this emphasizes the importance of all three dimensions in the praxis, and hence education, of the professional agriculturalist.

Philosophy-for-action

Perhaps the most obvious philosophical domain in the above logic is logic itself. The conventional science and technology of agriculture are both dominated by the logics of deduction and induction, which in turn reflect the notion of linear and causal relationships. Most of the argument of this chapter, however, has been based on mutual and recursive interrelationships, and, tacitly at least, on what Bateson (1972) refers to as abductive logic. This is the logic of metaphor and analogue, which allows us to invent educational systems, agricultural systems and hierarchies of levels of learning. This sort of logic can provide some wonderful insights into the nature of complex situations and thus provide many pointers with regards to the constitution of improvements. It also allows us to embrace non-rational thinking and to integrate it with reason: it allows the synthesis of the logic of the poet with that of the physicist, and it imbues discussions about aesthetics with a logical respectability! Thus in addition to the reason of rationalism, there are the many insights borne of non-rational intuition, value-grounded beliefs and cultural mores.

The talk of improvement highlights another vital area of philosophy-for-praxis, for ultimately, improvements can only be grounded in 'that which is ethically defensible', to use the elegant expression of Churchman (1971). Professional agriculturalists already recognize many ethical dilemmas with respect to such issues as land stewardship, land rights, animal welfare, consumer rights, genetic pool diversity, and so on. Their praxis must not only heighten the consciousness of this philosophical domain, but also embrace competencies which emancipate those to be affected by decisions to participate in the debate about that which is 'ethically defensible'.

And finally, and crucially, there are philosophical aspects of views about the nature of the world and about the ways one can know that world: about ontological and epistemological assumptions, respectively. It is often a shock for those born of a tradition in the physical or life sciences, to discover that there are those who dispute the positivist view that there is only one 'true', knowable reality 'out there'. It is even more shocking for them to discover that there is increasing scientific evidence to support the contention that the physiology of our perception is influenced by our psychology and that, therefore, we cannot access the world objectively in any way. All that we see we construe!

And so to curricula

The thinking above has been 'brought forth' over the years as we have been developing our own praxis as agricultural educators, while helping our co-learning students to develop theirs. The curriculum has become reconstrued as a dynamic learning system which is in constant evolution with the environments which surround it, as theories and experiences are brought to bear to inform our practices. Educational strategies, which facilitate the development of different ways and different levels of learning, emerge, are transformed, disappear and re-emerge in novel forms. Abductively, the faculty is like a bubbling cauldron; first liquid, then gas, then precipitate – to borrow a powerful metaphor offered by Samples (1976).

Our students learn how to improve situations across an enormous range of complexity, through their involvement in 'real world' projects which start on the first day they enrol. Their enquiries-for-action involve them in science and technology and philosophy, in propositional, practical and experiential learning, and with a range of intents from technical to emancipatory. They learn how to improve their ways of improving through reflection on the actions they take, and on the theories and philosophies they use to inform these. They learn how to work in collaboration with others at the same time that they are developing as autonomous learners. They also learn how to solve some problems.

References

Bateson, G (1972) *Steps to an Ecology of Mind*, New York: Balentine.
Bawden, R J, Macadam, R D, Packham, R G and Valentine, I (1984) Systems

thinking and practices in the education of agriculturalists, *Agricultural Systems*, 13, 205–225.

Checkland, P B (1981) *Systems Thinking, Systems Practice*, New York: John Wiley.

Churchman, C W (1971) *The Way of Inquiring Systems: The Design of Inquiring Systems*, New York: Basic Books.

Habermas, J (1972) *Knowledge and Human Interests*, London: Heinemann.

Reason, P and Heron, J (1986) Research with people: the paradigm of cooperative experiential enquiry, *Person-Centred Review*, 1, 457–476.

Samples, R (1976) *The Metaphoric Mind: A Celebration of Creative Consciousness*, Reading, Mass: Addison Wesley.

Chapter 33

The Limits of Problem-based Learning

John Drinan

For many of us, the preoccupations and anxieties accompanying early experiences of problem-based learning are potent distractions from questions about what lies beyond it. Yet it is fundamental that if we seek to engage students in problem-based learning, we should also emulate its processes in reviewing, refining and developing it further. Constant reflection on our observations and the building of new concepts can lead to the improvement of the learning environment and the extension of our own understanding of how we learn. This journey might happily challenge the very foundations of our understanding, and can deepen and enrich our lives as co-learners with our students. This is the ultimate goal which, I believe, currently lies beyond the purposes of most problem-based curricula.

It is instructive to try to distil what it is that teachers using problem-based learning are trying to achieve, even though it would be wrong to believe that all are seeking the same generic capabilities in their graduates (see Part IV for examples). However, it seems that many educators are attempting non-traditional approaches to education in the hope of creating active, interdependent and independent learners; holistic, divergent, creative thinkers; people who can solve problems or improve situations; better communicators; people who are able to entice the best from others; people who are aware of their own talents and who are confident in using them. They believe that problem-based learning is an approach to the attainment of these goals.

The possible permutations and combinations of design variables in problem-based learning are endless (Barrows, 1986). It is an amalgam of teaching strategies, not all of which are employed in all problem-based forms. Typically, they include an activity that addresses a challenging or problematic situation in a particular context. The situation is multi-faceted; much of the activity is conducted with small groups of students; and students are expected to participate actively in their own learning – ie four different strategies. The term problem-based learning does not seem to be restricted to the first of these but to the totality. It is important that this is recognized, because each of these strategies needs independent and contextual consideration in the design of the curriculum, if the full potential is to be realized.

Not all forms of problem-based learning seem capable of developing all of the qualities listed above, even through their inclusion of potentially powerful strategies. Indeed, some problem-based learning becomes mechanical in practice, destined merely to train students to solve problems and acquire the knowledge needed for this. In these cases, the potential for stimulation of deeper, holistic and creative thought is lost through prescribed problem-solving pathways and processes: The opportunity for development of interpersonal and communication skills disappears in proportion to ill-chosen or non-intervention by teachers, and innate independent learning skills wither through lack of stimulation by teachers who find it difficult to resist the urge to give of their knowledge and wisdom.

It might be helpful to confine the term 'problem-based learning' to a defined territory of learning purposes. This restriction might be made through a distillation of the essences of problem-based learning forms and derivatives and ordering them from the original, to those that have emerged with growth of understanding.

1. Motivation for learning through use of professionally relevant material.
2. Developing the ability to make decisions.
3. Acquisition of, or exposure to, a body of knowledge.
4. Raising awareness of the complexity of real-world issues.
5. Developing the capacity for self-directed learning.
6. Developing the ability to extend learning beyond the presented situations into new ones.
7. Generating the desire and ability to think deeply and holistically.
8. Generating an enthusiasm for learning from all of life's experiences in personal, professional and community development.
9. Encouraging a search beyond one's own preconceptions, so becom-

ing ultimately innovative and positively critical with respect to self and one's profession and society.

The term problem-based learning might be restricted to curricula embracing purposes 1–5 above, where the desired or attainable end-point is the acquisition of relevant information and its organization into making decisions, and the capacity to go on learning independently. This does not necessarily require the reflection and conceptualization that would mark attainment of the full set.

Restriction of the term problem-based learning requires that another be used to include those forms which additionally embrace the higher purposes (6–9) above, as described, for instance, by English *et al* (1994). 'Experiential learning' seems to accommodate them all, and requires fulfilment of all stages of the cycle so well elucidated by Kolb (1984). Thus, reflection and conceptualization on any experience, whether contrived or real, a problem or opportunity or life happening, should involve a depth and breadth of thought which might ultimately lead to the freedom to challenge, rework and appreciate one's most cherished fundamentals. Perhaps all forms of education founded on problem-based learning might have this endpoint, but such a goal would be unrealistic. We should be more precise in our terminology so that we understand and can signal to others the purposes of our curricula.

There is also a need to resolve a number of pragmatic issues that currently stand in the way of effective and efficient adoption of problem-based learning. Prominent among these is student assessment, but the relative importance of the process and content of learning, age and experience differences among students, and resource requirements, are also important barriers.

It can be too easy in problem-based courses for students to believe that they are only required to solve a problem and so guess their way from problem to solution without seriously engaging either sources of information or mental facilities! This deficiency should show if student assessment clearly reflects the purposes of the curriculum. That it sometimes does not is an example of the lack of appreciation of the need for different approaches to assessment in problem-based learning, and/or of the difficulty in devising such approaches.

Most forms of assessment used in conventional courses are designed to test recall of information and ability to apply it in intellectual or physical processes. There are particular difficulties in transplanting these forms of assessment to problem-based curricula, based as they are on different conceptions of knowledge (Hager and Butler, 1994). *Inter alia*, the body of information is more diffuse and less prescribed, relationships are as important as the bits and pieces, problems are complex and often non-linear, and awkward matters such as personal values and belief systems intrude. Clearly, conventional assessment methods are of limited value, and the future progress and credibility of problem-based learning depends heavily on encouragement of innovative thinking and practice in this respect.

Exponents of problem-based learning argue that the process by which students learn is of critical importance in helping them to conduct themselves appropriately in their future professions, and that they will acquire the information they need as they need it. My experience shows that students can and do access information according to need, but that their capacity to do so outside a directive curriculum is dependent on age and motivation, which themselves appear to be related. I doubt the capacity and motivation of many students who emerge direct from school into tertiary education, and we do them a grave injustice if we do not support them with facilitators who care to watch, challenge, encourage, constructively criticize and retrieve them from the holes into which they occasionally fall.

The need for facilitation seems to be somewhat less for the students who have left school for some time, as they generally have better considered purposes in selecting a particular course. However, perhaps this group needs a different type of facilitation, with emphasis on challenge and critique. Facilitation requires attributes that are substantially different to the usual ones on which academic staff are hired. A genuine and personal care for students, a real enthusiasm for learning and a commitment to modelling the principles inherent in experiential learning, are probably the most crucial qualities in such persons. There are not enough quality facilitators, perhaps because our traditional education systems are unlikely to encourage the desired characteristics.

The above remarks are also relevant in the extent to which teachers may feel comfortable about 'letting go' of their focus issues and moving on to fully experiential learning. The construction of most problem-based curricula involves much work in developing and packaging a series of focus problems or case studies. Having invested so much effort, teachers are understandably reluctant to change the issues or seize the opportunity to immerse students in real-time issues in the real world. This spells danger because the issues become stale and increasingly irrelevant, and the richness and stimulation available to students and teachers alike in the real world is forgone. Teachers who are willing to respond to learning opportunities, who trust themselves in the real world, who are capable in the theory of the target profession, and who truly care for their students should be an objective and outcome of all problem-based curricula.

Curriculum designers quickly collide with the realities of resource availability, and none more so than those who seek to use problem- or experience-based approaches. The apparent 'efficiency' of large groups of students being lectured stands in stark contrast to the seeming 'inefficiency' of small groups groping for information and understanding, supported by teachers who are never quite sure what they may be asked to do next! Obviously, such appearances are misleading, because the foundations and purposes of the two approaches are so different. Nevertheless, the development of the better graduate we seek through experience-based learning can be more expensive, but it need not be so with imagination and good management – Alverno College (Chapter 29) is a good example. If it *is* more expensive, this is not unreasonable in view of the superior quality of the graduates. However, evidence on the latter claim remains somewhat equivocal (eg, Schmidt *et al*, 1987), though care should be taken in interpreting comparisons to ensure they address the criteria sought in experience-based programs.

The resource squeeze of the nineties constitutes a major obstacle to problem- and experience-based curricula. Greater student:staff ratios, increased proportions of non-tenured and less experienced teachers, and fewer discretionary funds constrain curricular innovation. Administrators perceive them as being more costly, and teachers whose futures in the institution are short do not have the time or incentive to invest in curriculum redesign. If they are junior staff, their reluctance to innovate may be reinforced by lack of confidence and senior support, as well as by the damaging emphasis given to research over teaching in university pronouncements and recruitment and promotions practices. On the other hand, the implications of quality assurance might counterbalance this, alongside growing awareness of the need to focus on learning rather than teaching, and of the relativity or contextualization of knowledge. Thus might student learning gain priority over institutional and staff concerns.

There are other developments which may be used to good effect in the quest for learning beyond problem-based learning. For example, systems theory and practice (eg, Checkland and Scholes, 1990) and the allied field of complexity science (eg, Waldrop, 1993) have much in common with experiential learning, and many insights to offer. The World Wide Web has the potential to remove the last plank supporting those who see teaching as an information providing exercise and the resultant disturbance should create fertile ground for the further development of experiential and even better approaches to learning.

Cowdroy (1994) has exposed many of the constructivist notions that are inherent, though often unrealized, in problem- and experience-based learning. Illumination of the constructed or contextual bases of individual and community knowledge has posed an enormous challenge to the 'certain facts' on which much teaching is based. Taken to its extreme, constructivism can logically invalidate all knowledge, yet we know we live and breathe, grass grows and aeroplanes fly.

Despite raising difficulties like the above paradox, one of the benefits of constructivism is that it has reaffirmed values as fundamental to meaning in human existence, and the different perspectives they bring to understanding existence. For Western societies, where belief in the non-material has declined as science and technology have ascended, this is another significant challenge. Yet the ability of humans to draw exquisite creations out of material and non-material things, and our capacity to be enraptured by the beauty of these and natural things, are reminders of a dimension which is not easily described through the mechanistic world-view of Western society.

Nor are reminders confined to these examples: the insights of meditation, the serendipity of discovery and the powers of non-medical healers also point to the dimension that is most explicitly stated in the sacred books of many traditions. It has been distinctly unfashionable to entertain belief in a spiritual or, at least, non-material dimension but many are beginning to suspect that this has been a major limitation to our wholeness as individuals and as societies. Education, in general, has gone along with the prevailing view and, in any case, has probably not been capable of seriously addressing things which can be 'known' or experienced but not easily taught. By its nature, experiential learning has the capability to allow this dimension to inform and flavour the rational processes of reflection and conceptualization. Out of this could come a richer, more harmonious society.

There is much evidence that our world is at a turning point. Realization is dawning that the world-views that have underpinned technological progress have also undermined the health of our society and our environment, to the point that collapse of both is possible. The turnaround can happen if we adopt new paradigms that involve a view of the world as an organic unity, where diversity is valued as fundamental to creativity and in which relationships among all things are recognized to be as important as the constituent parts. Such a turnaround is happening at the grassroots, where all significant change begins, and governments, business and educators will inevitably be forced to acknowledge and support it. Education must anticipate this change and rapidly move to its own reform to allow it to develop the people who will bring our society into a new world. New approaches are needed to bring forth creative, constructive thought and endeavour in societies that care for the individual, communities and the environment. Experiential learning offers a powerful choice for the future.

References

Barrows, H S (1986) A taxonomy of problem-based learning methods. *Medical Education*, 20, 481–486.

Checkland, P and Scholes, J (1990) *Soft Systems Methodology in Action*, Chichester: Wiley.

Cowdroy, R M (1994) Concepts, constructs and insights: the essence of problem-based learning. In *Reflections on Problem Based Learning*, Campbelltown, NSW: Australian PBL Network, 45–56.

English, B, Gaha, J and Gibbons, J (1994) Preparing social workers for an uncertain future. In *Reflections on Problem Based Learning*, Campbelltown, NSW: Australian PBL Network, 279–296.

Hager, P and Butler, J (1994) Problem based learning and paradigms of assessment. In *Reflections on Problem Based Learning*, Campbelltown, NSW: Australian PBL Network, 35–44.

Kolb, D (1984) *Experiential Learning: Experience as the Source of Learning and Development*. Englewood Cliffs, New Jersey: Prentice-Hall.

Schmidt, H G, Dauphinee, W D and Patel, V (1987) Comparing the effects of problem-based and conventional curricula in an international sample. *Journal of Medical Education*, 62, 305–315.

Waldrop, M M (1993) *Complexity – The Emerging Science at the Edge of Order and Chaos*, London: Viking.

Index